ACTION RESEARCH PRACTICES IN K-12 CLASSROOMS

ADEL T. AL-BATAINEH, EDITOR
KENNETH F. JERICH, EDITOR

ACTION RESEARCH PRACTICES IN K-12 CLASSROOMS

ADEL T. AL-BATAINEH, EDITOR
KENNETH F. JERICH, EDITOR

COMMON GROUND

First published in 2013 in Champaign, Illinois, USA
by Common Ground Publishing LLC
as part of The Learner Book Series

Library of Congress Cataloging-in-Publication Data

Action research practices in K-12 classrooms / Adel T. Al-Bataineh, editor.
     pages cm
 Includes bibliographical references.
 ISBN 978-1-61229-210-6 (pbk : alk. paper) -- ISBN 978-1-61229-211-3 (pdf)
 1. Action research in education--United States. 2. Teaching--United States. 3. Educational change--United States. I. Al-Bataineh, Adel T.

 LB1028.24.A35 2013
 370.72--dc23

                                  2013018061

Cover image photo credit: Emma Ann Deluhery

Table of Contents

Foreword

Adel T. Al-Bataineh & Kenneth J. Jerich

Action Research Practices in K-12 Classrooms

The improvement of teaching is a perennial concern for teachers, administrators and government agencies and perhaps the responsibility for improving teaching is one of the most debated educational issues in the United States. Educational reforms which have been raging for over a millennium are abundant with ideas and plans to improve teaching. In recent years, reforms have been focused on making teachers more accountable for students' learning. Consequently, preparing highly qualified teachers has become a main concern for stakeholders.

In 1986, The Carnegie Forum on Education and the Economy released a major report, "A Nation Prepared: Teachers for the 21st Century," that advocated the creation of a non-profit, private board to oversee the improvement of teaching. The Forum, like many professional organizations and researchers before and after the release of this report, recognized the importance of effective teaching and the necessity of entrusting teachers with restoring the quality of our educational system.

Furthermore, the Carnegie Forum on Education and the Economy (1986) have called on higher education institutions to work closely with teachers throughout their careers, to conduct research on teaching in P-12 classrooms, and to advance teachers professional careers. Accordingly, the idea of advancing the professionalization of teaching is broadly accepted in our society among chief executive officers of major U.S. corporations, the heads of teachers' unions, state governors and progressive educators in a variety of roles. As early as 1992, the National Society for the Study of Education reiterated this need. In 2005, Darling-Hammond and Bransford developed a framework for promoting the professionalization of teaching. They stated that:

> All professions at some point in their development have worked to achieve consensus about the key elements of a professional education curriculum: the building blocks of preparation for all entrants into the occupation....Meanwhile, great strides have been made in our

> understanding of learning and the teaching practices that support it. Over the past two years, the National Academy of Education, through its Committee on Teacher Education (CTE), has been considering the implications for the curriculum of teacher education of what the field has learned about effective learning and teaching, as well as about the learning of teachers. (Darling-Hammond and Bransford, 2005, p. vii)

As we begin the second decade in the 21st century, teacher development is being referred to as the professional learning of teachers (Wei, R., Darling-Hammond, L., Andree, A., Richardson, N. & Orphauos, S. (2009). The key features related to the professional learning of teachers include improving students' academic achievement and the transformation of schools in order to meet federal and state requirements, and public expectations. Consequently, teacher skills and knowledge need to match with diverse learner needs. To accomplish this, high quality professional learning for teachers should be sustained throughout their teacher preparation programs and throughout their careers as teachers. Preservice and inservice teachers should be prepared for a variety of roles that include; but is not limited to, the construction of instructional units, curricular rationales, lesson planning, teaching models and strategies, and assessment and evaluation techniques.   Additionally, purposeful observation and reflection should be integrated with meaningful and significant teaching practice (simulation and real life) and must be linked to the teacher preparation curriculum that incorporates pedagogical skills for teaching and learning. Preservice and inservice teachers should be provided with opportunities for active learning experiences that incorporate factual knowledge, replicative knowledge and motivational creation throughout the curriculum of their teacher education programs.

Additionally, professional teacher education programs should transcend teaching approaches that primarily emphasize the role of procedure-oriented and rule-based routinized patterns which potentially constrict practitioners from having opportunities to make responsible decisions about the complex world of teaching as they develop as teacher-researchers.

Professional teacher education programs should be based on a greatly enriched capacity for knowledgeable and responsible decision making on the part of teachers. The challenge is to create new teacher education programs that will support teaching strategies appropriate for every learner in order to achieve higher levels of learning. Teacher training should seek to create practices that are client-oriented and knowledge-based. To professionalize teachers and teaching means that the teacher is not merely responsible for "covering the curriculum" but for connecting it to students in ways that actively help them to construct and use their knowledge in real life. By doing so, students are able to make logical-based informed normative knowledge-based value judgments that reflect societal norms. It means that teachers must be able to meet students on their own terms, at their own starting points, assess their prior interests and knowledge, and provide them with a wide range of strategies to support their success.

Moreover, if we are to prepare teachers for a changing world, then teaching must be recognized as a profession. Teachers ought to be able to conceptualize that teaching is a profession that is clearly linked to democratic purposes in societies that embrace such principles. Teacher qualifications do make a difference in the lives of the students whom they teach. Teachers do matter in the lives of their students and highly qualified teachers do make a substantial positive difference in the education of youth.

Likewise, a professional teacher education program should be organized around a conception of effective teaching that is both content and context-specific. This approach to teaching proposes that teachers must achieve congruence between teacher and students' thinking about the meaning and significance of subject-matter. The development of content and context-specific conceptions of effective teaching and learning through the use of action research is a key component of graduate level teacher education programs. Lieberman (1992) eloquently summarized the shift of focus in research on teaching from focusing on teachers behaviors to the focus on the context of teaching. She stated: "research on teaching, long dominated by a view that attempted to link particular behaviors of teachers to student achievement and thus find generic rules for teachers, is now in the process of shifting its focus to observing the context of teaching, recognizing that diversity rather than uniformity may be the norm" (p. 21).

Similarly, Darling-Hammond & Bransford (2005) shared that standards for learning are higher than ever before and that gaining an education is vital for the success for a nation's citizens to flourish in the 21st century. They stated:

> To meet the expectations they now face, teachers need a new kind of preparation--one that enables them to go beyond "covering the curriculum" to actually enable learning for students who learn in very different ways. Programs that prepare teachers need to consider the demands of today's schools in concert with the growing knowledge base about learning and teaching if they are to support teachers in meeting these expectations. (p. 2)

Accordingly, teachers, administrators, and researchers have been engaged in a variety of activities to improve teaching and students' learning in conjunction with teacher education programs in higher education. This includes looking at the ways teacher education program curricular and outreach service initiatives advance the professional development of teachers. These initiatives range from providing quality professional development to conducting research. Among these initiatives are ways in which teachers can advance their knowledge and professional development through active study and participation in action research as well as outreach efforts offered in higher education. One paradigm of research that was intended to improve teaching is also known as, teacher as researcher. In an effort to promote research by teachers, we provide the reader with exemplary action research studies that teachers conducted in the last two years.

The action research studies that are presented in this book focus on three thematic concepts. These themes are (a) curriculum and schools, (b) instructional strategies and practices, and (c) teacher preparation, professional development and career satisfaction. This book contains fourteen chapters related to these themes that, in particular, showcase teachers' action research projects at the graduate studies level. These chapters cover a variety of educational topics that impact teaching and learning in k-12 settings in the 21st century. It is our desire to share these chapters to contribute to the ongoing emerging knowledge base for teacher education programs representative of the education needs for the 21st century.

References

Darling-Hammond, L. & Bransford, J. (2005) Preparing Teachers for a Changing World: What Teachers Should Learn and Be Able to Do, Jossey-Bass, San Francisco, CA.

Lieberman, A. (1992) Office of Educational Research and Improvement (1992). Secretary's Commission on Achieving Necessary Skills (SCANS). U.S. Department of Education. Washington, D.C.

Carnegie Forum on Education and the Economy. (1986). "A nation prepared: Teachers for the 21st century." Washington, D.C.: The Task Force on Teaching as a Profession. ED 268120.

The National Society for the Study of Education (1992). Yearbook of the National Society for the Study of Education, Chicago, Illinois.

Wei, R., Darling-Hammond, L., Andree, A., Richardson, N. & Orphauos, S. (2009). Professional Learning in the Learning Profession: A Status Report on Teacher Development in the U.S. and Abroad. National Staff Development Council, Stanford University.

Chapter 1: Comics and Graphic Novels: Making Literacy Connections

Kate F. Springer

Introduction

What constitutes a text? Is it just a book? Or is it anything that can be read? Educators today are forced to grapple with this issue. Although many teachers grew up reading books that were checked out from the library, today middle school students spend a majority of their time reading texts online as they browse websites or play online games. In fact, watching movies, scanning trading cards, and reading comic books have recently been placed in the category of text—popular culture text (Xu, Perkins, & Zunich, 2005). Some of these popular texts that students interact with every day may not seem like texts to educators due to the fact that they contain very small amounts of print. However, even texts which demand students to depend on visual skills can help build literacy skills. According to McVicker (2007), "due to the ease and access of information gathering on the Internet, children must have visual literacy skills to comprehend" (p. 85). Therefore in order to help students become literate members of society, educators must address the multimodal, visual aspect of texts today (McVicker, 2007).

Many teachers hold the action of reading books in high regard. Those who teach reading enjoy reading, love to curl up with a good book, and feel that if others just find the right book they too will be hooked. However the truth is that many adolescents do not share teachers' loyalty to reading. Rather, many of these students are loyal to their favorite bands, video games, and celebrities (Alvermann & Hagood, 2000). In fact, as it was reported in the National Assessment of Educational Progress results, only 43% of fourth graders said they read for fun and only 19% of eighth graders reported that they read for enjoyment (Padak & Rasinski, 2007). This is nowhere near where literacy instructors would like the percentages to be! For many young adolescents in the middle grades, the traditional act of reading has taken a backseat to movies, video games, and online activities.

Regardless of what texts are used in teaching, there is still the issue of how students feel about the texts they enjoy reading. In a study conducted by Norton (2003), a student expressed that he felt a text was not a legitimate or school-worthy if it was considered to be fun. Furthermore, children involved in the study felt that adults viewed texts such as comics as a "waste of time" (Norton, 2003, p. 142) when compared to other traditional texts. Studies have shown that many students equate the terms "school text" with "not fun", which has no doubt had detrimental effects on students' perceptions as successful readers in school. Therefore it is important that teachers help pull students back into reading and attempt to use students' interests in popular culture media as a chance to legitimize students' out of school literacy activities (Morrison, Bryan, & Chilcoat, 2002). Additionally, as expressed by Norton (2003) by using media that grabs student interest, teachers can again "reclaim literacy as a meaning-making practice" (p. 140).

Due to young adolescents' interest in popular media, it is clear that students' interests and teachers' interests can be dramatically different. So how can educators validate students' interests and at the same time help them develop the skills they will need to be effective readers? Instead of asking students to leave their interests behind, teachers can implore popular media to help students think critically about the world and texts around them. As stated by Morrison, Bryna, and Chilcoat (2002), "there is no denying that popular culture is popular" (p. 759). It is what students enjoy and what grabs their interest. Therefore why not take the media that students are so interested in, the popular culture texts, and bring those into classroom activities? After all, recent research concludes that bringing popular media into the classroom can spark interest and work towards reaching the standards in a way that grabs students' attention (Xu, Perkins, & Zunich, 2005). Rather than forcing students to leave their interests at home, educators must find ways to pull students back into reading—to make reading instruction relate to the multimodal aspect of students' everyday lives and help literacy instruction become more cohesive for students (Rowsell, 2006).

One popular culture text that has been debated by educators and researchers alike is the comics. Even before World War II, comics and comic strips were popular. American politics have been portrayed in comics, the United States Postal service has issued stamps of famous comic characters, and comic strip text has even been read into the Congressional Records (Wright & Sherman, 2006). As stated by Wright and Sherman (2006), "comic characters such as Popeye, Superman, Batman, Peanuts, and Garfield have become American icons" (p. 165). These comic book characters are not bound by the ends of the pages, rather they can be found on television, apparel, toys, and advertisements (Wright & Sherman, 2006). Presently, comic books have become all the frenzy due to their tie in with popular movies and the surge of Japanese animation (Bitz, 2004).

From an educational standpoint, comics may range anywhere from a first a grade to a high school reading level (Wright & Sherman, 2006). Similarly, the content can be as innocent as a kindergarten scene or geared towards adults with a political motive. Wright and Sherman (2006) conducted a study to analyze fifty-eight comic strips in order to gain more information about the structure of comics.

The researchers sought to identify the number of sentences and syllables per comic strip, readability estimate, and orientation of the comic. Of the comics studied, nineteen percent had a story line and eighty-one percent were humorous with a joke theme. Regardless of the orientation of the comic strip, it was found that comic strips were certainly at the readability level of both elementary school and high school students (Wright & Sherman, 2006).

Children and adults alike sift through the paper to read the funnies or go online to view comics. With the shift towards online newspapers and methods of print, many comics are available in an online format as well (Wright & Sherman, 2006). Moreover, there are now new hardcover and paperback collections of comics; in fact, the numbers of hardcover and paperback collections are highest they have ever been in America (Wolk, 2000). Another comic-based text of interest is graphic novels. Graphic novels are longer than comics and usually have a beginning, middle, and end. As stated by Haynes (2009), "one form of graphic novels collects complete story arcs that first appeared in comic book form, but that type is only a subset of the overall graphic novel universe" (p. 10). Most graphic novels are dependent on both pictures and text. A particular group of graphic novels that are quite popular now is manga, or Japanese comics. Many of these texts are published in their original form, which means they are read from back to front and right to left, and are translated into English. Graphic novels have become quite popular among adolescents recently. In fact, YALSA (a division of ALA) now publishes a "Great Graphic Novels for Teens" list each year in order to select the top graphic novels (Haynes, 2009).

Just as the comic genre has been around for over a half of a century, the controversy regarding comics has also been long-lived. Those in favor of using comics in the classroom welcome the chance to further develop visual literacy skills and use comics as a method of improving comprehension and grammar skills (McVicker, 2007). These teachers feel that comics can be used to pique student interest in another form of text. Thinking that perhaps comics can provide an alternative avenue for some students who have "tuned out" the idea of reading for fun, there are teachers welcome the idea of incorporating comics into the classroom (Cleaver, 2008). On the other hand, those opposed to using comics as a teaching genre feel that all the graphics in comics are a distraction. Moreover, it is thought that both the plot and characters are left underdeveloped. In a study conducted by Norton (2003), some pre-service teachers have expressed that they would prefer to use "actual books" (p. 141) over comics because they believe comics are not very educational and do not focus what they feel are the important elements of literacy.

Rationale for the Study

Despite the numerous articles reporting comics being read by the American public and the interest of graphic novels being at its peak, little research has explored how children view these particular texts. While there is evidence suggesting that these texts are popular culture texts, there is little evidence that suggests whether or not students would want to have these texts integrated into their school curriculum. Likewise, research done to explore the fact as to whether or not students feel comics and graphic novels are indeed a form of reading is lacking. One study conducted by Norton (2003) provided an example when a student felt that comics were not considered real texts because comics were fun

(Norton, 2003). But are there other reasons students do not consider comics as texts? It is possible that students view comics as something dramatically different than what we are doing in school when we discuss fictional stories. Perhaps students are not seeing the connections that adults have drawn without the ties being described explicitly.

Additional information also needs to be collected when it comes to analyzing how students interact with comics they read. Do they just read them and then put them in the recycling bin? Or are students hooked in a series of graphic novels and discuss them with their peers? All of this information will help educators have a better idea of how students interact with the popular culture text of comics. Gathering data with regards to students' ideas about comics and how they relate to material read in school will help teachers effectively integrate comics into the curriculum. After all, if educators are to integrate popular culture texts into the curriculum, it must be done in a way that follows suite with students' perceptions about comics and ways of interacting with the text.

Statement of the Problem

In response to No Child Left Behind and the push to continue to make adequate yearly progress, there is no doubt that educators feel a pull to meet the standards. However, research has shown that part of becoming a strong reader involves reading a lot of text. With only 43% of fourth graders and 19% of eighth graders reporting that they read for fun (Padak & Rasinski, 2007), it is clear that we must do something to not only engage students in reading activities outside of school, but also find a way to connect home and school literacy experiences (Morrison, Bryan, & Chilcoat, 2002). Teachers must be aware of what students in their classrooms are reading for fun and why they are reading it. For example, are the students interested in a particular theme, genre, or style of writing? It is critical that teachers are aware of this so that they can help scaffold other fun literacy experiences. For if the ultimate goal is to create lifelong readers, we must build upon the foundation students have already constructed. Learning more about this foundation—unveiling further information about student interests—is a way for educators to set the scene for future literacy development.

Due to the fact that "the structure of a comic book is similar to that of a storybook in terms of story elements" (Xu, Perkins, & Zunich, 2005, p. 107), the purpose of my study is to explore the perceptions students have about comics. I would like to learn more about how students view comics with regards to reading and whether or not comics count as "real reading" for the students in my class. Another equally important purpose is to explore whether or not the fifth graders are able to verbalize any connections they see between comics and fiction stories. Students describing perceived connections (or lack thereof) will allow insight as to whether or not the home reading of comics is being connected with concepts in the academic setting.

A minor purpose of my study is to try to examine the perceptions students feel adults have with regards to comics. Perhaps one of the reasons why students are not making connections between texts at school is due to the fact that they feel adults would not fully appreciate the genre of their particular interest. With reading for fun happening so infrequently among middle school students, it is imperative that educators are aware of students' ideas about home reading interests and popular culture texts as well as ways in which these texts can be infused into everyday literacy lessons (Xu, Perkins, & Zunich, 2005). It is my goal through this research that I will be able to provide educators with some insight into the realm of comics and how it pertains to students at the upper elementary grade levels.

Literature Review

The comic genre has been alive for nearly one hundred years, yet the popularity of comics has changed dramatically throughout the last century. Should comics remain only in the Sunday newspaper? Or should they continue to branch out on more websites and be bound into new books? With fewer people purchasing daily newspapers, the fate of the comic genre remains unclear (Wright & Sherman, 2006). Regardless of what the future holds for this genre, children, adults, and especially educators, must stop and consider what the comic genre can currently provide for students. What impact can comics have on children and their literacy growth? The question to ponder is not what will come of comics, but rather, how these comics can positively influence the children of the future. Research has shown that comics are indeed influencing students, which may be shaping both home and school literacy experiences.

Bridging the Gap between School and Home

In school, students spend time reading texts that their teachers have chosen. As was described by a participant in Norton's study (2003), students often feel that texts read in school have a prescribed meaning which allows little wiggle room for creativity. For example, while at school students feel they must look up words that they do not know or ask an adult if something in the story seems unclear. As they read school texts, students often feel that there is one concept they must take away from the story-one right answer that only those who are studious or "good readers" will find after profound digging (Norton, 2003). The process described by the participant in Norton's interview (2003) almost seemed like the method of searching for the buried treasure; it was something that only those who worked really diligently could find.

If the situation described previously is indeed how a majority of our students in public schools are feeling, then they are left wondering what steps to take and what they should be saying rather than truly relating to the text and creating individual experiences. It seems that some students may be left wondering what the right answer is and believe that the teacher holds the solution to the story—or the key to the buried treasure. As stated by Norton (2003), "school-authorized literacy practices have, for many of them, become rituals in which teachers define "good," "proper," and "challenging."" (p. 145). This feeling that there is only one right way to read and interpret the story can easily create a power struggle between student and teacher as the student may have negative consequences for not producing an accurate response or interest to the text (Norton, 2003).

At home students may choose texts that are dramatically different from those required during school hours. Some children are required to read silently at home while others may read along with their parent(s). Still, some children choose to not even pick up a book after school hours. Many students would rather watch television, play video games, or browse the Internet than read a book from the teacher's suggested book list. Nonetheless, when children choose to engage in literacy activities at home, chances are these activities are quite different from those at school. At home children may read magazines, hypermedia texts, or comic books (Xu, Perkins, & Zunich, 2005). Furthermore, when children come across an unfamiliar word, they are more likely to skip it or ask a family member (Norton, 2003). Therefore the literacy activities students engage in after school hours may vary greatly from those practiced within classroom walls.

Alternative Texts and Critical Literacy

This gap between school reading and home reading can be seen clearly in students' responses regarding texts. During Norton's (2003) study, a child expressed that home reading was fun, and school was not. That comment alone screams out that something must be done! Why is it that students perceive school reading to be less enjoyable and so automatically different? Although some adults would not view surfing the internet, playing video games, or looking at a comic book as a literacy experience, it is imperative that we step back from the situation and inspect what it is exactly that children engage in during these out of school activities. Students do not need to be holding a book in order to be practicing literacy skills. When reading a magazine, children must decode and comprehend; as they browse the internet, children must decode and make meaning from texts and illustrations, all while determining the significance of information found (Xu, Perkins, & Zunich, 2005). Lastly, when looking at a comic strip, children must interpret the many layers of the text-words, visual, and pictorial-and analyze their meaning as these three relate together (Cleaver, 2008). Children are in fact applying reading strategies as they engage in these activities.

So are these after-school activities truly problematic for children? Or must we as adults change our idea of literacy? Many researchers in the field have indeed changed their view of literacy to include these popular culture texts that children readily interact with outside of school. According to Xu, Perkins, and Zunich (2005), "a popular culture text often is made up of print and nonprint text" (p. 5). These popular culture texts may include items from the following areas: videos, films, Internet websites, music, trading cards, comic books, and video games (Xu, Perkins, & Zunich, 2005). Rather than dissuade students to engage in these alternative literacy experiences, educators must capitalize on similarities between popular culture texts and traditional texts (Cleaver, 2008). Just as some adults may hold particular texts to a high regard, students also hold their video games, comic books, or trading cards—their alternative texts—to a high regard (Alverman & Hagood, 2000).

The difference between the texts at school and alternative texts at home can create quite the gap in literacy experience for students. At school students engage in one type of task, and at home it may seem completely different; thus creating quite dissonance! As stated by Semali (2003), "the gulf between education inside the classroom, which remains heavily print based, and outside of school continues to grow" (p. 275). It is important to question then the type of impact this abyss has on students. Researchers have found that this gap between the two causes students to struggle with literacy concepts. However it is not just students who are low in reading skills who struggle. Students who have the ability and the skills could still fall behind in school activities due to the dissonance between activities; what appears to be a knowledge gap in a student could instead be a fissure in experiences (Pressley, Billman, Perry, Reffitt, & Reynolds, 2007). Debruin-Parecki and Krol-Sinclair (2003) explained that "there is good evidence that some children fail not because they lack intellectual ability or motivation to learn, but rather, at least in part, because their home and school lives lack congruence" (p. 25).

So then what can educators do in order to close the gap and diminish the incongruence? Rather than keeping school and home literacy distant, educators can tap into what students are already learning naturally at home (Cleaver, 2008). It is beneficial for teachers to use the texts that students engage in outside of school and find a way to fuse some of these alternative texts into the curriculum (Morrison, Bryan, & Chilcoat, 2002). Bringing alternative texts into the curriculum will help students take ownership of literacy experiences. When students see how the text and concepts taught at school fit into their everyday lives, the literacy experiences will allow them to be truly "meaning making" (Norton, 2003, p. 146). As stated by Morrison et al. (2002), "popular culture is integral to the lives of most middle school students. Use of popular culture can, therefore, diminish the disparity children perceive between their lives in and out of school by legitimizing many of their after school pursuits" (p. 758-9). It is in this process that students will begin to understand that literacy skills taught at school are not abstract. Contrary to their belief, concepts discussed within the classroom walls do relate to their lives! Reading is not just a ritual with a teacher holding the answer key, but rather a process that can be unique to each individual (Norton, 2003). By bringing texts that are integral parts of the students' lives into the classroom, we can begin to show young adolescents just how essential reading is to their future.

Equally important is the idea that students will become critical users of the media around them. This means that students will start to become aware of the elements of alternative texts they engage in independent reading. Students should be encouraged to ask questions about what they see or read—whether the text is a book, website, or graphic novel (Semali, 2003). Asking students to analyze everyday texts will encourage students to be active readers and more importantly, to take ownership! Norton (2003) describes that "if children are to engage meaningfully with a text, they need to have a sense of ownership with the text, and it is from this sense of ownership that pleasure derives" (p. 146). It is every literacy teacher's goal that his/her students will take ownership and enjoy texts read both in and out of school.

How must the reading curriculum change in order to promote students to think critically about the texts around them and take ownership of these experiences? Researchers such as Norton (2003), Xu et al. (2005), and Cleaver (2008) propose that we must bring these alternative texts into the classroom. Alternative texts such as ones from the comic genre have so much to offer students! While this may seem a little odd at first, it is important to remember the responsibility the reading curriculum has to each student. As described by Au, Carroll, and Scheu (1998), the reading curriculum should be "tailored to the strengths, needs, and interests of the students, community, and teachers" (p. 71). Therefore it is the educator's responsibility to make sure the curriculum is equally tied to standards and students' interests. Building on prior and home literacy experiences can give educators an advantage. Dewey (1998) stated long ago that "the beginning of instruction shall be made with the experience learners already have; that this experience and the capacities that have been developed during its course provide the starting point for all further learning" (p. 88). So it makes sense then that educators tie in texts from literacy experiences students have at home in order to strengthen the connection between school and home literacy development. After all, it is this connection that will improve the likelihood that students become lifelong learners and readers.

Since there are so many alternative texts out there, it may be more beneficial to focus on one genre-the comic genre. It is important to analyze how this genre can be used to bridge the gap in literacy experiences. Comics can be seen in the daily newspapers, magazines, online, and even posted on walls of workspaces. Comics are readily accessible and free. Additionally, they can be a daily representation of real life. Comics represent the world around us as it changes, and they have captured the interest of both adults and children alike (McVicker 2007).

Elements of Comics

At first glance a comic strip may appear to be merely graphics with a smattering of a few words. However, the comic genre truly contains a text structure with a story to tell! In order to read and comprehend comics, the reader must blend the print and graphics. After reading just a few frames, it becomes evident that readers must possess visual literacy skills (McVicker, 2007). Items from the comic genre may be expository, narrative, or historical fiction (Morrison et al., 2002). Not all comics are cartoons; in fact, many comics can be quite complex (Rowsell, 2006). The content for some comics has been derived from everyday experiences, politics, romance, and crime. While other comics—some of the most successful comics—push reality. A larger group of comic plots go beyond the truth and contain superheroes, super powers, and science fantasy (Xu et al., 2005).

In order to delve deeper into the structure of comics, Wright and Sherman (2006) completed a readability study of fifty-eight comic strips. Surprisingly, the comics analyzed all fell within a first through seventh grade reading level with a majority of them falling well within a fifth grade reading level (Wright & Sherman, 2006). This statistic alone indicates that comics can be "a viable literacy source for classrooms" and that "newspaper funnies are suitable for school age children" (Wright & Sherman, 2006, p. 168). While 81% of the comics examined had a humorous orientation, 19% actually had a storyline that readers could follow (Wright & Sherman, 2006). This storyline statistic indicates that there are instances when readers must follow a plot, just as readers would follow a plot in other texts. When comic series are gathered in chronological order, the text structure begins to look more like the text structure in a storybook in terms of story elements such as character and setting as well as plot problem and resolution (Xu et al., 2005).

Also in the comic genre are graphic novels. Graphic novels are a long form of a comic book (Morrison et al., 2002). Graphic novels can encompass the humor, fantasy, mystery, science fiction, and even nonfiction genres. Like comics, graphic novels depend on both pictures and text (Haynes, 2009). Some argue that graphic novels' texts with pictures and other elements unique to the comic genre may require more skills than genres that solely depend on text. For pieces in this genre require readers to understand dialogue, point of view, how color affects emotion, and also how the layers of the text fit together (Schwarz, 2002). The graphic novel genre contains more than just superheroes or super heroines; these texts also have plot structures similar to those accepted texts in the fiction genre (Xu et al., 2005).

Both comics and graphic novels can be part of a series that connects a body of readers. However a difference between the two is length—graphic novels are longer, bound in book form, and contain a complete story. One can see that graphic novels have multiple panels or pictures on each page (Haynes, 2009). A graphic novel essentially tells a story in comic form. There is a problem and resolution with all the elements that one would find in a narrative story (Xu et al., 2005). Additionally, graphic novels "have become much more prominent in popular culture in general" (Haynes, 2009, p. 10). A few examples of graphic novels that have recently been popular are *Jimmy Corrigan, the Smartest Kid on Earth*, the *Bone* series, and the *X-Men* series (Wolk, 2000). In his article, Wolk (2000) states that "every couple of years there's a graphic novel so strong that it pulls in tens of thousands of new readers who haven't looked at comics in decades" (p. 38). What makes the pull even stronger is the media connection. Many of these graphic novels are paired with movies or television series (Rowsell, 2006). *X-Men* is a great example of a graphic novel that can be seen on the big screen, in the toy store, and also in the graphic novel section (Wolk, 2000).

Another specific text in the comic genre is m*anga*, or Japanese comics. These comics are bound in the traditional Japanese way with the spine of the book on the right side. The unique binding requires readers to flip pages from the left, almost as if you had turned a traditional American book over and read it back to front. Characters in this genre tend to wear bright clothes, have pointy hair, and must rely on problem solving and mathematics throughout the plot (Rowsell, 2006). The plots can be almost like a soap opera and *manga* tends to attract a multicultural audience (Wax, 2002). Some examples of *manga* comic books are *Sailor Moon, Dark Horse,* and the *Pokemon* series. Manga comics are quite commercialized too—with television shows, movies, trading cards, and action figures (Wolk, 2000).

Student and Adult Perception

With the abundance of intriguing features, it is clear to see why young adolescents are so captivated with comic genre texts. Comic books, graphic novels, and *manga* can really draw students into the frames! In Norton's study (2003) it was documented that children who like comics often read them together, discuss latest releases, and debate about the texts. As she interviewed *Archie* comic readers, Norton (2003) found that there is a sense of "literate underlife" (p. 144) as students swap comics, engage in texts, and share insights with friends regarding particular comic books. There is in fact "an unofficial curriculum in which much learning, debate, and engagement take place (Norton, 2003, p. 144). Is this not the same debate that teachers try to create in their literacy classrooms every day? Many teachers try, without avail, to engage students in discussions with school readings.   However, there is research to show that students automatically engage in these discussions with texts they enjoy (Norton, 2003). Why is it that connections are not made between the comic curriculum and our school literacy curriculum? Perhaps educators could see different results if these connections were made!

The omission of comics in school literacy lessons has fueled students' belief that texts which are interesting and entertaining are not the ones classified as "school" texts. Students believe that reading comics is fun, and therefore comics cannot be a legitimate selection for reading lessons. In Norton's study (2003) participants explained that when they read for fun they have a certain amount of control in the reading process; something they must not feel while reading school texts (Norton, 2003). Perchance comics seem to be too much fun to bring into school; however it is unfortunate that school and home texts are so disconnected. If something why is it automatically (in a student's mind) not a school lesson? The notion that school texts cannot be fun, but rather a process or ritual is quite alarming for today's educators (Norton, 2003).

Additionally, adult perceptions of comics have most likely enhanced the dissention between home and school. Whether or not it is true, children believe that many adults feel comics are a waste of time (Norton, 2003). If students feel this way, then it makes sense that they would draw a dividing line between comics and school reading. Some teachers have been quoted saying that they believe "students will become distracted by the pictures" in comics (Norton, 2003, p. 144). However if students are already reading comics, it only seems natural to build on this activity. Research has shown that comics have the power to pull in even the most reluctant readers. Why then would educators diminish that literacy activity at school? It makes sense rather that teachers should capitalize on the literacy experiences that are connected to students' lives (Cleaver, 2008).

It may be that it is time to throw out the idea that some texts are "proper" (Norton, 2003) and just try to build on what it is that students are naturally interested in reading (Morrison et al., 2002). Not to mention that the literacy skills addressed in school could help students become stronger consumers of the media outside of the classroom. It is our job as educators to help students ask questions about what they see and read with regards to texts and media both inside and outside of the classroom (Semali, 2003). It seems fitting then that discussing alternative genres such as comics would help students become better-rounded in analyzing the print media world that surrounds them.

Finding a Place for the Comic Genre

Some school districts have made the connection between school and alternative texts in order to answer the call to tie comics into the school curriculum. Bitz (2004) reports that a school district in New York City created a Comic Book Project where 733 children at 33 after-school sites met to brainstorm, sketch, write, and create their own comic books. The goal of this program was to motivate children to attend program sessions and take pride in their work. Academically speaking, the program aimed at aiding children who had limited English proficiency or were struggling in the school environment build textual and visual concepts. The project also allowed its participants to "explore their own social worlds when they read and write" (Bitz, 2004, p. 575). The comic clubs met 1-2 times a week and walked children through the steps to create a comic book. Students had the option to write about their own life and the instructors were trained on how to facilitate students through the writing and illustrating steps (Bitz, 2004).

As one can imagine, the task of creating a comic book was not necessarily easy for the children involved in the Comic Book Project. However, with much help and guidance, children started taking ownership of their work. Comic books were written about the hard realities of these children's inner-city environment: drug abuse, gang violence, difficult family situations, and other real life stories. The final project produced was meaningful to each student, and it helped build literacy experiences. One site coordinator from the study (Bitz, 2005) stated,

> I think kids were skeptical at first about the project because they didn't believe they were going to be able to make their own comics. But after spending some time talking about what was going to happen, and also seeing that they could really do it, they got really excited. We have kids who are normally bouncing off the wall, but this really helped them focus. And some of those kids produced incredible work. (p. 577).

The instructors and students participating in the Comic Book Project were surveyed upon its completion. According to Bitz (2004), students responded that as a result of the comic book project, 88% of them would look at pictures in order to find clues for the story, while 92% stated that they liked to write their own stories. Moreover, an instructor responded that "This was the first time that I got my kids to write without complaining about it" (Bitz, 2004, p. 582). Lastly, it is important to note that this project helped students meet the local standards in untraditional, and perhaps unexpected, ways (Bitz, 2004). The Comic Book Project was clearly a positive way to tie something students enjoy into literacy experiences.

The inclusion of comics in the school activities does not need to be limited to after school programs. Rather, it would make sense that educators infuse the comic genre into classroom activities within the school day. While students could create texts of the comic genre during core subject activities, it also makes sense that students have the chance to read alternative texts during literacy blocks. In his article, Ranker (2007) describes a classroom that infused comics into the curriculum via read-alouds. In this study the second grade classroom teacher read comics out loud just as she would read other pieces of literature. The goal of reading texts such as *Spider Man, Wild Girl,* and *Hulk* aloud was to increase reading comprehension as well as recognize problem and resolution in narrative text structures. The classroom teacher also explored character traits through comics (Ranker, 2007).

Ranker (2007) reports that as the classroom teacher opened the comic book to read students cheered and the characters immediately caught the children's attention. For those students who have read comics, it was most likely a warming experience to see their home texts placed in the school setting! Yet in this instance the comics were not just heartwarming, they were a useful academic tool. Watching students think critically about character traits and plot, Ranker (2007) reports that comics gave the students in Ms. Stephen's classroom interesting, motivating reading material that she used to engage them in learning various aspects of reading processes—as well as opportunities to write, think, and discuss texts as they learn new literacy practices. (p. 304).

Additionally, students were made aware of the fact that they could read many alternative texts with a more critical perspective (Ranker, 2007). In the grand scheme of reading, is this not what we want our students to achieve? By using multiliteracy texts educators can help students begin to analyze character development, plots lines, and storyboards in all the media they choose to engage in outside of school (Wax, 2002).

Another important aspect that comic books bring to the classroom table is the possibility of drawing in reluctant readers. Not only can comics be seen as a learning tool (Bitz, 2004), but they are a great way to "pique reluctant readers' interest and challenge those students who are fluent in more traditional literature" (Cleaver, 2008, p. 28). The humor in comics can help reluctant readers enjoy reading. In a way, it can be thought of as an "ingenious hook" (McVicker, 2007, p. 86). Those students who might find school texts boring could be drawn in by the bright graphics and dialogue. However, comics should not be limited to re-teaching and lessons with low readers! Comics have something to offer to all students (Cleaver, 2008). Just as comics can be used for lessons on development of characters and plot, teachers may also use comics to help reinforce comprehension, grammar, and literacy text structure (McVicker, 2007) or irony and foreshadowing (Wright & Sherman, 2006) in a way that makes students feel successful. The texts that teachers pull for literacy exploration do not have to be all upper level texts. Rather, educators can pull alternative texts that children find less intimidating (and more interesting) in order to reinforce the idea that literacy is all around us and is something students can be successful at! Allington (2006) reports that "tasks completed with high rates of success were linked to greater learning and improved student attitudes toward the subject matter being learned" (p. 58). So why not create situations where children can work with comics and enjoy literacy activities in a genre they feel comfortable with? Better yet, if students are not familiar with the comic genre, why not expose them to another form of literacy? There is nothing to lose with infusing a little bit of fun and success into our literacy curriculum!

Whether it is helping students make connections between comics and the fiction genre, practicing a grammar skill or working on comprehension of a science lesson, comics do indeed have a place in the classroom. It is imperative that educators start realizing the niche of the comic genre in order to capitalize on students' prior knowledge and boost students' literacy skills. In today's world where students engage in multimedia texts outside of school, we must begin to bridge the gap between school and home experiences (Xu et al., 2005). For if we do not address the hole, the dissonance between school and home experiences will continue to widen—thus making school texts seem more like a ritual than an experience (Norton, 2003). Regardless of the debate over comics, educators must continue to look into student perceptions about popular culture text, especially the ever so popular comic genre.

While many tie-ins to school literacy experiences have been proposed, few results have been documented.

It is clear that more research must be done in this area. The children of our country's future deserve a chance to express how they perceive comics, and educators must document new approaches with alternative texts in school literacy activities. This is an area of new research that certainly warrants the need for a closer examination and it is my personal goal to delve deeper into this part of research! For if we are unable to connect students home and school experiences, we will indeed fail to create a body of lifelong readers who think critically about the world around them. Instead, we will allow students to remain stagnant in this area of dissension where school and home learning do not mesh. It is clear that researchers must dig deeper in the area of critical literacy—for this may be an exceptional way to build positive and meaningful literacy experiences throughout the school curriculum!

Methodology

Participants

This study was conducted in a Midwestern school district in Illinois. The district population is approximately 1,050 students of which 95 students are at the fifth grade level. This study involved a sample of 21 fifth grade students, which is one of the four sections of fifth grade. Typical class size ranges from 16-26 students among all grade levels Kindergarten-12th grade (Northern Illinois University, 2009).

Socioeconomically, students in this school district range from lower to upper class with the majority of students being in the mid-high range. The low income rate of students is about eight percent. Just as there is little diversity in socioeconomic class, there is also little diversity in the area of ethnicity. The demographics are as follows: 95% Caucasian, 2% African American, 1% Hispanic, 1.5% Asian, and less than 1% Native American. The high school graduation rate is 97% and the mobility rate is very low (Northern Illinois University, 2009. Although the majority of the students within the district are Caucasian, students come from many different home backgrounds.

The participants of this study are fifth graders in one of the four homerooms at Tri-Valley Middle School. Children range from ages 10-12 and all students in the homeroom were invited to participate in the study. The homeroom contains 24 students; more specifically, 11 boys and 13 girls. None of the students have been asked to repeat fifth grade and all students started the school at the same Middle School.

Instruments

The intention of this study was to gather information regarding how often students read comics and how they feel about the legitimacy of the comic genre as a text. For this reason, the researcher conducted a survey to collect data from all the students in the study regarding their feelings about comics. The survey was created by the researcher and worded in student-friendly language so that fifth graders could easily answer each question. For the purposes of this study, the survey was a great way to gather this data because the researcher is looking to describe trends, interests, and opinions about comics and how comics relate to school reading (Creswell, 2005). The survey used in this project has twelve questions. The first five questions ask students how much they read at home and how they feel about reading comics. The last seven questions have a Liker scale and ask students to rate how much they agree with statements about comics.

After the initial survey, there was a follow-up focus group. Using the information students gave on the survey, the researcher interviewed the four students who responded to reading comics most frequently. This way the students in the focus group truly were the ones who are most familiar with comics and have had the most interactions with the comic genre. The interview questions were created by the researcher and aim at digging a little deeper into students' perceptions of the comic genre as well as any connections that students might see between comics and fiction reading in school. The interviews were done one-on-one with the four students selected based on the survey results and will be conducted by the homeroom teacher—who is also the researcher. The one-on-one interviews were helpful to gather more information from students as they allow students to "provide comments that go beyond the initial questions" (Creswell, 2005, p. 361).

Lastly, the study involves gathering the four students interviewed for a small group discussion. In the discussion, students used a Venn diagram to compare and contrast a comic strip with a fiction story the class has read in school. All four students were familiar with both texts; they were provided at school and read by all students. During the small group discussion students considered the similarities and/or differences between the two genres. The researcher collected data during the discussion as well as analyzed the notes students write on the Venn diagram.

Research Questions

1. Do fifth graders feel comics are a legitimate text to read?
2. Are fifth graders aware of any similarities between comics/graphic novels and stories from the fiction genre? The primary focus for this question is in regards to literary elements; however any suggested commonalities will be noted for research purposes.
3. How do fifth graders perceive adults feel about comics as a reading genre?

Definitions of Terms

Alternative texts - texts that are not traditional books or basal readers

Comics – texts that have frames, cartoons, or speech/thought bubbles to convey a message to the reader

Fifth grade – students ages 10-12

Graphic novel – a longer book that has comics and pictures to convey meaning to the reader

Popular culture text – texts that exist in students' lives outside the school walls, texts that a student willingly engages in without school requirements

Limitations of the Study

The researcher has identified the following limitations that could impact this study:

- The small groups of students participating in this study are all from the same homeroom in the same small school district. Therefore the information gathered from this study is most relevant to other students in the same school district around the same age group. It would not be accurate to generalize the results of this study to all fifth graders across the state or the country because the research sample is so small and the participants were not randomly selected.
- The researcher is the homeroom teacher for the group of students participating in the study. This may influence students' participation in the study as well as the responses on the survey, interviews, and discussions.
  - Students have been exposed to comics as a genre in Language, Math, and Science already in the school year. This is a normal part of the fifth grade curriculum at their school; the curriculum was not altered in any way for this study.

Data Analysis

For the purposes of this study, there are several different types of data collected: the survey given to all students, the interview of the four selected students, and then the Venn diagram created by those four students in a small group. The survey data gathered was analyzed using SPSS. The researcher looked for means and percentages as they relate to students' responses. It is important to look at the mean and standard deviation in student responses on the initial survey in order to gather data about how a large sample of fifth graders in the school district feel with regards to how the comic genre relates to what they consider "legitimate" texts. It is also imperative that the researcher learns how students perceive adults feel about their reading interests. Tables and graphs will be created to represent students' responses in order to depict trends in the data analyzed.

The data collected in the interviews was recorded and analyzed to delve further into students' perceptions regarding the comic genre. This data was categorized and the researcher looked for emerging themes. Emerging themes and the Venn diagram created by students were recorded and recreated in order to present it in the research findings of this study. The researcher triangulated the data to find out if the qualitative responses support the quantitative data conclusions.

Only those four students who read comics were part of the interview and diagram data sets in order to insure that the data is truly taken from avid comic readers. Lastly, the qualitative data taken from these two instruments were not analyzed using SPSS because the purpose for this data was to look into a few unique cases rather than draw broad conclusions.

Results

Participation

Of the 24 students asked to participate in this study, 21 agreed to participate and took the survey. The 87.5% participation rate makes the data collected in the survey a strong representation of the researcher's homeroom class. Although it would have been ideal to have all students in the class participate, the 87.5% participation rate is considered acceptable by most research standards (Creswell, 2005). Out of those responding to the survey, 57% were girls and 43% were boys. While more girls participated in the survey than boys, the sample is still a fair representation of the researcher's classroom population because the researcher's homeroom consists of 13 girls and 11 boys. The four students who responded to the survey as reading comics most often were also interviewed by the researcher. This group consisted of two girls and two boys and these four students worked together to complete the Venn diagram. These four students had been in the same homeroom for seven months of the school year and had worked together many times during the current school year.

Survey Results

The second question on the survey asked students to identify texts they read at home from the following group: magazines, newspapers, recipes (either in books or on cards), books, comics (either in books or in the newspaper), websites, trading cards, and advertisements. Students were allowed to check as many texts as were true for them. Figure 1 shows student responses to this survey question and also compares responses by gender. In response to the question regarding texts read at home, 54.5% selected magazines, 27.3% selected newspapers, 13.6% selected recipes, 59.7% selected books, 36.4% selected comics, 54.5% selected websites, 9.1% selected trading cards, and 18.2% selected advertisements. Furthermore, girls had higher response rates to the magazine, newspaper, book, comic, website and advertisement categories while boys had higher response rates to the recipe and trading cards categories. It is important to note, however, that the whole class response rate did not exceed 60.0% for any category.

When students were asked how often they read comics at home, the responses were as follows: 4.5% read comics every day, 9.1% read comics several times a week, 13.6% read comics several times a month, 27.3% read comics several times a year, and 45.5% responded that they never read comics. These comparisons can be seen in Figure 2. Students selected to be interviewed and participate in the Venn diagram discussion came from the "Everyday", "Several times a week" and "Several times a month" categories.

Figure 1: Texts read at home responses

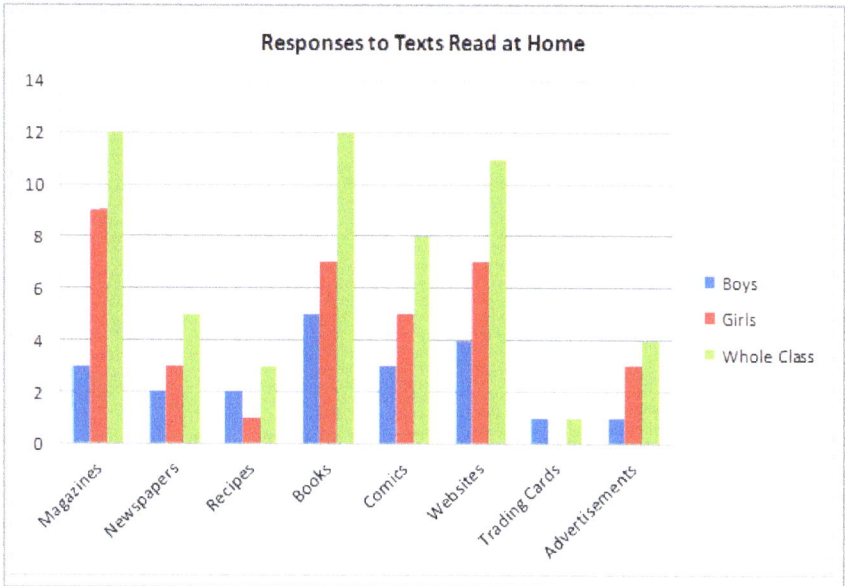

Figure 2: How often comics are read
The next two questions on the survey were about students' perceptions of how

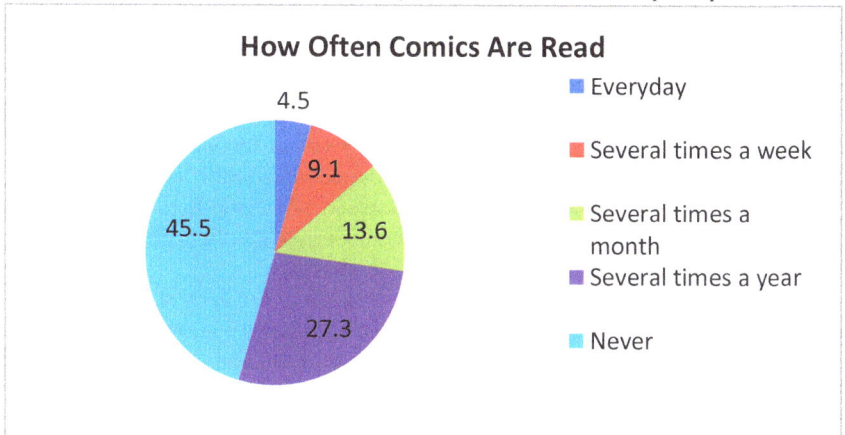

their parents and their teachers would feel about them reading comics; this data is presented in Table 1. No student thought that their parents or teachers would strongly disagree with their choice to read comics. However, 4.5% of students thought their parents would disagree with them reading comics and home at 22.7% of students thought their teachers would disagree with them reading comics at school. In their responses, 81.8% of students thought their parents would not care if they read comics at home and 36.4% said their teachers would not care if they read comics at school. Only 4.5% of students said their parents would agree with them reading comics at home and that corresponded with 27.3% stating they felt their teachers would agree with them reading comics at school. Lastly, 9.1% of students said their parents would strongly agree with them reading comics at home and 13.6% said they felt their teachers would strongly agree with them reading comics at school.

Table One: Student Perception of Adult and Teacher Feelings

Survey item	How do you think your parents would feel about you reading comics at home?	How do you think your teachers would feel about your reading comics at school?
Strongly agree	9.1%	13.6%
Agree	4.5%	27.3%
Not care	81.8%	36.4%
Disagree	4.5%	22.7%
Strongly Disagree	0.00%	0.00%

For the last half of the survey, students were given a set of statements and asked to indicate how much they agreed or disagreed with the statement. The following scale was used for student responses: 5 means you strongly agree; 4 means you agree; 3 means you are indifferent; 2 means you disagree; and 1 means you strongly disagree. Table 2 shows the mean and standard deviation for student responses to each question. When asked if comics were a legitimate text and if reading comics can be classified as reading, the average response was "indifferent" or "agree". Students were also averaging in the "indifferent" area when asked to take a stance to the statement, "I use the same strategies when I read comics and when I read stories." More than half of the students agreed on some level that comics are fun to read.

But students were quite divided with the statement, "I would prefer reading comics more than reading a book." Students were again divided in regards to whether or not they would like to read more comics at school. There was not a strong response for students who like to get comic books at the library, bookstore, or book fairs. Lastly, when students were asked to responds to the statement, "Comics are like the stories we read at school during Reading class," the mean response was between "disagree" and "strongly disagree".

Since the sample size was smaller, the frequency for each student response can also show quite a bit about student responses. Figure 3 shows the frequency of each student response for seven of the survey questions. About 40.9% of students stated that they agreed reading comics can be classified as reading, just like reading a book is classified as reading. Students' responses were more divided as to whether or not "book reading" strategies are used when comics are read. A majority of students responded that they agreed or strongly agreed when that comics are fun to read. With regards to what text they would prefer and whether or not they would like to read more comics at school, students were again quite divided on the issue as the chart on the next page clearly shows! Figure 4 shows exactly 50% of students responded that they were "indifferent" as to whether or not they like getting comic books from the library, bookstore, book fair or book orders, with 22.7% of students saying that they would *not* like to get comics to read. A final interesting data piece is that 77.3% of students strongly disagreed or disagreed that comics were like the stories they read at school. Only one student responded that comics were like the stories read at school!

Table Two: Average students responses

Research Question	Mean	SD
Reading comics can be classified as reading, just as reading books can be classified as reading.	3.50	1.144
I use the same strategies when I read comics and when I read stories.	3.14	1.207
Comics are fun to read.	3.77	1.193
I would prefer reading comics more than reading a book.	2.77	1.602
I would like to read more comics at school (either on your own or during subjects).	3.00	1.602
I like getting comic books from the library, book store, book fair, or book orders.	2.24	0.944
Comics are like the stories we read at school during Reading class.	1.95	0.844

One final way to interpret the survey data is to analyze students' responses with respect to how often they read comics. In doing this, possible trends between those students who read comics daily, monthly, weekly, yearly, or never can be revealed. These are the same questions as reported in the table on page 34, however Table 3 shows that standard deviation tends to be smaller when data are grouped by students' response to how often they read comics.

Figure 3: The frequencies of students' responses

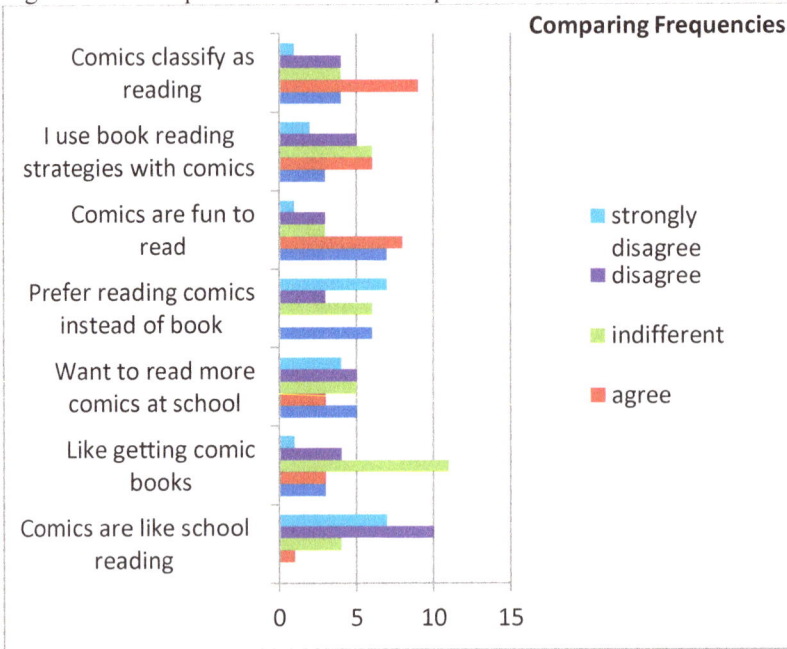

Table Three: Comparing Averages by how often students read comics

	Comics are a legitimate text.	I use similar strategies.	I would like to read more comics.	Comics are fun to read.
Comics read weekly	Mean: 4.5 SD: 0.707	Mean: 5.0 SD: 0.00	Mean: 4.50 SD: 0.707	Mean: 5 SD: 0.00
Comics read monthly	Mean: 4.33 SD: 0.577	Mean: 3.67 SD: 0.577	Mean: 4.33 SD: 0.577	Mean: 4.33 SD: 0.577
Comics read yearly	Mean: 3.33 SD: 0.816	Mean: 2.67 SD: 0.816	Mean: 2.83 SD: 1.329	Mean: 4.17 SD: 0.753
Never read comics	Mean: 2.40 SD: 1.578	Mean: 2.4 SD: 1.578	Mean: 1.80 SD 0.789	Mean: 3.00 SD: 1.247

Interview Results

The four students interviewed responded that they read comics from 1-7 times a week. Some factors that influenced how often comics were read were whether or not they got the paper before their mother, whether or not they are currently reading a book, and if they were at their grandma's because they no longer subscribed to the daily paper. Students responded that they read comics either at home or at their grandma's house. When I asked if they remembered how they started reading, all students named someone who shared their interest in comics and read comics with them when they were younger; students mentioned a mother, grandmother, grandfather, or teacher who handed them a comic book and captivated their interest in comics. All four students reported that they liked to read comics that build on one another and had characters they were able to get to know by reading the comic series.

Mellissa* said that her favorite comic is *Peanuts*. She said that she likes this one because it is funny when you know what *Peanuts* is about and you know the characters. She especially likes Snoopy! Melissa described that she usually reads the comics by herself but she sometimes will show her dad. She described that reading *Peanuts* is similar to reading some books like the series with *Ramona* because those books build on each other just as *Peanuts* comics can build on one another. However, she said that comics are different from books because books do not have as many picture or thought bubbles. When I asked Melissa if she thought reading *Peanuts* was like reading a book she said it "kinda depends." She explained how a page comics isn't equal to a page in a book because sometimes a book has more details.

Teddy* also enjoys reading the *Peanuts* comic strip. He often reads *Peanuts* and *Garfield* at home because they are funny. When asked what comics and books have in common, Teddy explained that sometimes he has to go back and read a comic frame again in order to understand the comic, just as he often will go back and re-read a paragraph or page to understand a story. On the other hand, he said comics were different from books because comics are really quick—"like 30 seconds"—and books take longer to read. I asked Teddy if there was anything he did differently when he read comics that he didn't do when he read books and he said that when he reads comics he really has to look at the pictures to see what type of character they are. Teddy described how if the character was a person he would look closely to see what they were wearing because the clothes could often tell him a lot about the character. For example, if they were wearing business clothes they would probably be different a different type of person than a character wearing baggy clothes. Teddy explained that the appearance of each character would help him understand the story line of the comic.

Ella* explained how she likes to read any comic that looks interesting! Ella said she likes reading comics that are about things that could really happen, and she usually tries to keep up with *Family Circus*. Ella really enjoys the funny things that the kids and adults say in *Family Circus* and she says she can imagine the scenes in this comic happening in real life. When her family got the paper every day, she would try to beat her mom to the paper so that she could see them first. However, her family does not get the daily newspaper anymore, so she catches up on the comics when she goes to her grandma's once a week. Ella explained how after she reads the comics she talks to someone in her family about them—either her grandpa, grandma, mom, or dad. When asked what the two genres had in common, Ella described how she read books and comics in order—left to right, and top to bottom. When asked how the two genres were different, she explained that the "pictures mean a lot to comics." Ella really has to see the pictures in comics and think about the words more in order for the comic to make sense. Sometimes, she described in a low voice, she even has to re-read them! On the contrary, when she reads books, often there aren't pictures and the book just "flows"…she rarely goes back to reread the text when she's reading because it makes sense to her the first time.

The fourth student interviewed, David*, was very interested in the *Fox Trot* comic series. He described that he has three *Fox Trot* books that are over 200 pages each and he likes to read these books over and over again. David described the family—Jason, Paige, Peter, Andy and Roger—in great detail. He described at least 3 attributes for each character and chuckled when he described how bad of a golfer Roger was. David explained that he often talks to his brother, mom, and dad about *Fox Trot* and he especially likes this one because it can make him chuckle in a way other books cannot. David explained that both books and comics can be realistic fiction; they can both be about a "10 year old super nerd" like the one in *Fox Trot*. In contrast, books have "lots of pages" while comics have "squares" and "don't have chapters." After listening to David's excitement about *Fox Trot*, I asked him if he would rather read comics instead of a book. David eagerly replied, "If comics were AR [Accelerator Reader] I'd prefer those!"

Small Group Results

The final phase of this study was to gather all four students together to compare and contrast a fiction story and a comic strip. In order for all students to compare the same texts, the texts were selected in advance and students read these texts prior to the meeting (if they had not already read the pieces for class requirements). The fiction text was a fiction story the class had read earlier in the year titled *The Hot and Cold Summer*. The comic was a series of *Peanuts* comics centered on baseball and Valentine's Day. The ideas Melissa, Teddy, David, and Ella recorded can be seen in the Venn diagram on the following page. One interesting tidbit from their discussion is that the group did not feel *Peanuts* was realistic because when a baseball flew past the pitcher's mound the characters spun in the air, and that doesn't happen in real life. Another area of difference was the formatting of each; the fiction story has paragraphs and indents and rarely has speech bubbles. On the contrary, the comic strips have cartoonish people drawings with speech bubbles and comics are usually broken down into short segments rather than chapters. Students were also quick to point out that the comic strip had more humor than the fiction story! However, the group agreed that both the fiction and the comic texts were written to entertain the reader, they both have main ideas, and they could both be found in the fiction genre because they stories are created by the author. The Venn Diagram discussion results can be seen in Figure 4.

Figure 4: Comparing and Contrasting Comics and Fiction Sections

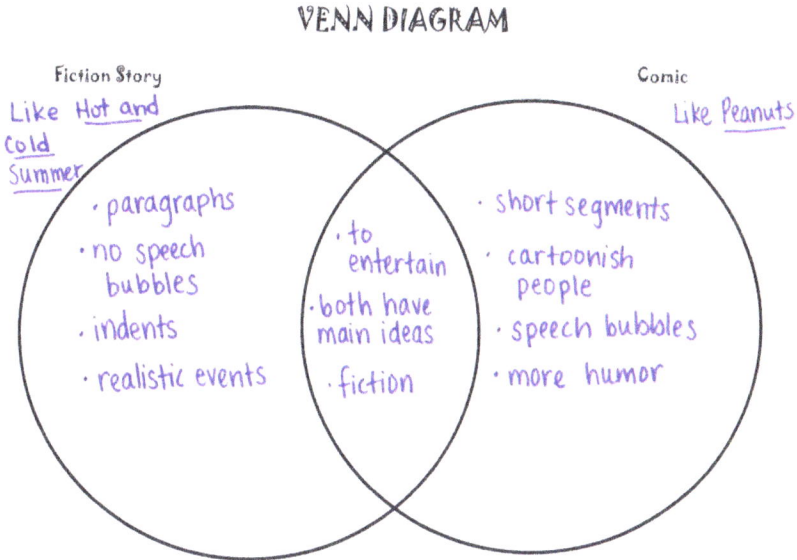

VENN DIAGRAM

Fiction Story

Comic

Like Hot and Cold Summer

Like Peanuts

- paragraphs
- no speech bubbles
- indents
- realistic events

- to entertain
- both have main ideas
- fiction

- short segments
- cartoonish people
- speech bubbles
- more humor

Summary

In sum, nearly half of my class said that they never read comics. Of those who read comics, on 13.6% read them on a weekly basis. Students were more likely to think their teachers would agree with them reading comics compared to their parents. Although nearly 30% of my class would rather read comics than read a book, 57% of my students felt that comics and school reading are not similar. On the contrary, when averages are compared between students who read comics weekly, monthly, yearly, and never, those who read comics more often tend to be more likely to agree that they use the same strategies when reading comics and school texts.

The Venn Diagram in Figure 4 shows that students who read comics often are able to point out similarities between comics and the fiction genre. Students were able to list literary and formatting elements that were similar in the two genres. Students were also able to list differences between the two. It was concluded through my interviews that some students would rather read comics than the books they feel forced to read for the Accelerated Reader program. Other students expressed that they like to read both texts and it would just depend on the subject matter or what they were "in the mood" for.

Analysis

The results obtained were different than those the researcher had projected. One difference was that many students in sample were not reading comics. In fact, many students reported they were not reading much of anything at home! Only 50% of the class reported reading magazines and books at home...something that the researcher predicted would be much higher! Therefore even though only 30% of students reported reading comics at home, that is still more than the percentage of students who reported reading newspapers, recipes, trading cards, or advertisements. One explanation is that students in the sample do not read much at home. This finding is consistent with the National Assessment of Educational Progress results that only 43% of fourth graders and 19% of eighth graders read for fun (Padak & Rasinski, 2007) Another explanation would be that students do not feel looking at the newspaper, recipes, trading cards, or advertisements truly qualifies as the act of reading. As reported by Norton, students may not classify these processes as reading or worthy to be reported as reading in a school context because they are fun (2003).

How students perceive adults feel about them reading comics is another interesting area. Only 4.5% of students thought their parents would disagree with them reading comics; however 22.7% thought their teachers would disagree with them reading comics. This shows that a small percentage of students in the sample believe adults would feel reading comics as a "waste of time"; this finding was also reported in a previous study (Norton, 2003). Is this because school places such an emphasis on textbook reading? Do teachers tend to value the texts they use when they teach? I wonder if many classroom libraries even have comics in them as an option. The classroom chosen for the sample did not have any comic texts in the classroom library at the time of this study. However, the school library had several comic series for students to check out. If teachers stocked their libraries with comics, would this number go up? Morrison, Bryan, and Chilcoat (2002) propose that we must find a way to connect school and home literacies. The number of students who feel their teachers would disagree with them reading comics proves that students are not clear on whether or not the comic genre is a legitimate text and could benefit from teachers making connections between home and school literacy experiences (Morrison, Bryan, & Chilcoat, 2002).

On the other end of the spectrum, only 13.6% of students reported as believing their parents would agree or strongly agree with them reading comics at school, which 40.9% reported they felt their teacher would agree or strongly agree with them reading comics at school. Is this because teachers are constantly pushing students to read any material they can get kids to pick up? After seeing the low percentage rates with regards to what texts students pick up at home, this could certainly be the case! Teachers should capitalize on what students are naturally interested in reading and build from these experiences (Morrison et al., 2002).

The higher standard deviations for questions 6, 7, 9, and 10 on the survey show students'' responses were dispersed among the five answer choices. Therefore a trend in that sample response cannot be statistically proven. This shows that student responses varied greatly on whether or not comics are a legitimate text, if they use the same strategies when they read comics and stores, if they would rather read comics over a book, and if they would like to read comics at school. Some of the dispersal of responses could be contributed to the fact that all fifth graders are unique and have different preferences. It could also be that some students had never considered these ideas and were more likely to choose the indifferent category rather than choose a side on the issue.

The mean response for "Comics are fun to read" was 3.77 and only 18.5% of students disagreed with the statement. This shows that the majority of the student sample would not mind reading comics, even though only 30% choose to pick up a comic to read when they are at home. The difference in those percentages could be that students do not have access to comics at home. Ella reported that her family no longer subscribed to the local newspaper so she did not get to read comics as often now. This is consistent with previous study findings by Wright and Sherman (2006) that fewer people are purchasing daily newspapers. Although David owns several comic books, maybe the majority of students so not ask to purchase comic books. The mean response to the statement, "I like getting comic books from the library, book store, book fair, or book orders" was 2.24—that falls between "disagree" and "indifferent". In fact, the most frequent response was "indifferent". If so many students' reported that comics were fun to read, why do they not want to purchase them? Are students today not interested in buying books? Perhaps books are losing the race as they compete with so many other after school activities and other hypertext media (Xu, Perkins, & Zunich, 2005). Or, it could be that students have not yet been introduced to comics and the interesting world of graphic novels!

The average score to the statement, "Comics are like the stories we read at school during Reading class" was 1.95, which falls in the "disagree" category. This statistic reinforces that students perceive the school texts to be unrelated to comics which was consistent with Norton's (2003) previous findings. However students often read fiction stories at school with characters, setting, and plot. And what do comics have? They have characters, setting, and plot! Although these elements might be presented in a different way, they are there! In fact, graphic novels can have a plot very similar to chapter books. This again shows the discrepancy students feel exists between comics and school stories. Which the difference between comics and nonfiction is larger, it is still imperative for students to see how their home texts fit in with school texts---something this survey reinforces teachers have not mastered.

The averages that glean even more light on the big picture are the ones shown in Table 3: Comparing Averages by How Often Students Read Comics. This table shows the trend that those students who read comics more often are noticing similarities between the two genres. When thinking about if comics are indeed a legitimate text, those who read comics weekly have a mean of 4.5 (between agree and disagree) and those who never read comics have a mean of 2.4 (closer to disagree). When asked if students use similar strategies while reading comics and fiction stories, those who read comics weekly strongly agreed and those who read comics yearly were indifferent. In response to the statement I would like to read more comics, those who read comics weekly had a mean of 4.5 (between agree and disagree) and those who never read comics…their mean fell between disagree and strongly disagree. It is also interesting to note that the mean for each answer was highest for those who read comics most often and lowest for those who read comics least often. Average student responses gradually decrease as the frequency of their time spent reading comics decreased! These statistics seem to conclude that those who are reading comics enjoy reading comics, want to read more comics, feel comics are a legitimate text, and use similar strategies. This supports Nortons (2003) findings that those who read comics are more aware of the similarities and discuss the plot of comics just as they discuss the plot of school texts. Those students who hardly even read comics are indifferent about whether or not comics are fun, do not really want to read more comics, do not feel they would use the same strategies with comics, and are not sure that they are a legitimate text.

Students who were interviewed and met in the small group seemed to follow the same trends. They were students who read comics daily, weekly, or several times a month and had a strong interest in at least one specific comic. Each student could name a comic title and describe characters and common plot themes. Wright and Sherman (2006) concluded that some characters "have become American Icons" (p. 165) and students from this study could identify many of these icons! The students could also describe commonalities between the two genres. Students described how different texts could be written to entertain and have main ideas; which shows that they are noticing similarities between school and home genres (Xu, Perkins, & Zunich, 2005). David described the story line of his favorite comics and this shows his understanding of how comics tell a story in a visual form (Xu et. Al., 2005)

When contrasting the two genres, students focused on the formatting of each: comics have frames, speech bubbles, and pictures whereas fiction books have more words and are organized in chapters. These were similar to the differences students presented in similar stories and that researchers presented in previous writings (Haynes, 2009). Teddy reported that he had to pay close attention to the pictures because the images would cue him into the plot. This shows that Teddy is aware of the multiple layers of comics—words, visual, and pictorial—and can analyze the meaning of all these layers put together (Cleaver, 2008). Students concluded that some comics like *Family Circus* are realistic, whereas others such as *Peanuts* (where kids are airbone at the pitcher's mound after a line drive and lose their hat, glove, etc.) are not realistic. This is proof that some students do indeed see comics as a daily representation of real life (McVicker, 2007). Students also commented that comics tend to have more humor and said that comics can make them chuckle out loud or really ponder word and character and how these elements affect the storyline as a whole Cleaver, 2008).

Summary

The trends from this study seem to support what teachers have hypothesized for years-that those students who enjoy reading read well and understand how their reading fits into their daily world. Although this study has more of a comic twist! It seems that those students who enjoy reading comics are able to see connections between the texts. Frequent comic readers are able to see similar strategies that they use while reading comics and fiction texts (Norton, 2003). They are also able to see how both genres can share a purpose and have themes related to real life.

On the contrary, those who do not read comics often do not see similarities between comics and school texts. Those students do not use similar strategies when they read comics and when they read school fiction texts. Is it just that some students have not been introduced into the world of comics? Or are they not interested? While some of it can certainly be based on interest—we all have genres we prefer to read—the statistics show that some of them may be worried to pick up comics because they feel the adults in their lives do not want them reading comics (Norton, 2003). Ella, Teddy, David, and Melissa all named an adult as the person who introduced them to comics. They also named someone older than them that they discussed these comics with. It is possible that a large portion of students from this study never had someone hand them a comic book. No one ever showed them a funny comic or talked about an interesting speech bubble. How can these students be expected to know about comics if they have not been introduced to the genre? It is also imperative that only 59% of students reported reading books at home. This compares with 54.5% reading magazines and 54.5% reading websites. Thus there could be many students who are not reading at home, and when they are at school, may not have the access or encouragement to read comics. It would be interesting to see if any of the students who reported as reading very little at home would be interested in comics after an adult sparked their interest.

Conclusion

Reading at home helps children build literacy experiences. Bridging the gap between home and school texts—including texts that may not be print based—helps students begin to see how everyday texts fit in with their classroom experiences (Semali, 2003). This study shows how the gap between home and school texts can be bridged by bringing comics into the curriculum. Students who read comics and were given time to discuss comics at school were able to find ways that reading comics can be like reading texts at school. When students stated the similarities, it shows how students are beginning to see the big picture of texts in their lives and how the gap between school and home has been made smaller.

Many students believe that school texts have a prescribed meaning and that the teacher holds the answer key (Norton, 2003). Incorporating texts students naturally read at home can help students enjoy the experience rather than search for what they believe is the correct answer. Incorporating home texts like comics can also spark interest among reluctant readers (Cleaver, 2008). Teachers are aware that students are not reading as much for enjoyment once they get to the upper elementary and middle school levels (Padak & Rasinski, 2007). Teachers must take the initiative to try to "pull in" students who might not otherwise read by offering students exposure to a multitude of genres. While exposing students to different genres such as comics, teachers can also address concepts required in state and national standards (Xu, Perkins, & Zunich, 2005). As students expressed in this study, they are interested in exploring different genres and enjoy reading comics; however, the amount of reading done at home is not extensive. Therefore teachers can pose some interesting home reading material through mini-lessons in order to bridge the gap between school and home literacy and offer students exposure with interpreting everyday texts (Cleaver, 2008). Allowing this exposure will provide students with another genre to choose from, help students see connections between genres, and new opportunities to read, write, and discuss texts. The exposure will also help students see adults interacting with different texts, not just the school texts which students feel have a prescribed meaning. It will also help students dismantle the notion of a "legitimate text" and the idea that texts different from the ones presented during traditional literacy lessons are not "truly reading".

Implications for Future Research

This topic is relatively new in literacy research and much more studies must be conducted. This study investigated the ideas of one class in one school of a very small district. It would be worthwhile to repeat the study in various schools across the state and/or country in order to draw more general conclusions about fifth grade perceptions of the comic genre. The possibility exists that this group of students was not the norm for fifth grade perceptions of comics and that other classrooms could be a better representation.

It would also be useful to look at this issue from the classroom teacher perspective. While surveying additional students, teacher perceptions could also be gathered in order to get the whole picture and understand what steps are being taken (if any) to bridge the gap between home and school literacy experiences. It would also be interesting to gather information regarding students' availability to comics at school and if comics are incorporated into classroom lessons.

Lastly, a longitudinal approach would be beneficial. It would be interesting to follow students through middle school and even high school to see what future connections students make between the two genres. Furthermore, it would be interesting to see if the students interviewed (the ones who reported as reading comics more often and were able to draw conclusions between the two genres) excelled in future literacy experiences or standardized testing. Did these students go on to be lifelong readers? Or were they just as likely to struggle in high school as their peers who did not make connections between school and home texts?

It is clear that this is a developing area of research. Although comics have been around for quite some time, the research surrounding comics and the impact they have on students and schools is quite new! This is an area that must be unveiled in order to provide positive literacy experiences to students and their families. For if teachers would like to see adolescents reading more, they must get to the bottom of what exactly it is that students look for in an alternative texts and find a way to address students literacy needs. By learning more about what students choose to engage in at home, teachers can learn more about the gap between home and school literacy and how to address this gap in order to provide students with experiences to help them become lifelong consumers of text—whether it is alternative texts or traditional ones!

References

Allington, R.L. (2006). What really matters for struggling readers: Designing research-based programs. New York: Pearson.

Alvermann, D. E. & Hagood, M.C. (2000, February). Fandom and critical media literacy. Journal of Adolescent & Adult Literacy, 43(5), 436-446.

Au, K.H., Carroll, J.H., & Scheu, J.A. (1998). Balanced literacy instruction: A teacher's resource book (2nd ed.). Norwood, MA: Christopher-Gordon Publishers, Inc.

Bitz, M. (2004, April). The Comic Book Project: Forging alternative pathways to literacy. Journal of Adolescent and Adult Literacy, 47(7), 574-586.

Cleaver, S. (2008, May/June). Comics & graphic novels. Instructor, 117(6), 28-64.

Crewsell, J.W. (2005) Educational research: Planning, conducting, and evaluating quantitative and qualitative research (2nd ed.). Columbus, OH: Pearson: Merrill Prentice Hall.

Debruin-Parecki, A. & Krol-Sinclair, B. (Eds.). (2003). Family literacy: From theory to practice. Newark, DE: International Reading Association.

Dewey, J. (1998). Experience and education: The 60th anniversary edition (2nd Ed.). West Layfayette, IN: Kappa Delta Pi.

Haynes, E. (2009, January/February). Getting started with graphic novels in school libraries. Library Media Connection, 10-12.

Hurwitz, J. (1984). The hot and cold summer. New York: William Morrow and Company, Inc.

McVicker, C. (2007, September). Comic strips as a text structure for learning to read. The Reading Teacher, 61(1), 85-88.

Morrison, T., Bryan, G., & Chilcoat, G.W. (2002, May). Using student generated comic books in the classroom. Journal of Adolescent & Adult Literacy, 45(8), 758-767.

Norton, B. (2003, October). The motivating power of comic books: Insights from Archie Comic readers. International Reading Association, 57 (2), 140-147.

Northern Illinois University. (2009). Interactive Illinois report card. Retrieved October 15, 2009 from http://iirc.niu.edu

Padak, N. & Rasinski, T. (2007). Is being wild about Harry Potter enough? Encouraging independent reading at home. The Reading Teacher, 61(4), 350-353.

Pressley, M., Billman, A., Perry, K.H., Reffitt, K.E., & Reynolds, J. (Eds.). (2007). Shaping literacy achievement: Research we have, research we need. New York: Guilford Press.

Ranker, J. (2007). Using comic books as read-alouds: Insights on reading instruction from and English as a second language classroom. The Reading Teacher, 61(4), 296-305.

Rowsell, J. (2006). Family literacy experiences. Portland, ME: Teahouse Publishers.

Schulz, C.M. (2000). Peanuts 2000. New York: Ballantine Books.

Schwarz, G.E. (2002, November). Graphic novels for multiple literacies. Journal of Adolescent & Adult Literacy, 46(3). Retrieved September 26, 2009 from
http://www.readingonline.org/newliteracyies/lit_index.asp?HREF=/newl iteracies/jaal/11-02_column/index.html

Semali, L. (2003, July/August). Ways with visual languages: Making the case for critical media literacy. The Clearing House, 76(6), 271-277.

Wax, E. (2002, May 17). Back to the drawing board: Once-banned comic books now a teaching tool. The Washington Post.

Wolk, D. (2000, October 16). Comics: Not just for specialty stores anymore. Publishers Weekly, 247(42), 36-43.

Wright, G. & Sherman, R.B. (2006, January). Comics redux. Reading Improvement, 43(3), 165-172.

Xu, S.H., Perkins, R.S., & Zunich, L.O. (2005). Trading cards to comic strips: Popular culture texts and literacy learning in grades K-8. Newark, DE: International Reading Association.

Chapter 2: Summer Reading Regression: Is It Really A Pain In the BAS?

Jennifer Deluhery & Ashley Marten

Introduction

In the school year of 2009-2010, our district implemented the Response to Intervention (RTI) program. By implementing this state mandated program, we, as a district, adopted the Benchmark Assessment System (BAS) created by Fountas and Pinnell. A Benchmark Assessment System is a series of tests that can be used to identify a student's current reading level and progress along a gradient of test levels over time. The word "benchmark" means a standard against which to measure something. We will be taking the BAS scores from the spring 2010 third grade class, and comparing it to the fall 2010 fourth grade scores. We will be concentrating on two, third grade classes from the 2009-2010 school year and we will be comparing them to the now fourth graders in the 2010-2011 school year.

Problem and its Background

At the end of the year, students leave their classrooms to begin their summer vacation and with this goes three months of their reading instruction. Summer reading regression occurs when students are out of school for three months and do not receive proper reading instruction. The problem with this situation is that when students return to school after their three month break of little to no reading instruction, their reading skills lack compared to the end of the prier school year. Richard Allington (2006) states *"that annual AYP testing assumes that any growth, or loss, can be attributed to the school. But summer setback occurs when school is not in session"* (page 23). This creates a dire reading problem within districts.

As two educators, we have observed low income students who are already struggling at the end of the year and fall even more than three months behind in the fall of the following year. According to the article "Stop the Summer

Reading Slide" low income students losses add up to two or more years which is 80-100% of the achievement gap between low income students and middle income students (Lundstrom, 2005).The purpose of this study was intended to determine if the summer break negatively affects students' reading in comparison to their reading scores which were obtained at the end of the school year prior to students' summer break.

Literature Review

Summer reading regression is not an uncommon issue in schools across America. However, the Benchmark Assessment System (BAS) is a newly developed universal tester that has not been around long enough for adequate research. Studies on BAS and the impact of summer break on students' academic achievement are limited. We have compiled a few articles that explain and answer questions within the Fountas and Pinnell RtI program. These studies will help educators assist and/or attempt to close the summer reading regression gap.

A Never-Ending Story: Action Research Meets Summer Reading

The purpose of this study was to find a new way of motivating students to read during the summer. At Barnstable High School in Massachusetts, a teacher, Carol Gordon, was unhappy with her students' performance on their summer reading book list. Her colleges had hoped that their students had at least read three books from their summer reading list. Instead all she heard were complaints about books that were chosen. She decided to do some research to see what other schools were doing. Gordon's research found that among the fifty-seven lists studied, two did not list titles, merely giving a reading assignment. The remaining fifty-five lists contained three to three hundred titles, usually organized by grade level. Annotation- mostly one-liners or short summaries- appeared on twenty-seven lists. Commonly, summer reading lists did not reflect student input: 43 to 92 percent of the titles were fiction, even though research studies from the authors Gurian, Henley, and Trueman reported that boys prefer nonfiction.

She shared the information with the English department chair. He suggested she work with five English teachers in order to revise the reading list. Before confronting the five English teachers, Gordon turned to a book entitled *The Power of Reading* by Krashen. It summarized research about Free Voluntary Reading (FVR). Students read independently and are involved in minimal accountability. It also showed that more reading leads to better writing. She presented her research information to the members of the reading committee at Barnstable High School. The committee accepted and agreed to the following guidelines:

1.   "People who say they read more read better" (Gordon 2008), therefore the primary purpose of the summer reading program is to encourage students to read more. In to encourage students to read more another primary purpose of summer reading is reading for fun.

2. Summer reading offers choices because choice is an important element in reading engagement.

From there she wrote up a questionnaire that English teachers administered to their classes to find out how students felt about summer reading, and to also collect student's recommendations for titles. She also included the staff at Barnstable High School by collecting their recommendations via e-mail. What the committee analyzed from the data collected from the questionnaire was the following information:

- Since "results suggest that schools can encourage children to read more by also requiring them to complete a short writing activity based on their summer reading activities... and students who fulfilled teacher requirements by writing about their summer book... are predicted to read more books than their classmates who did not complete these activities reading responses would include writing activities" (Gordon, 2008)
- In addition, student projects can accommodate multiple intelligences and thinking styles by providing options for reading responses that are graphic, visual, and auditory, as well as written.
- Reading response projects can reflect activities students enjoy in their spare time and are grounded in reading response described as the aesthetic stance to transactional theory.
- Reading choices can include nonfiction sections.
- The summer reading program can be web-based.

To conclude the article, Gordon found that students were reading more during the summer when they were allowed to choose the books they read and were given choices as to how to present the information that they had read about.

Bridging the Summer Reading Gap

The following article takes a look at different reading programs that are available to students during the summer and how important it is to get books into the hands of children during the summer.

In their article, Anne McGill-Franzen and Richard Allington, stated that regardless of other activities, the best predictor of summer loss or summer gain is whether or not a child reads during the summer. The best predictor of whether a child reads is whether or not he/she owns books.

They took a look at libraries. School libraries are closed during the summer, so most people think to go to the public libraries as a solution to closing the gap on summer reading regression. However, those students who are located in poor neighborhoods are often the first to close or restrict hours in a budget crunch. Even when public libraries are open, poor children may lack transportation. They also found that teachers and librarians in the poorest communities, are the least likely to allow children to check out books because their school cannot afford to risk the loss of the few books they have. Some suggestions they made in their article to help solve this problem were:

- Have the schools sponsor book fairs

- In schools serving low-income families, money might be allocated from the school budget or from federal program funds to pay for the books.
- Create a "Books for a Buck" program. Recycle donated paperback books and books purchased at garage sales or library sales. At a dollar or even twenty-five cents apiece.
- Create an "honor library" that provides a steady supply of new and used paperbacks. Place a cart outside the front doors of the school, or in another public place, where students can borrow books and leave books they've finished reading.
- Create a Summer School Voluntary Reading Program. Make popular reading books available to summer school students to listen to, discuss and read, and take home to share with family and friends.
- Allow students to check out school or classroom library books for the summer. Staff the library one evening each week during the summer so that children can return the books they've read and can select new ones.

In the end, McGill-Franzen and Allington found that their study suggests that children who read as few as six books over the summer maintain the level of reading skills they achieved during the preceding school year and when children are provided with 10 to 20 self-selected children's books at the end of the regular school year, as many as 50 percent not only maintain their skills, but actually make reading gains.

Summer Reading Loss

The purpose of this study is to combine statistics and an explanation on why reading loss is such a significant problem in education. The study also gives ideas on how to curb the reading loss, how important family participation is in their child's reading loss, and advice for families. Educators work so hard during the school year and then after three months of vacation, it is like starting all over again. Teachers find themselves spending the beginning of the year on mostly reviewing and re-teaching topics from last year. Summer reading loss refers to the decline in children's reading development that can occur during summer vacation times when children are away from the classroom and not participating in formal literacy programs (Allington & McGill-Franzen, 2003). Research has shown that summer reading loss affects students, but significantly those at-risk. Mraz states that it is the students who can least afford to lose the reading gains they've achieved during the school year, who fall the farthest behind when they return to the classroom after a summer break away from formal literacy instruction (2007). The achievement gap between high-socioeconomic and low-socioeconomic students has been a huge concern for educators as well as policy makers. This summer reading loss makes the achievement gap between these two groups even worse.

The method of this study is a combination of research articles that offer statistics and a solution to try to make the summer reading loss gap smaller. This study gives many reasons on why summer reading loss occurs and how easily students lose their reading development without direct instruction on a weekly basis. At the end of the study, the researchers have given ideas on how engaging families in participating in their child's reading development can have a positive effect on minimizing the summer reading loss.

The results of this study show that when students read, the better readers they become. However, the accessibility of reading materials has been a vital element in improving the reading ability of children (Allington, 2006). The research indicates also that students, on average, spend pitifully little time reading outside of school – about 10 minutes per day (Anderson, Wilson, & Fielding). Those students, who are already at-risk during the school year, normally have little or no opportunity past the classroom to receive any improvements in their reading development. If you think about it, wealthier communities have bookstores, libraries, and reading programs for students to be actively involved in throughout the summer. Even though students may not take advantage of these opportunities, they are still provided. Students in poorer communities don't have these resources and sometimes have a lack of parent awareness to the benefits of reading (Mraz and Rasinski, 2007).

In the article, the research concluded that there are a number of things that can be done to 'curb' summer reading loss.

1. The value placed on literacy in the home, time spent reading with children, and the availability and use of reading materials have been identified as important elements in children's reading success (Snow, Burns, & Griffin, 1998).

2. Schools can host workshops for parents in the weeks before the start of summer vacation in which teachers make the case for summer reading and share suggestions for keeping children engaged over the summer months (Mraz & Rasinski, 2007).

3. A summer reading list of proven favorites for children that will be accountable when school begins again. This may only be appropriate for some schools. Teachers have to make sure that the books are available at the local library or if the school library could be open a couple days a week for a few hours (Mraz & Rasinski, 2007).

4. Parent-Teacher Organizations can set up some type of reading program for the students to keep track of their minutes throughout the summer. When they turn their minutes, in they can add up the total amount the entire school read and present it at the beginning of the school year. This would be a way to kick off the new school year (Mraz & Rasinski, 2007).

5. The International Reading Association (1998) suggested that parents look for reading materials that relate to interests that a child enjoys. Also reasonable limits should be put on children watching television and video games. Even the daily routines such as cooking, using a phone book, reading the newspaper, searching the World Wide Web, reading directions or a brochure are more simple ways how children can be actively engaged with reading in day to day activities (Mraz & Rasinski, 2007).

6. Parents should be setting a good example to their children by reading for enjoyment as well. This can be a powerful way to help your child understand how important and enjoyable reading can be.

7. Reading on the way to a destination, at a park, or even waiting for an appointment. Also making a weekly routine to visit the local library or bookstores to check out or find books that seem interesting (Mraz & Rasinski, 2007).

This article was written in a way for educators, policy makers, and parents to be able to understand the concept of summer reading loss. Their statistics, explanations, and suggestions seemed to fit out districts situation similarly. At the end of the study, Mraz and Rasinski talked about what elements contribute to family literacy participation. We thought these things would be interesting to keep in mind when we encourage our parent/guardians to continuing reading throughout the summer. Here are the elements that are gained when parents are actively involved with their child's literacy.

1. An established sense of community between the families.
2. Teacher's effective interpersonal skills create good rapport with teacher-parent relationships.
3. Ongoing and varied communication between the parent and teacher. There can be face to face, phone calls, newsletters, emails, and classroom visits.
4. Consistent recruitment of family participation can encourage different families to interact and then more likely to participate in school programs.
5. Suggestions for a variety of literacy activities for the home, like the ones in this article.
6. Teachers understand more about family challenges.

Stop the Summer Reading Slide

The purpose of this study is to suggest how to keep children reading during the summer vacation, which will help them maintain their reading skills they learned during the school year. This article is written for teachers and administrators to help set up a relationship with parents to help them better understand and have the background knowledge to keep their child's reading development at peak.

The method of this study is qualitative study on other research that has been completed on summer reading loss and how to prevent the slide from happening. Meg Lundstrom has given ideas on how to keep books in children's hands and their skills at a peak (2005).

She focuses on four main points in her article.

1. The first is that teachers need allies. Different programs have started throughout the country such as a Connecticut giving their schools incentives if 60% of their students turn in reading logs from the summer months. Also, scholastic online has an online summer reading program that helps parents and teachers encourage their kids' reading. (Lundstrom, 2005)
2. The next concept is having books be closer to the students. Some ideas such as allowing the students to take home four or five books for the

summer. Also not locking up the school libraries all summer, and opening the school up one day a week to buy, check out, or exchange books. You can set up a 'take a book/leave a book' system at your school or community center. (Lundstrom, 2005)

3. Motivation is key to reading during the summer. The kids can pick up a book at the library, but the motivation of the actual reading is the most challenging part. They talked about required book lists and having a prize system for when they return to school. The best way to motivate kids on their own reading is to let them pick out their own books. They may find silly books with goofy titles, but all that matters is that they are reading! (Lundstrom, 2005)

4. Talking with parents and providing them with newsletters during the summer can boost the accountability at home. Giving them new ideas, websites, and new books that are being released is a way to encourage throughout the summer months. One teacher at Mercer Middle School in Seattle gives her students pre-stamped, plain postcards and when they finish reading a book they mail a summary and illustration to her. Then, she sends them a postcard back. This allows her to be one step ahead at the beginning of the year by knowing their level and interest's. (Lundstrom, 2005)

In conclusion, Lundstrom ended with facts about the summer slide. She explained that it is important for educators and teachers to understand the effects of the summer slide and how it can be helped. She used saying such as, 'kids who read, succeed', 'they've got to have the books', 'role models matter,' and 'make the time.' These little sayings are to encourage parents and teachers to continue communication with students throughout the summer months and to educate parents on ways to keep their child motivated and reading!

After reading this article, it made us realize how much more we can be doing in order to help our students and their parents succeed through reading throughout the summer. The most important part of this study was that it explained how important it is to keep a good rapport with your parents and to find ways to keep your students held accountable and motivated. Starting a school wide summer reading book list and reading goal would be a way for the whole school and administration to be involved. When things seem like a big deal to you the students are going to act like it is a big deal as well. This school wide goal can also give a great way to start off the new school year with, especially when beating the prior year's goal.

Methodology

Participants

In this research project, we conducted a quantitative study to examine the impact of summer break on students reading scores. The study participants consisted of students who were in third grade in the spring of 2010 and are currently in fourth grade in the fall of 2010. These students attend a school in Illinois which is a consolidated district that contains a primary, middle, and high school. The primary school, in which this research took place, contains grades Pre-Kindergarten through 5th grade. The primary school consists of 535 students of which are: 97% Caucasian, .7% African American, .4% Hispanic, .7% Asian Pacific Islander, .2% Native American, and .9% Multi-Racial/Ethnic. The building has a 44.7% low income rate and a 12.6% mobility rate. The attendance rate is at 94.4%. As of the first school day in May of 2009, the average class size in grade three was 17.3 students. In grade four the average was 21.3 students.

The research focused on 36 students, which is a mixture of instructional, inclusion, and mainstreamed students. This is a combination of two classrooms, which were decreased by the mobility rate. At the end of spring 2010, there were 38 students and at the beginning of fall 2010, two students had moved out of the district, which gave us 36 student participants.

Instrumentation

Our district adopted the Benchmark Assessment System (BAS) created by Fountas and Pinnell. These scores are recorded using a wall chart provided by our reading specialist team. This wall chart consists of grades K-5 and provides student information such as free/reduced lunch, reading level based on BAS score, AIMS Web fluency score, male/female, interventions provided, reading recovery, and if a child has moved into the district after Kindergarten. This wall is used by teachers, specialists, and administration to make decisions and provide a key visual in the growth and movement of our students. The wall changes three times a year after each BAS test administration has been conducted. The reading specialists take pictures and keep records through spreadsheets of the prior wall results.

Research Questions

Through our research we attempted to answer the following questions.

1. How many students met or exceeded the third grade target reading level for spring 2010?
2. How many students met or exceeded the fourth grade target reading level for fall 2010?
3. What is the percentage of mobility from third to fourth grade?
4. Was there an overall drop in BAS scores from spring 2010 to fall 2010?

Definitions of Terms

RtI: According to Batsche (2005), RtI response to Intervention or otherwise known as RtI, is a general education initiative, which requires a collaborative effort from all district staff. It provides high-quality instruction and interventions matched to each student's needs and abilities, measures the student's rate of improvement over time through ongoing assessments to make important instructional decisions for interventions, and identifies specific and effective research-based interventions for individual students. (p. 5)

The RtI model that our district is/will be implementing is a "Three Tiered Model". The three tiers consist of the following:

- **Tier 1:** Core instruction interventions for all students, which is both preventative and proactive provided by regular classroom teacher. This includes differentiated and small group instruction. This should be about 80% of students.
- **Tier 2:** Supplemental group, one-on-one, or one-on-two interventions for at-risk students. Duration of intervention is based on student's needs and student's response/progress. This should be about 15% of students.
- **Tier 3:** Intensive individual and one-on-two student interventions, which are assessment-based and of longer duration. This should be about 5% of students.

BAS: According the Fountas & Pinnel's website, the Benchmark Assessment System (BAS) is a series of tests that can be used to identify a student's current reading level and progress along a gradient of test levels over time.

Results

Research Question #1: How many students met or exceeded the third grade target reading level for spring 2010?

According to our data gathered by the Benchmark Data Management System, we found that four students met the benchmark and 21 exceeded the benchmark. This means that out of the 36 total students tested four students were at level P reading level and 21 of the 36 were above the P reading level. This leaves 11 students below the reading level of P. The spring 2009/2010 reading level results are displayed in figure 1.

Figure 1: Spring 09/10 Reading Level Results

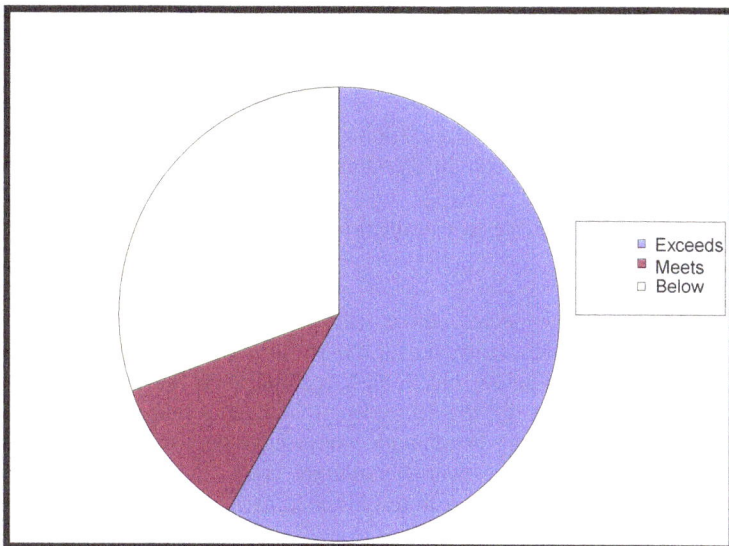

Research Question #2: How many students met or exceeded the fourth grade target reading level for fall 2010?

According to our data gathered by the Benchmark Data Management System, we found out that no students met the reading level P, which is the benchmark for the beginning of fourth grade. After testing, there were 20 students who exceeded the benchmark for entering fourth grade, which leaves 16 students below benchmark. The Fall 2010/2011 reading level results are shown in figure 2.

Figure 2: Fall 10/11 Reading Level Results

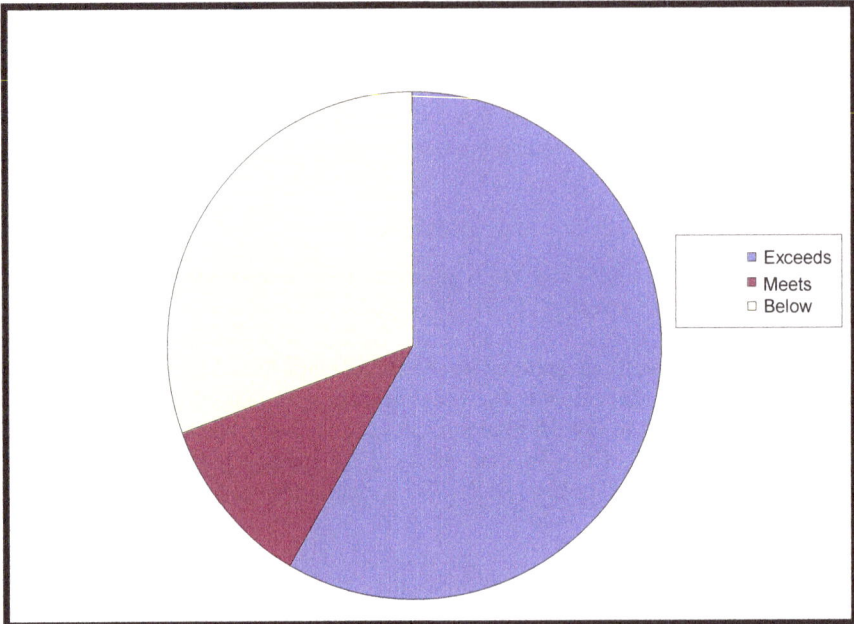

Research Question #3: What is the percentage of mobility from third to fourth grade?

The mobility percentage of our population, which started out at 38 students and decreased to 36 students between third and fourth grade is 1.05%.

Research Question #4: Was there an overall drop from BAS scores from spring 2010 to fall 2010?

According to our data collected, there was not a significant drop in the overall scores of the population. However, of the 36 students tested, there were 5 more students who dropped below benchmark reading level in the transition between third and fourth grade. Of the 36 students, 5 students who were meeting and exceeding third grade reading benchmark would have been ready for fourth grade reading curriculum. Instead, over the summer break, these five students' reading levels dropped to below the fourth grade benchmark.

Discussion

After completing and collecting all the data for our research project, we looked back at our research questions to compare. We did expect a drop in reading levels over the summer months between third and fourth grades. Therefore, we were not surprised when we looked at the data and saw that between our two classes there were students who went backwards. The research was expected, especially from the past research we have read about. Even though our prediction to our research was correct, we were actually expecting more of a drop from more students. Only having a percentage of 14% of our population drop levels, was a little bit surprising. Our research still answered our research questions, and our predictions and outcomes were similar.

In our research, the results turned out because of the summer reading regression. The reason why students dropped reading levels is because of the lack of reading instruction during the summer months. After students leave our classrooms in the beginning of June, they are set free from any school activities and instruction. There are programs in the community, which we will be discussed later, that students are involved in but sometimes that just isn't enough for some students. There are students who will read all summer and have an "inner voice" or reasoning in their minds as they read. Students like this comprehend as they are reading, and if they don't understand they will go back and reread or use other strategies that we have taught in the classroom. Those students, more than likely didn't participate in that summer slide. However, there are students who do read during the summer but don't read for meaning and instead just read in order to complete the program. These students usually need more teacher-lead instruction as they are reading at their level. It is great that these students are still reading, but they seem to still fall back a little in their reading level. Lastly, there are the students who don't read anything all summer and those students are the ones who will fall significantly behind. The research that we found agrees with our data and shares our knowledge of the different kinds of students that we let loose in the summertime. Every piece of literature that we read had the same outcome as ours. The most difficult problem in summer reading regression is that students don't receive the reading instruction after they leave our buildings. This is also a difficult problem to fix because we all know that we can't go home with them!

There are some slight validity concerns with the Benchmark Assessment System tool. The classroom teacher administrates the BAS test, therefore depending on the teacher may depend on how the child is scored. At the end of the third grade year, we gave the test and scored the students. Every new school year the students are switched around when entering the next grade. This means that the students that we had last year are broken up into three different classes instead of two. Then there were three different fourth grade teachers that administered the test. Each teacher may score their students a little differently, some may score hard and some easy. This could alter the validity of the universal test.

Conclusions & Implications

According to Richard Allington (2006), that annual AYP testing assumes that any growth, or loss, can be attributed to the school. But summer setback occurs when school is not in session" (page 23). Our district uses the Benchmark Assessment

System (BAS) created by Fountas and Pinnell to identify our students' current reading level and progress along a gradient of test levels over time. Through our research, we have taken a look at our third grade classes form the 2009-2010 school year, and compared them to their scores as fourth graders in the 2010-2011 school year. By the end of third grade, it is expected that all third grades end the year at a level P reading ability. When they enter fourth grade they are still expected to be at a level P reading ability. At our district, it is only through the BAS testing that we are able to prove the gains and losses of our students reading abilities after the summer months.

Our results have uncovered that although our students have had three non-school instructed summer months off, only a small percentage of the students tested dropped below grade level reading benchmark. When looking beyond these results, we can conclude that the BAS, testing system does show gains and losses, however it is just one assessment tool. This tool is used by every single teacher in our district and each teacher has his or her own way of using it. This creates an inconsistency in the BAS testing system. If we as a district were to adopt another standard based assessment tool to accompany the BAS then it might create a more tightened and more accurate testing system. There are many unanswered reasons as to why the students who were at the end of third grade reading at grade level dropped below grade level when they began fourth grade. Maybe they didn't have access to books? Maybe they just didn't read at all over summer break? Maybe they didn't have anyone at home to read with or to them? Whatever the reasons may be, there are some things that in our community that can help those struggling reading during the summer.

Being a large consolidated district that is compiled of many small towns, there are very few summer activities that are offered within those towns that can help readers stay strong readers. However, there are many things that we as teachers can suggest to parents/guardians to participate in throughout the summer months. These suggestions are inexpensive ways to keep children reading: have your children read anything to you, be it the back of a cereal box to the direction on bubble bath and turn your T.V. to mute and put the subtitles on so that they must read what they are watching. Some other activities that the "larger" towns and cities offer are Vacation Bible School, Boys and Girls Scouts.

In conclusion, our research was intended to determine if the summer break impacts students' reading scores at the third grade level. The findings show that there was a slight drop in reading scores. Future studies should examine all grade levels to determine if summer break conclusively impacts students reading scores.

References

Batsche, G., et. Al. (2005) Response to Intervention: Policy Considerations and Implementation. Alexandria, VA: NASDSE.

Fountas, I., Pinnell, G. (2001) Guided Readers and Writers: Grades 3-6. Portsmouth, NH: Heinmann

Gordon, C. (November/December 2008). A Never-Ending Story: Action Research Meets Summer Reading. *Knowledge Quest, v. 37 no. 2,* 34-41.

Illinois State Board of Education (2008, January 1). The Illinois State Response to Intervention (RTI) Plan. Retrieved March 19, 2008, from http://www.isbe.net

Lundstrom, M. (2005). Stop the summer reading slide. *Instructor*, 114(8), 20.

McGill-Franzen, A., Allington, R. (May/June 2003). Bridging the Summer Reading Gap, *Instructor, v. 112 no. 8*, 17-18.

Mraz, M., & Rasinski, T. (2007). Summer reading loss. *Reading Teacher*, 60(8), 784.

Chapter 3: Word Study versus Traditional Spelling Approach

Amber Thomas & Marci Whitford

Introduction

After years of research surrounding spelling instruction, many teachers are still struggling with how to best teach it in their classrooms. In addition students are failing to correctly transfer words from a weekly spelling test to their daily work. Although many educators use what is deemed a traditional approach to spelling, there is research that suggests more effective methods exists that can improve students' spelling ability. Word Study may be one of these methods, and it is our goal to determine if this way of instruction improves our students' spelling.

Through research we have found that spelling instruction has undergone many changes. In the 1950s and 1960s, language arts was based on teaching basic skills. More time was spent on phonics drills and practice worksheets than actual reading and writing. In order to make education more meaningful, the whole language movement began in the 1970s. This movement suggested that teachers instruct reading and writing through real-life writing experiences and rich literature. Due to conflicting views in the 1980s, people felt that phonics and spelling were being ignored and demanded that schools abandon the whole language approach to return to phonics drill and spelling practice. Current research shows that both of these methods can exist together to provide a balanced spelling curriculum (Degeneffe & Ward, 1998). Even more recently, Zutell, a professor of Elementary Education and Reading best known for his research on word sorts and word webs, states

> Now the challenge is to develop focused approaches that not only help students become fluent spellers, but also are systematically connected to the writing processes. These new approaches should be consistent with language and literature-based instruction and with child-centered, active approaches to student learning. (2009, p.1)

Often teachers forget how important spelling is to students' daily work. In places where educators had eliminated spelling instruction, they found that test scores dramatically lowered and the schools began to see failure within their literacy program (Gentry, 2009). Research shows that learning to spell is a developmental process. Good spellers use many strategies in their work while poor spellers use a small amount of strategies. A major goal of spelling is to have students improve the range of strategies used when spelling unfamiliar words (Chase-Lockwood & Masino, 2002). It can also be used to improve students' abilities and confidence as productive readers and writers.

It is found that although students can spell correctly on weekly spelling tests, this does not ensure they are spelling words correctly in written work (Johnson & Marlow, 1996). According to Allred (1977), spelling ability affects a writer's creativity. He continues by saying "good spellers are able to express their thoughts on paper freely while poor spellers are hampered in their ability to communicate in writing" (p.5). Spelling errors can cause the reader to devalue the message of the writer. Difficulties in spelling can also interfere with the implementation of other processes of composing. When students have to concentrate on how to spell words as they write, it exhausts their processing memory which causes them to forget ideas and plans for their writing. Difficulties in spelling can even influence the words students choose to use as they write, as they are unlikely to use words they cannot spell (Graham et al., 2008).

Spelling is also important to all stages of a child's reading. Phonics instruction, often taught as a component of spelling, will help students decode words and improve word recognition. To become better readers, students must be able to identify words quickly and accurately. When students are able to recognize large amounts of words, their reading fluency improves and increases the ease at which students read the text. As children no longer have to struggle with decoding words, they can pay more attention to making meaning of what they read (Blevins, 2001).

Research shows that many teachers use a traditional test/study/test method of teaching spelling, which is a conventional approach. Using this method, teachers give a test at the beginning of the week, and the words missed usually become the spelling list for the students to study. A post-test is then given at the end of the week (Murphy, 1997). This approach has been found to have little impact on students' spelling ability. It does not require children to apply the words on their weekly spelling lists to their daily work. When taught through spelling lists, children focus on the individual words rather than learning strategies that can be applied to many words. As a result they are memorizing words for the test, but not truly learning them or learning how to use them (Degeneffe & Ward, 1998).

The traditional approach often teaches words in isolation which contradicts the main purpose of spelling which is to connect it to writing. Research shows that teachers have become frustrated with pre-packaged spelling programs that do not impact students' writing because the high frequency words are not being mastered (Chase-Lockwood & Masino, 2002). Also, students may not see a reason to make correct spelling an important part of their writing. Many children continue to spell words phonetically, even when a word has already been taught and mastered on a spelling test. The focus of spelling needs to be moved from simple memorization to recognizing and correctly spelling the words they see daily in their reading and writing (DuBois, Erickson, & Jacobs, 2007).

Often teachers choose to use the more traditional approach because of the lack of training in best spelling practices. One national survey reported that some teachers did not even teach spelling (Graham et al., 2008). In order to be proficient in spelling instruction, teachers need proper training. Due to this lack of training, many teachers treat spelling as a separate subject from other literacy instruction (Chase-Lockwood & Masino, 2002).If teachers were more familiar with alternative methods of spelling instruction, we would not have to rely solely on the traditional approach.

Student disengagement and boredom are often the consequences of the traditional approach to teaching spelling. Much of the time student motivation is low and spelling is thought of as unimportant. Many seem to resent this rote way of learning how to spell words (Angelisi, 2000). This may be because teachers do not spend as much time teaching it as they do testing it (Johnson & Marlow, 1996).

Word Study is an alternative approach to spelling instruction that moves away from memorization as the focus (Williams, Phillips-Birdsong, Hufnagel, Hungler, & Lundstrom, 2009). Through spelling instruction, students have the chance to investigate and manipulate word parts. This model assesses a learner's knowledge of words and then gives spelling instruction in phonics, spelling, and vocabulary based on the learners' developmental stage (Massengill-Shaw & Berg, 2008). These levels can be determined by giving a quality spelling inventory which is a list of approximately twenty words or by using a list of words organized by developmental spelling levels (Templeton & Morris, 1999).The results of this assessment are used to group students for more individualized spelling instruction.

The word study approach is beneficial to students in many ways. It helps children quickly and accurately recognize word patterns within our written language. When students rapidly recognize words it provides more opportunities to engage in meaningful reading. Using this approach, children can compare and contrast characteristics of words and discover similarities and differences among them. This will help students not only learn about our language and its function, but also to improve comprehension of the words they read. Research states that word study is developmentally appropriate for students. "That is, word study differentiates word-level instruction according to students' demonstrated levels of orthographic awareness; it authentically integrates word-level skills with reading and writing vocabulary; and the activities are student-centered" (Invernizzi, Abouzeid, & Bloodgood, 2004, p.12). When students are actively involved in their instruction and are taught at their own individual spelling levels, they are more engaged and encounter less boredom than when taught with a more traditional approach.

Importance of the Study and Statement of the Problem

Spelling is one of the most researched areas in language arts, yet many teachers are still struggling to determine the most effective methods of teaching it. Many educators continue to use a more traditional approach to spelling. However, current research is showing that word study may be a more effective method. We believe that spelling instruction at the intermediate school level is an area of concern for teachers. As educators, we see our students continually spell words correctly on weekly spelling tests yet not transfer them to their written work. This research was intended to give educators insight to the outcome of a traditional method of spelling instruction versus a word study approach. Gathering this data provided teachers with information that would help them make more informed decisions about their own spelling program in order to better meet the individual needs of their students. The purpose of this study was to determine if the word study approach to teaching spelling is more effective than the traditional approach.

Literature Review

Historical Trends

Research has shown that spelling has gone through various instructional trends through the years. Throughout the 1950s and 1960s, language was based on teaching basic skills. It was directed by scope and sequence charts and phonics drill and practice worksheets. During the 1970s, the whole language movement became the new trend in spelling instruction. Reading and writing was taught through the context of genuine literature and real-life writing experiences. Researchers wanted to replace drill and practice worksheets. Degeneffe & Ward (1998) indicated that in later years people felt whole language ignored phonics and spelling, and they wanted basic phonics taught again. Current research shows that both methods should coexist. Direct instruction of spelling is necessary within the context of meaningful experiences now and in the future.

Many researchers have found that for decades teachers have struggled with how to best teach spelling. With increasing focus on reading instruction, spelling has not been a key priority. "Unfortunately, much of the time teachers are not provided with the adequate training and support that would make their teaching truly effective" (Degeneffe & Ward, 1998, p. 20). Most teachers treat spelling as a subject away from language arts. Teicher (2005) explains that schools often settle for reading book supplements that contain word lists without guidance for teaching spelling, because it is not in the budget to purchase effective spelling curricula. Others use textbook series and neglect fundamentals of how English works and spelling pronunciations. Many teachers think memorizing is the key for good spelling. Students are expected to memorize words, but not use them on a daily basis or in their writing (Chase-Lockwood & Masino, 2002). Teachers focus too much on weekly spelling tests and do not teach with other subject area connections. Instead, they need to learn the developmental stages of spelling and be trained in phonics awareness in order to help students visualize the conventions of spelling words (DuBois, Erickson, & Jacobs, 2007). The combination of the above mentioned causes seem to indicate why students do not spell as well as they could and should.

Importance of Spelling to Reading

Research shows that the more students understand about the structure of words and their spelling, the more efficient and fluent their reading will be (Templeton & Morris, 1999). Countless research studies have been done on phonics instruction which is taught as a component of spelling. All children can benefit from instruction in common sound-spelling relationships and syllable patterns in English (Blevins, 2001). When students come across unfamiliar words in reading, they can apply their knowledge of word patterns to understand the sound of these words. By learning phonics, students make faster progress in attaining key literacy skills. "Phonics instruction is therefore an essential ingredient in reading instruction, as it teaches children how to read with accuracy, comprehension, fluency, and pleasure" (Blevins, 2001, p.12).

There is a direct connection between spelling and students' reading stages. Research has found that there are different phases of reading that cover a range from pre-readers to mature readers. Researchers have described how these reading stages connect to students' spelling. As students advance through the stages, their spelling is also improving. During the emergent stage children may spell with random letters that have no phonetic relationship to the words they believe they are writing. Students may read words they recognize, because it starts with a certain letter. They do not have a true understanding of how the alphabet works. A student in the beginning stage has moved from pretend reading to real reading. They begin to use letter sounds to identify and store words in their memory (Bear et al., 2008). As they spell, children begin to obtain a more complete knowledge of letter sounds and they will often include, but confuse, vowels in the words they are spelling. Transitional readers begin to recognize patterns or chunks of words when reading and spelling. Students begin to recognize and use initial consonants, blends, and diagraphs and then focus on the vowel and the rest of the letters that end the word. They do continue to use, but confuse, the vowels in words. Intermediate and advanced readers have automatic word recognition, and their minds are free to think rapidly as they read and spell new words. However, students in this reading stage may still have difficulty spelling the endings or final syllables of words (Bear et al., 2008).

Importance of Spelling to Writing

Research has also shown that when students are strong spellers, it will improve the quality of their writing. In a study done by Johnson and Marlow (1996), second grade students from two different schools located in the suburbs of Chicago, Illinois, were unable to retain and transfer weekly spelling words to their written work. In order to improve their students' spelling in writing, a pre-test was given to show students' errors and writing samples were collected. In School A, 42% of the words on the pre-test were spelled correctly. In School B, 28% of the words were spelled correctly. School A spelled 51% of words correctly on their writing sample, while School B spelled 26% of the words correctly on their writing sample.

The goal of this study was for students to be able to apply spelling words in writing assignments. Johnson and Marlow (1996) also wanted students to learn to apply strategies for spelling words and identify errors in their writing. The students were taught spelling strategies and shown how to apply them in their writing assignments. They also developed student and class spelling dictionaries. A spelling trend assessment form was used to help students identify misspellings found in written work. Writing samples were kept during the study, and spelling tests were given along the way to track students' progress.

After four months a post spelling test was given, and a writing sample was written by students to determine if these interventions were successful. Results showed that School A spelled 86% of their words correctly on the spelling post-test (a 44% increase from their pre-test score), and School B spelled 68% of their words correctly on the spelling post-test (a 40% increase from their pre-test). On the writing samples, School A spelled 86% of words correctly (a 35% increase), and School B spelled 650lo of words correctly (a 39% increase). The researchers' conclusions showed that students significantly increased in retention and transfer of words to their writing.

Another study was conducted by Chase-Lockwood and Masino (2002) because their fifth grade classes, with clusters of learning disabilities, were having difficulty transferring spelling skills into their written work. At the beginning of the study a pre-test was given as well as a writing assessment. In Classroom A, 11% of students spelled the words at a mastery level (90% or better), 50% spelled at a partial mastery level (70-89% right), and 39% spelled at a non-mastery level (below 70%). In Classroom B, 30% of students spelled the words at a mastery level, 40% spelled at a partial mastery level, and 30% spelled at a non-mastery level. In Classroom C, 5% of students spelled the words at a mastery level, 33% spelled at a partial mastery level, and 62% spelled at a non-mastery level. In the written assessment an average of 14% of the words, in all three classrooms, was misspelled. A variety of spelling strategies were used for five months in these fifth grade classrooms.

Students created personal spelling dictionaries where they could add words they were learning. Then, they could refer to this dictionary while they were writing. The classrooms also participated in word sorts. Individual words were printed on cards, and students were asked to group and categorize them according to specific features. Students became active in their learning rather than just memorizing spelling words. In addition, breaking words activities were used in these classrooms. Students were taught to look for small words within words to help them spell longer words.

At the end of the study, a post test and writing prompt were administered. The results showed that in Classroom A, 56% of students spelled the words at a mastery level (90% or better), 37% spelled at a partial mastery level (70-89% right), and 7% spelled at a non-mastery level (below 70%). In Classroom B, 46% of students spelled the words at a mastery level, 43% spelled at a partial mastery level, and 11% spelled at a non-mastery level. In Classroom C, 20% of students spelled the words at a mastery level, 60% spelled at a partial mastery level, and 20% spelled at a non-mastery level. In the written assessment an average of 11% of the words, in all three classrooms, was misspelled. This shows an improvement of 3% from the first writing sample.

In a third study conducted by DuBois, Erickson, & Jacobs (2007), kindergarten, first, and third grade students were not consistently using spelling words in their daily work. They were spelling them correctly in isolation, but not transferring them to their writing. A pretest and a

Gentry Developmental Spelling Inventory were given at the beginning of the study. In this spelling inventory, each word given is categorized into levels of developmental spelling. These levels begin at the precommunicative level and move through the stages of semiphonetic, phonetic, transitional, and conventional. On the pretest, kindergarten students spelled 15% correctly, first grade students spelled 23% correctly, and the third grade students spelled 74%

correctly. On the Gentry Spelling Inventory, 32% of the students in the three classrooms were at the precommunicative stage, 23% were at the semiphonetic stage, 23% were at the phonetic stage, 23% were at the transitional, and 13% were at the conventional stage.

The goal of this study was to help students develop skills that would enhance their ability and confidence as effective writers and communicators (DeBois, Erickson, & Jacobs, 2007). They worked during a period from September through December. Spelling instruction consisted of a minimum of seventy-five minutes per week. They taught high frequency words from the Dolch Sight Word List. They also used multisensory spelling methods that included writing words with shaving cream, on sand paper, and with magnetic letters. Students were also taught to sort words by vowels, word patterns, blends, and chunks. Additionally, they were taught to self-correct and edit their writing and use word walls.

The researchers concluded that the instructional adaptations were successful. A post-test and the Gentry Developmental Spelling Inventory was given at the conclusion of the study. On the post test, kindergarten students spelled 67% correctly (a 52% increase), first grade students spelled 68% correctly (a 45% increase), and the third grade students spelled 94% correctly (a 20% increase). On the Gentry Spelling Inventory, 0% of the students in the three classrooms were at the precommunicative stage, 18% were at the semiphonetic stage, 22% were at the phonetic stage, 23% were at the transitional, and 37% were at the conventional stage.

Traditional Approach to Teaching Spelling

Research shows that most teachers use a traditional test/study/test method to teach spelling in the classroom (Murphy, 1997). This method is deemed the conventional approach. Most often students are given a pretest at the beginning of the week. Misspelled words become their list to study throughout the week, and then they are given a test on Friday. Many times spelling words are also practiced by completing various assignments throughout the week.

More recently there has been an increase in research surrounding spelling. "Many of the traditional approaches have proven to be ineffective at helping students become proficient spellers"(Johnson & Marlow, 1996, p.23). Spelling is a subject often taught in isolation, and it is not used as a tool for reading and writing. Due to this lack of connection, students do not recognize the primary purpose of needing to spell correctly. Johnson and Marlow (1996) state that many words used in traditional spelling programs are unfamiliar to students and not frequently used as part of their speaking and writing vocabulary. Many times the number of words presented to students weekly can be overwhelming. Often children are placed in spelling programs according to their grade level. This placement does not take into consideration students' individual developmental levels.

Consistently, educational literature is reporting that the traditional approach to spelling is not effective for many students (Teicher, 2005). The findings show that children are not retaining and transferring words from their weekly spelling lists into other areas of the curriculum. There are many probable causes as to why this is occurring (Johnson & Marlow, 1996). Teachers are not being provided with adequate instruction on best practices. In addition, poor spelling resources are being used, and there is overdependence on commercial materials (Beirn-Smith & Riley, 2009). Furthermore, current spelling programs are not requiring students to use words outside of the spelling lessons, and the traditional approach lacks the teaching of strategies that are needed to be successful at spelling the words in the English language (Johnson & Marlow, 1996). These "are among the many factors that can jeopardize the ability of any student to learn to spell" (Beirm-Smith & Riley, 2009, p.171).

There is also a lack of motivation by the students to learn spelling when taught with the traditional method. In a study by Angelisi (2009), the traditional spelling method was compared to other methods of spelling instruction. She conducted a three week long study comparing three different spelling strategies in her third grade classroom. Prior to teaching her spelling lessons each week, a pretest of words was given in order to determine students' knowledge of those words. A lesson test was administered at the end of each week. She taught one group with phonemic awareness strategies including the use of flashcards, syllable tapping, and discovering rhyming patterns for words. A second method used word recognition to help students spell words. They used basic sight words they already knew to help them learn to spell more difficult words. The final method used a more traditional drill and write strategy. The students wrote words three times each, found the definition for each word, wrote sentences using the words, and completed work book pages for each lesson. Students were split into three groups. For three weeks the groups would rotate in order to be taught by each different strategy one at a time.

The findings showed that the phonemic awareness groups scored between 95-100% on their post-test each week, the word identification group scored 100% on their post-test each week, and students using the drill and write method scored between 88- 100% each week. These scores prove that the drill and write learning style was least successful in engaging students' attention and memory by the end of each week. However, the scores do show that the drill and write method did not lose out by much when compared to the other two (Angelisi, 2000).

Angelisi's (2000) study also indicated how students felt when using each of these spelling strategies. Through discussions and observations with her students, she found that the drill and write method caused all three groups to feel more frustrated when completing the sentences, definitions, and work book pages independently without any other sources to help them. They seemed bored when performing these tasks, and this technique did not strengthen students' attention or memory spans. Even after students wrote sentences using their words, they had difficulty determining the meaning of them. They merely completed the tasks they were given without comprehending the meaning of each word. Using the phonemic awareness and word recognition strategies, proved more successful in holding students' interest. They were able to work more independently on their tasks and use resources they were provided to spell words. Students seemed to absorb this strategy and improved when decoding words. Angelisi (2000) concluded that when students were asked to use the traditional method, their love for learning diminished. She believed that they deserved to be taught in ways that encouraged their love of learning and held their interest.

Zone of Proximal Development

Often with the traditional method of teaching spelling, the same spelling lists are given to all students. These spelling lists may not meet the needs of all students. The lists can be frustrating to children who have difficulty with spelling, and those who excel in spelling may be bored with their list and need something more challenging (Chase-Lockwood & Masino, 2002). To determine how best to teach spelling with each child, educators need to focus on each students' developmental spelling level. This level is also called the zone of proximal development (ZPD) which was developed by the Russian psychologist, Lev Vygotsky. "This concept suggests that there is a tie between instruction and a child's development and that the best instruction moves children to higher levels of independence" (Gentry, 2004, p.32).

Educators can learn how to engage students in their learning about word features in a developmentally appropriate way. Students can build on what they already know, to learn what they need to know next, and to move forward (Bear et al., 2008). Instruction is useful when it is moved ahead of development and scaffolded by an adult. Eventually the level of assistance decreases, and the learner can work more independently. "If instruction takes place outside of a learner's ZPD, nothing will be gained as the child is beyond the scope of his understanding and development" (Elliott & Rietschel, 1999, p.4).

Word Study Approach to Teaching Spelling

In research conducted by Bear, Invernizzi, Templeton, and Johnston (2008), word study was found to be an important method for teaching spelling. Teachers can differentiate effective instruction in phonics, spelling, and vocabulary. The wordy study program teaches students necessary skills and engages their interest and motivation to learn about how words work (Bear et al., 2008). This approach provides students hands-on opportunities to manipulate word features and create groups of words that are spelled the same way. Word study teaches students how to look at words so they can construct a deeper understanding of how spelling words represent sound and meaning.

Word study is important, because it helps students develop a general knowledge of English spelling. A teacher provides the class with opportunities to learn the regular patterns and conventions of English orthography, which is the correct sequence of letters in the writing system. Word study also increases specific knowledge of a word's spelling and meaning. It helps to examine words to show consistencies in our written language in order to help students master the recognition, spelling, and meaning of specific words (Bear et al., 2008).

"Word study also comes from what we have learned about the orthographic structure of written words" (Bear et al., 2008, p. 5). There are three layers of English orthography and each layer builds on the one before. The alphabetic layer represents the relationship between letters and sounds. The pattern layer is above the alphabetic layer. Our language does not have a single sound for each letter all of the time. Sometimes sounds are spelled with more than one letter and can be affected by other letters that don't stand for any sounds themselves. This means that we must search for patterns within words. The third orthographic layer is the layer of meaning. This is where students learn that groups of letters can represent meaning.

Developmental spelling research shows that students' growth in knowledge of words move through ordered stages. As students move through the orthographic layers, they develop knowledge of specific word features. An emergent speller produces large scribbles that are basically drawings and they can sometimes add pretend writing next to their pictures. During this stage children begin to learn letters and pay attention to sounds in words. The next stage is alphabetic spelling. Students use the names of letters to represent the sounds they want to use. They also learn to segment sounds within words and match the correct letters or letter pairs to these sounds. Children will often spell the first sound and last sound to represent the entire word. Later in the stage long vowels, which say their names, begin to appear in children's spelling, and students learn to use consonant blends. Additionally, spellers begin using short vowel sounds and digraphs. Students in the word within word pattern spelling stage can read and spell words correctly due to their knowledge of letter sounds and short-vowel patterns. They move away from the sound-by-sound approach of letter names and begin to think of patterns or chunks of letters to spell words. They also begin to look more closely to vowel patterns. A speller in the syllables and affixes stage will still be using patterns and words, and also learning how prefixes and suffixes affect word meaning and spelling. A student in the derivational relations spelling stage is in the last stage of the developmental model. This stage continues through adulthood and can begin as early as fourth or fifth grade. In this stage students begin to examine how words share common derivations and related base words and word roots (Bear et al., 2008). They also expand their knowledge of vocabulary by learning words with Greek and Latin origins.

At the start of a word study program the teacher will begin working with groups of students at their developmental level. Groups are created after the teacher administers the Elementary Spelling Inventory, and determines students' spelling stages. Words are then learned by comparing and contrasting their features and discovering similarities and differences between them. Rather than rote memorization, word study encourages active exploration and examination of word features. Children create their own understanding about how word features work. Through active practice, students begin to internalize word features which will become automatic when spelling (Bear et al., 2008).

Word sorting is a key component of word study.

> When students sort words, they are engaged in the active process of searching, comparing, contrasting, and analyzing. Word sorts help students organize what they know about words and to form generalizations that they can then apply to new words they encounter in their reading. (Bear et al., 2008, p. 51)

Word sorts provide a hands-on opportunity for children to manipulate words. Students must pay attention to words and make decisions about their sound, pattern, and meaning as they place them in columns. They determine similarities and differences among features of words, and use higher level thinking skills to place words into categories. Sorts can be teacher-directed so that the columns for sorting words are already set up before students begin putting words into them. Sorts can also be more student-centered where the categories are created by those working in the group.

In a study conducted by Degeneffe and Ward (1998) strategies were used to improve the spelling of first and third grade students. Student progress was measured through writing samples and report card grades in spelling. A student attitude survey was also given. During the study, students were taught visual spelling patterns. They hunted through their reading for words that fit certain spelling patterns, and also sorted various spelling words into particular sounds. Writing samples were taken from students every two weeks during the intervention. At the end of the study, a final writing sample was collected. Students showed a marked improvement in the correct spelling of words on this assessment. "The most significant change was in the attitude toward spelling in general; students in both targeted groups showed an increase in the levels of perceived importance of spelling words correctly" (Degeneffe & Ward, 1998, p. 36).

A second study conducted by Massengill Shaw and Berg (2008) evaluated the impact of word study on the spelling ability of adults with limited literacy proficiency. Ten participants from an adult literacy center in Midwestern City were chosen to participate in this study. None had more than a high school education, and they attended the literacy center to receive help with the basics of reading and spelling simple words. These ten students were divided in half so that five were in a control group and five were in an experimental group. A developmental spelling analysis was given at the beginning of the study. This test showed what features of words students knew and their knowledge of spelling patterns and sounds. The pretest showed that the traditional (control) group had a mean score of 25 words spelled correctly and that the word study (experimental) group had a mean score of 10 words spelled correctly.

Participants in the word study group participated in word sorting activities. They were presented with twenty word cards that contained two to four different spelling features. They were told to sort the words in whatever way made sense to them. Once words were sorted into categories, participants made a guess about sounds they heard in each word group. After this knowledge was mastered, the adults could apply it to new and unknown words during future lessons. Participants in the traditional group used more traditional spelling methods. They were assigned five to six sight words and then had to write these words multiple times. The teacher in this group also provided them pages of spelling rules for support and explanation. Participants were then tested at the next session. When words were spelled correctly, new words were presented.

Post-test results showed that the traditional spelling group had a mean score of 28 words (an increase of 3 words) spelled correctly. The word study spelling group had a mean score of 32 words (an increase of 12 words) spelled correctly. An interview was conducted with participants of the word study group at the conclusion of this study. Results indicated adults had an increased awareness of phonics, a greater amount and heightened sense of self-efficacy, and an appreciation of the convenience of the method (Massengill Shaw & Berg, 2008).

A third study conducted by Elliott and Rietschel (1999) examined the effects of word study on second grade students' application of spelling and phonics in their independent writing. These researchers worked with nineteen students. Seven children are ESL (English Second Language), seven children are Strategies/LRE (Least Restrictive Environment), and five students were in the general population. The Strategies/LRE group consisted of students who qualified for special education services, students who were tested and did not qualify for special education services, and those who were currently being monitored for special education in the future.

Several methods of data were collected including the Elementary Qualitative Spelling Inventory and independent writing samples. The Qualitative Spelling Inventory gives students a set of twenty five words to spell. A teacher then analysis the words spelled incorrectly to determine each student's developmental stage of spelling. Writing samples were taken from students' journals to assess their transfer of spelling into their writing. Pretest scores showed that students in the general population spelled 36% of words correctly, students in the Strategies/LRE group spelled 12% of words correctly, and children in the ESL group spelled 8% of words correctly.

Elliott and Rietschel (1999) divided the class into four different developmental spelling groups after administering the Qualitative Spelling Inventory. Small groups of students worked for seven months and explored patterns in words and learned to apply them to new words. They also participated in student discovery activities including word hunts, word softs, and making words.

At the end of the study, the Qualitative Spelling Inventory was again given to students. Post test scores showed that those in the general population spelled 56% (an increase of 20%) of words correctly, students in the Strategies/LRE group spelled 28% (an increase of 16%) of words correctly, and children in the ESL group spelled 36% (an increase of 28%) of words correctly. In addition, students' spelling in their writing improved during the course of this study. The researcher's concluded that based on the findings of their study, organized wordy study has positive effects on spelling performance, particularly the ESL population (Elliott & Rietschel, 1990).

Summary

Literature and research conducted on spelling instruction has revealed that it has changed through the years. Despite all of this research, teachers still are not certain of best spelling practices. Spelling is known to improve students' reading and writing. However, children are failing to transfer words learned into other areas of the curriculum. Current research is showing that the traditional method is not the most effective way to improve students' knowledge of the English language. Recently, it has been found that teaching students at their developmental spelling level may be more appropriate at helping them improve mastery of word knowledge. Word study has been found to be a more effective method of spelling instruction. This research study will attempt to determine if the word study approach is in fact more beneficial than the traditional approach.

Methodology

Participants

This study was conducted in an Intermediate School in Central Illinois. The participants of the study were selected from the Intermediate School. This district is made up of one preschool, six primary schools, two intermediate schools, and two junior high schools. Based on district boundary lines within the city, approximately 500 students from the various primary schools were enrolled at the Intermediate School.

Socioeconomically, the population of the Intermediate School has a low income rate of 39%. The school population is made up of numerous ethnicities including Caucasian (95.8 %), African American (0.2%), Hispanic (1.4%), Asian/Pacific Islander (0.2%), Native American (0.8%), and Multi-racial/Ethnic (1.6 %).

The Intermediate School is made up of seven fourth grade classrooms, one fourth grade Special Education classroom, six fifth grade classrooms, seven sixth grade classrooms, and one fifth/sixth grade Special Education classroom. The Intermediate School also has one Emotional Disorder classroom. The average class size for the 2008-2009 school year was nineteen students in fourth and fifth grade and twenty students in sixth grade.

There will be forty five students participating in this spelling study with ages ranging from nine to ten years old. They were selected from two of the seven fourth grade classes and all vary in ability levels. The Traditional Approach Classroom consists of twenty-three students with thirteen being male and ten female. Ethnic backgrounds include Caucasian (92%), Multi-racial/Ethnic (< 1 %), and Asian (<1 %). The socioeconomic make-up of the class is 39% low income. This classroom has two students with a 504 plan. The plan for one student allows her extra time to manage her medical needs due to diabetes. The other student has modifications to allow her extra time with her school work, as needed, due to ADHD. One student from this classroom receives speech services. The Word Study Approach Classroom consists of twenty-two students with nine being male and eleven female. Ethnic backgrounds include Caucasian (95%) and Multi-racial/Ethnic (<1 %). The socioeconomic make-up of the class is 39% low income. This classroom has two students with a 504 plan. The plan for one student allows him extra time to manage his medical needs due to diabetes. The other student has modifications to allow her extra time with her school work, as needed, due to ADHD. One student from this classroom receives speech services.

Instrumentation

Action research will be part of our research design. "Action research is a model of research that has, as its focus, the improvement of practice" (Parsons & Brown, 2002, p.6). It guides teachers in making decisions or improving their teaching methods. It also gives teachers a method for viewing their decisions in a systematic and rational way. Action research is valid and reliable because it involves designing research questions and hypotheses. Teachers determine a problem and decide possible actions that will lead to improvement.

> In action research these actions will be implemented, and data depicting their impact will be collected, reviewed, and employed to improve the understanding of the problem. In this way, teaching decisions are not only shaped by theory and research, but in turn help give shape and new

directions to educational theory and research. (Parsons & Brown, 2002, p.7)

Quantitative data collection will also be a part of our research design. "Quantitative research employs methods that attempt to categorize and assign numbers to an experience or event" (Parsons & Brown, 2002, p.50). Data can be compared with data collected from another time as a way of assessing the value of the teaching strategies used. The data can be manipulated with statistical measures. Descriptive statistics will be used to organize and describe our data collected and inferential statistics will help to observe the difference between the two groups. Descriptive statistics work best for our research, because it helps to simplify large amounts of data in a way that is easy to understand, and inferential statistics benefits our research since it can be used to observe differences between two groups (Trochim, 2006).

The instrument used in this research study was a pre and post spelling test administered in both the Traditional and Word Study Approach Classrooms. This test is a spelling inventory consisting of words that represent a variety of spelling features and patterns of increasing levels of difficulty. "Spelling inventories are quick and easy to administer and score, and they are reliable and valid measures of what students know about words" (Bear, Invernizzi, Templeton, & Johnston, 2008, p. 29). They assess students' knowledge of key spelling features that are most helpful in identifying a student's spelling level and planning instruction. These features range from first through sixth grade and can help track students' spelling growth over time (Bear et al., 2008).

This pre and posttest was not given for grading purposes and students did not study the words before or during spelling instruction. Thirty minutes was set aside to administer the inventory, and students numbered their papers to twenty-five. The class was told they would be asked to spell some words and that they would not be graded on them. Some of the words would be easy, and others would be more difficult. The purpose of this assessment was to show how well students spelled and where to begin their instruction. Each word was pronounced naturally without drawing out sounds or breaking it into syllables. The word was said aloud, a sentence was read using it in context, and then the word was repeated (Bear et al, 2008). After all twenty-five words were read students' papers were collected.

The teachers from both classrooms graded each student's spelling pre and posttest by marking the words spelled incorrectly. A score showing the number of words spelled correctly out of twenty-five total words was given. On the pretest the Word Study Approach Classroom used a Spelling Inventory Feature Guide (see Appendix B) to further divide students into groups based on their test results. The results of the pre and post spelling tests were compared between both classrooms to determine which method of spelling instruction benefited students the most.

Words for the pre and post spelling tests came from the Elementary Spelling Inventory (ESI) (see Appendix A). This inventory came from the book *Words Their Way: Word Study for Phonics, Vocabulary, and Spelling Instruction* published by Pearson Education Inc. Test results were recorded into Excel spreadsheets which were then imported into the SPSS Statistics software.

During this study measures were taken to reduce bias and achieve objectivity. All students were asked to spell the same twenty-five words from the Elementary Spelling Inventory. All words were pronounced in the same way for every student. Each class received the same amount of time to complete the test on a day when all students were present. Teachers in both classrooms did not provide extra help to their students during these tests. In order to further reduce bias and achieve objectivity, the teachers from the Traditional and Word Study Approach Classrooms exchanged tests and scored each other's.

Teaching Methods

In the Traditional Approach Classroom, spelling was taught weekly. The words were chosen in a variety of ways. Often, most students had the same words and same number of words. When students had the same spelling list, the words were compiled from the curriculum and stories currently being taught and read in this classroom. Students that struggled with the regular spelling list were given a reduced number of words. On most weeks, the list was introduced on Monday with a test following on Friday.

Some weeks, in an attempt to personalize and make spelling more meaningful, students would be allowed to choose their own words from a variety of reading material. They were instructed to go through their current independent reading books to collect words that they did not know how to spell. Students would compile a list of as many words as they could. If they needed more words to complete their lists, the teacher would provide misspelled words from their writing journals in order to create a list of twenty words. On weeks that each student had a different list, they were paired up on test day to give each other a spelling test.

Throughout the week, in the Traditional Approach Classroom, students would study and practice their spelling words a few different ways. At the beginning of the week activities were assigned and given a due date. To practice the spelling words, students would be asked to write a sentence using each word, complete word searches, draw comic strips using the spelling words, write the words multiple times, and study with a partner using a small white board.

In the Word Study Approach Classroom, spelling was taught on a weekly basis. After giving students the Elementary Spelling Inventory, their words were transferred to an Elementary Spelling Inventory Feature Guide. This guide helped determine the types of spelling words students should practice and be tested on each week. Children were then grouped according to their spelling level. Two groups of five students were at the word within word spelling level, five students were in the syllable and affixes spelling level, and six students were at the derivational relations level of spelling.

Two teachers met with small groups of students three times a week for fifteen to twenty minutes to work with assigned spelling words at each group's developmental level. On Monday, all groups did an initial word sort into categories. For example, one group may be sorting a list of words into the -ee (long e) category, -ai (long a) category, and the -oa (long o) category. Students are first introduced to the categories and discuss the key word given to help students remember what sound these letters make. Then, twelve words that fit into one of these categories are introduced and there meanings are discussed. Afterwards, students do a word sort and write these words below the categories they think match them. These word sorts are graded and students make any corrections to their sort. A spelling list is then given to students that sort the words into categories that they can take home to study during the week.

After the first spelling test, the teacher noticed that students did not seem to understand how to take a spelling test where they had to use categories to spell words. As a result, a lesson was taught that gave students a chance to practice their words by taking a spelling pretest. The test had the spelling categories listed at the top of the page with the key word to help students remember how to say each pattern. As words were given, students were guided about how to think about each word as they decided how to spell it. They had to determine what sound cach word made and then spell it correctly using the categories at the top of the test to assist them. Students had to make sure they used the pattern listed at the top of the test in the spelling of their word.

On Friday, students were given a spelling test within their spelling group. These tests were graded not only for spelling but also assessed if students were putting words into correct categories and using the patterns provided for them. Students who were not successful with their spelling tests were given more direct instruction about how to use the categories on their tests to help them spell words correctly.

The derivational relations spelling group had more difficult words and patterns for students to study. There initial Monday discussion of words and sort took them more than one class period to complete. Therefore, these students practiced their words for two weeks before they took a test. After their sort was complete, these students played games with their word patterns or looked up the meaning of words they were unfamiliar with to promote further understanding of them. These students then took their test after two weeks of practice.

Spelling lists for the next week were then determined based on the next word patterns for students' spelling levels given in the book *Words Their Way: Word Study for Phonics, Vocabulary, and Spelling Instruction*. The teacher in the Word Study Approach Classroom taught using these methods for the duration of the study.

Research Question

- Is the word study approach to teaching spelling more effective than the traditional approach?

Results

Data Analysis Procedure/Plan

The Social Packet for Social Sciences (SPSS) statistical software was used to analyze the data from both classrooms. SPSS comes with many useful features for data handling and manipulation and statistics and data managing. It is also useful for graphical output. Data can be put directly into the program in order to produce high quality graphs.

Using the scores from the pre and post-tests, a data table was created displaying the means and standard deviations for the pre and post test scores. It also shows the means of the differences (the amount of increase or decrease in students' scores) between the pre and post tests for the Traditional Approach and Word Study Approach Classrooms. Having the data displayed in this way allows the results to be easily compared between the two classrooms.

The mean of the pre and post test scores was used to analyze the data. "The mean is arithmetic average and, as a measure of central tendency, is computed by summing all of the individual scores and then dividing by the number of scores" (Parsons & Brown, 2002, p.5l). A mean describes a set of test performances for groups of students. After the pre and post spelling tests were conducted, an Excel file was used to record the data. The file was then downloaded to SPSS where the means were calculated for both the pre and posts tests and differences between them, for each classroom. Bar graphs were created to display the results.

The standard deviation was also calculated using the SPSS software. It is a measure of variability that refers to how far out scores are from the mean on a normal distribution. A normal distribution shows that more scores are concentrated in the middle. The standard deviations for the pre and post-tests, and differences between them, are displayed in the data table.

Creating t tests was the final method used to analyze the data. "The t test assesses whether the means of two groups are statistically different from each other. This analysis is appropriate whenever you want to compare the means of two groups, and especially appropriate as the analysis for the post test-only two-group randomized experimental design" (Trochim, 2006, p. l). The Excel file containing the data from the Traditional Approach and the Word Study Approach classrooms was downloaded to the SPSS software. From this file, SPSS was able to conduct multiple t tests which compared the means of each classroom's pre and post test scores as well as the means of the differences between the two classrooms.

Research Findings

Over the years we have found that students are not transferring the words they spell correctly on their spelling tests into their daily work. The goal of this research was to determine if the word study approach was more effective than the traditional approach to teaching spelling.

Our research took place in two different fourth grade classrooms at the Intermediate School from January 4, 2010 to February 26, 2010. We began by sending out a parent permission letter. Once they were all returned, a student assent letter was handed out to the students whose parents said they could participate in our research. This was read aloud and explained to students by a reading teacher who works in both fourth grade classrooms. In the Traditional Approach Classroom all parents and students agreed to participate in the research study. In the Word Study Approach Classroom two parents did not wish for their student to participate in the research study, and one student did not agree to participate.

Prior to the start of our research a pre-test of words from the Elementary Spelling Inventory (ESI) was given to students. This inventory contained words with increasing levels of difficulty, and helped us determine how well our students could spell. Based on this assessment, one teacher taught with the traditional approach to spelling, while the other teacher used the word study approach.

The teacher using the traditional approach to teach spelling gave lists of words on Monday followed by a test on Friday. Words were chosen based on the classroom reading selections and current curriculum being taught. A variety of ways to study and practice the words were assigned each week. Reduced lists were created for students with a much lower spelling ability.

The teacher using the word study approach to teach spelling divided students into groups based on the results from the ESI. Word sorts were done on Mondays where students had to place their words into categories based on the spelling pattern within each word. During the week, students were taught how to think about the spelling of their words in order to place them in the correct category on their test. They were also taught to use the patterns in those categories to correctly spell each word. A test was given on Friday, and a new list was created for the following week based on the next level of spelling in *Words Their Way: Word Study for Phonics, Vocabulary, and Spelling Instruction.*

For a post test at the conclusion of our research, we again gave the Elementary Spelling Inventory. These tests were scored to determine how many words students spelled correctly. We then compared the pre and post test scores to determine if there was an increase or decrease in these scores.

Twenty one students participated in the Traditional Approach Classroom, and eighteen students participated in the Word Study Approach Classroom (see Table 1). Our data shows that the mean of the Traditional Approach post-test was 16.62 with a standard deviation of 4.00, which indicates an increase from the mean of the pre-test score of 15.86 with a standard deviation of 3.67. There is not a significant increase between these two means. The mean of the Word Study Approach post-test was 17.17 with a standard deviation of 4.59, which shows an increase from the mean of the pre-test which is 14.44 with a standard deviation of 4.57. This indicates a more noticeable difference between the pre and post-test means than there is with the traditional approach to teaching spelling.

Table 1: Elementary Spelling Inventory Pretest and Post Test Results

Items	No.	Mean	Std. Deviation
Traditional Approach Pretest	21	15.86	3.67
Traditional Approach Post Test	21	16.62	4.00
Traditional Approach Difference	21	.89	1.78
Word Study Approach Pretest	18	14.44	4.57
Word Study Approach Post Test	18	17.17	4.59
Word Study Approach Difference	18	2.72	2.74

Table 1 also shows the mean of the differences between the pre and post tests for both the Traditional and Word Study Approach Classrooms. The mean of the difference for the Traditional Approach Classroom is .89 with a standard deviation of 1.78. For the Word Study Approach Classroom the mean of the difference is 2.72 with a standard deviation of 2.74. This indicates a large significance in the amount of words students spelled correctly between their pre and post-tests within the Word Study Approach Classroom.

The data in Figure 1 shows the mean of the pre-test and post-test in the Traditional Approach Classroom. There is an increase in the mean from 15.86 to 16.62. This indicates an increase of 0.76, which is not a significant gain between the pre and post test scores. Figure 1 also shows the mean of the difference which is the amount of increase or decrease from students' pre to post test scores. The mean of the difference for the Traditional Approach classroom is 0.89.

Figure 1: Traditional Approach Classroom Results

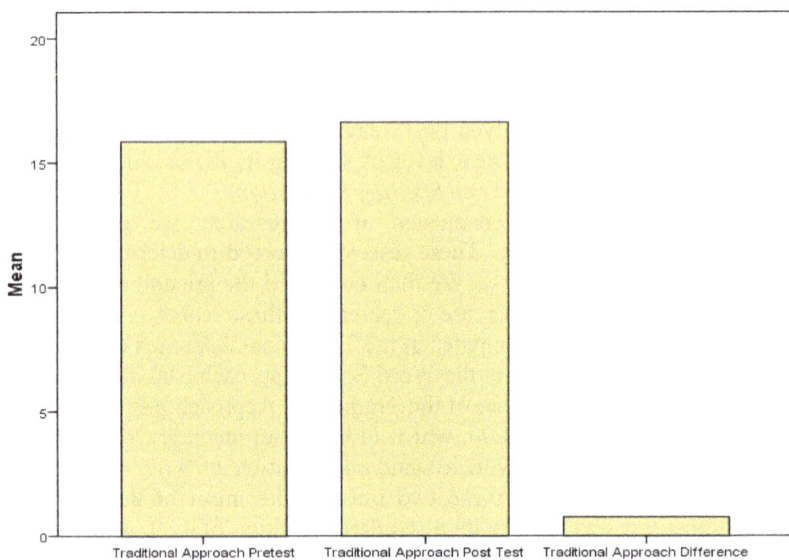

The data in Figure 2 displays the mean of the pre-test and post-test in the Word Study Approach Classroom. There is an increase in the mean from 14.44 to 17.17. This shows an increase of 2.73, which is a significant gain between the pre and post test scores. Figure 2 also shows the mean of the difference between both tests. The mean of the difference for the Word Study Approach Classroom is 2.72.

Figure 2: Word Study Approach Classroom Results

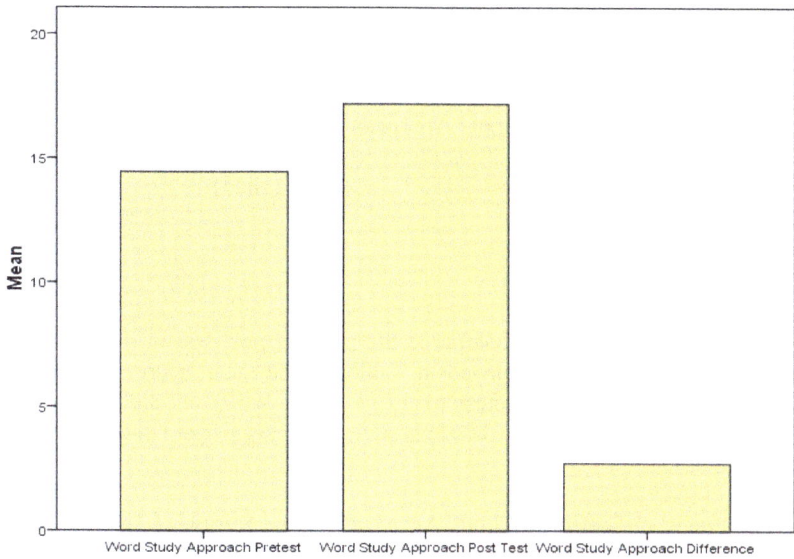

The mean of the difference in the Traditional Approach Classroom is 0.89 (see Figure 3). In the Word Study Approach Classroom, the mean of the difference is 2.72. There is noticeable increase in the amount of progress students made in the Word Study Approach Classroom when compared to the Traditional Approach Classroom.

Figure 3: Traditional and Word Study Approach Differences

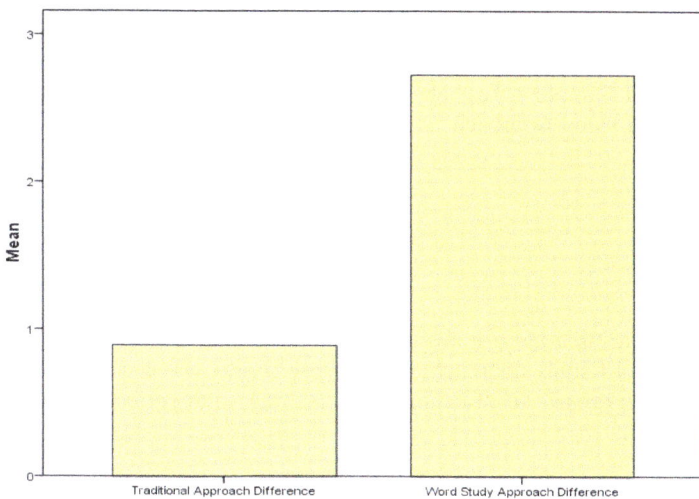

The results of the t test that compared the pre and post-test in the Traditional Approach Classroom are shown in Table 2. The mean score increased slightly, from 15.86 (sd = 3.68) on the pretest to 16.62 (sd = 4.00) on the post test. The difference between the means (0.076) is not statistically significant at the 0.05 level (t= -1.86, df = 20).

Table 2: Pretest & Post Traditional Approach-Paired Samples *t* Test

t	df	sig. (2-tailed)
-1.869	20	.076

The results of the t test that compared the pre and post-test in the Word Study Approach Classroom are displayed in Table 3. The mean score increased from 14.44 (sd = 4.57) on the pretest to 17.17 (sd = 4.59) on the post test. The difference between the means (0.001) is statistically significant at the 0.05 level (t = -4.21, df = 17).

Table 3: Pretest & Post Word Study Approach-Paired Samples t Test

t	df	sig. (2-tailed)
-4.215	17	.001

The results of the t test that compared the differences between the pre and post test scores in the Traditional and Word Study Approach Classrooms are displayed in Table 4. The mean of the differences in the Traditional Approach Classroom is 0.89 (sd = 1.78). The mean of the differences in the Word Study Approach Classroom is 2.72 (sd = 2.74). The difference between the means (0.038) is statistically significant at the 0.05 level (t= -2.25, df = 17).

Table 4: A Paired Sample *t* Test Showing the Difference between Traditional Approach & Word Study Approach

t	df	sig. (2-tailed)
-2.254	17	.038

This evidence proves that more students were successful with their spelling when taught with the word study approach. Given these results, we can conclude that the word study approach to teaching spelling was more effective than the traditional approach.

Discussion

The results show that the traditional approach to teaching spelling is not the most effective way to improve students' spelling. The data in Table 1 shows that there is not a significant increase between the means of the pre and post-tests. The mean of the difference, which is the amount of increase or decrease from students' pre to post test scores, also did not increase by a significant amount. The t test conducted using the mean scores from the pre and post-tests in the Traditional Approach Classroom shows that the difference between the means is not statistically significant. While students' scores did improve slightly, the results did not indicate a considerable increase in their spelling progress.

The results of this research, regarding the traditional approach to teaching spelling, are consistent with the results of other studies. Johnson and Marlow (1996) concluded that the traditional approach has proved to be ineffective at helping students become proficient spellers. When spelling is taught in isolation, it is not a useful tool for reading and writing. Many of the words used in traditional spelling programs are not frequently used as part of their vocabulary.

In a study conducted by Angelisi (2009), the traditional approach was compared to other methods of spelling instruction. One method used was the traditional drill and write strategy where students wrote words multiple times and wrote sentences using each word. Like our results, Angelisi (2009) also found that the traditional approach to teaching spelling was the least effective method.

Our results show that the word study approach to teaching spelling is a more effective way to improve students spelling than the traditional approach. The data in Table 1 shows that there was a considerable increase between the means of the pre and post-tests, and the mean of the difference increased by a significant amount. The t test conducted using the mean scores from the pre and post-tests in the Word Study Approach Classroom showed that the difference between the means is statistically significant. The t test that compared the means of the differences in both classrooms also shows that the difference between the means is statistically significant. This further proves that the word study approach is a more effective way to teach spelling.

Other spelling studies have shown similar results to our research findings. In a study conducted by Chase-Lockwood and Masino (2002), fifth grade students were having difficulty transferring spelling skills into their written work. Word sorts were conducted for five months so that students could become active in their learning, rather than just memorizing spelling words. A post test was conducted at the end of the study where students showed marked improvement in their spelling on written assessments.

In a second study conducted by DuBois, Erickson, & Jacobs (2007), students were not consistently using spelling words in their daily work. For four months children were taught to sort words by vowels, word patterns, blends, and chunks. At the conclusion of the study, a post test was given where students showed a significant increase in the number of words they spelled correctly.

In a study done by Angelisi (2009) the traditional spelling method was compared to other methods of spelling instruction. One approach to teaching spelling used word study activities such as discovering patterns in words. Students had more success on their post tests using this method than with the traditional approach.

Another study, by Degeneffe and Ward (1998), showed that students made progress while taught with the word study approach. During the study children were taught visual spelling patterns and hunted for words in their reading that fit these patterns. At the end of the research, a final writing sample was collected, and students showed marked improvement in the correct spelling of words on this assessment.

Massengill Shaw and Berg (2008) evaluated the impact of word study on the spelling ability of adults with limited literacy proficiency. Five students were taught with the traditional approach to teaching spelling, while five others were taught with the word study approach. At the conclusion of the study a post test was given. The word study spelling group had an average increase of twelve words spelled correctly, while the traditional approach group had an average increase of only three words spelled correctly.

In a study conducted by Elliott and Rietschel (1999), they examined the effects of word study on second grade students. Students were divided into spelling groups at their levels. For seven months they participated in word hunts, word sorts, and making words activities. At the end of the study, a post test was given where students showed a significant increase in the amount of words they were spelling correctly.

In light of these studies conducted on spelling, the word study approach has proven to significantly improve students' spelling. Based on the presentation of our results, we can also conclude the importance of using the word study approach to teaching spelling. We have found that there is a greater significance in students' spelling improvement when they are taught with the word study method than when taught with the traditional approach. We believe the results were in favor of the word study approach, because students were taught at their spelling ability level. This approach is student-centered, engaging, and meaningful. In addition, students are more able to transfer spelling patterns they have worked with into their daily work than with the traditional approach. Our study continues to prove the success of the word study approach to teaching spelling.

Limitations of the Study

Throughout the course of our research, there are a few implications that might have impacted our study. Within both classrooms students transferred to other school districts. The

Traditional Approach Classroom had two students move, and the Word Study Approach Classroom lost one student due to a transfer. The loss of students may have impacted the scores in both classrooms. The students who moved could have increased or decreased the means of pre and post-tests. There were also three students within the Word Study Approach Classroom who did not participate in the study. Their scores could have also impacted the scores on the pre and post-tests.

The overall academic ability of the students of each classroom was not taken into consideration for this study. When creating class lists, the Intermediate School tries to create balanced classrooms of varying abilities such as high grade level, at grade level, and low grade level. It was our assumption that both classrooms involved in this study were of balanced abilities. However, we did not verify that both classrooms had the same amount of students at each ability level.

If one classroom had a higher or lower overall ability level than the other class, scores could have been significantly affected.

Conclusions and Recommendations

After examining the data we collected, we can conclude that the word study approach to teaching spelling is more effective than the traditional approach. We noticed that there was a more significant increase in the means between the pre and post-test in the Word Study Approach Classroom than in the Traditional Approach Classroom. While many students in both classrooms increased their post test scores, some students in the Word Study Approach Classroom had more considerable gains.

Teaching with the word study approach has proven to be an effective method to teach spelling. Grouping students according to their developmental spelling levels allows the teaching of patterns and rules so that students can make more progress at their appropriate level. Once students have mastered the patterns and rules at their level, they can make progress towards higher developmental spelling levels.

In order for the word study approach to be most beneficial to students it is recommended that only three new spelling patterns be taught each week. When completing weekly word sorts students should have four words that fit with each spelling pattern. Lower level spelling groups will need additional support so they can be taught how to use the patterns to spell their words. Higher level spelling groups should be given more challenging activities that can be used to learn their words. Spelling tests will need to have patterns listed at the top of the page so that students can use them to spell their words.

Implications for Future Research

While our study provides detailed evidence that the word study approach is more effective than the traditional approach, it does not take into consideration students' interest and attitudes toward the way they were taught spelling. If students were provided an attitude survey that asked their views on how they were taught spelling this year, we could have a clearer view of which method students preferred. Future research in this area is suggested in order to find out whether the word study approach or the traditional approach to teaching spelling is most enjoyed by students.

Other suggested research in this area could require a longer period of time to compare the two approaches to teaching spelling. If more time was spent teaching with these methods in both classrooms, there could have been an even greater significance between the scores on the pre and post-tests. Future research can be done to verify if this significance would be evident.

The results of our research study have proved to us that the word study approach to teaching spelling is more effective for our students. Because of the success we have seen, we plan to further educate ourselves on this method and use it with future classes. As a part of our school's leadership team, we plan to share the results of our research with other staff. It is our hope that our research will provide more information on best spelling practices that will lead to overall improvement of students' spelling abilities.

References

Allred, R.A. (1977). *Spelling: The application of research findings. The curriculum series.* (ERIC Document Reproduction Service No. ED135003)

Angelisi, M. A. (2000). *Teaching spelling: Which strategies work best.* (ERIC Document Reproduction Service No. ED440395)

Bear, D.R., Invernizzi, M., Templeton, S., & Johnston, F. (2008). *Words their way: Word study for phonics, vocabulary, and spelling instruction* (4th ed.). Upper Saddle River, NJ: Pearson.

Beirn-Smith, M. & Riley, T.F. (2009). *Spelling assessment of students with disabilities. Assessment for Effective Intervention*, 34(3), 170 -177.

Blevins, W. (2001). *Teaching phonics & word study in the intermediate grades.* New York: Scholastic Professional Books.

Chase-Lockwood, R., & Masino, M. (2002).*Improving student spelling skills through the use of effective teaching strategies.* (ERIC Document Reproduction Service No. ED465190)

Degeneffe, L., & Ward, L. (1998). *A constructivist approach to spelling strategies.* (ERIC Document Reproduction Service No. ED420848)

DuBois, K., Erickson, K., & Jacobs, M. (2007). *Improving spelling of high frequency words for transfer in written work.* (ERIC Document Reproduction Service No. ED496700)

Elliot, J., & Rietschel, K. (1999). *The effects of word study on students' application of spelling and phonics in their independent writing.* (ERIC Document Reproduction Service No. ED429301)

Gentry, J.R. (2004). *The science of spelling: The explicit specifics that make great readers and writers (and speller!).* Portsmouth, NH: Heinemann.

Gentry, J. R. (2009). The right connections, the right results: Five questions teachers ask about spelling. Interview posted to http://www.zaner-bloser.com/educator/ products/spelling/index.aspx?Id=4824 &view=article

Graham, S., Morphy, P., Harris, K.R., Fink-Chorzempa, B., Saddler, B., Moran, S., et al. (2008). Teaching spelling in the primary grades: A national survey of instructional practices and adaptations. *American Educational Research Journal*, 45(3), 796 -825.

Interactive Illinois report card. (2009). Retrieved October 16, 2009, from http://iirc.niu.edu/ Invernizzi, M.A., Abouzeid, M.P., & Bloodgood, J.W. (1997).Integrated word study: Spelling, grammar, and meaning in the language arts classroom. *Language Arts*, 74(3), 185-192.

Johnson, P., & Marlow, P. (1996). *Improving spelling skills through the use of activities focusing on retention and transfer.* (ERIC Document Reproduction Service No. ED397401)

Massengill Shaw, D., & Berg, M.A. (2008). Effects of word study intervention on spelling accuracy among low-literate adults. *Adult Basic Education and Literacy Journal*, 2(3), 131-139.

Murphy, N. (1997). *A multisensory approach vs. conventional approach to teaching spelling.* (ERIC Document Reproduction Service No. ED405564)

Parsons, R.D., & Brown, K.S. (2002). *Teacher as reflective practitioner and action researcher.* Belmont, CA: Wadsworth/Thomson Learning.

Teicher, S. A. (2005). Spelling makes a comeback. *Learner.* Retrieved September 26, 2009, from http://www.csmonitor.com/2005/051/pl2s02-legn.html

Templeton, S., & Morris, D. (1999). Questions teachers ask about spelling. *Reading Research Quarterly*, 34(1), 102-112.

Trochim, W.M. (2006). *Web Center for Social Research Methods.* Retrieved October 17, 2009, from http//www.socialresearchmethods.net/

Williams, C., Phillips-Birdsong, C., Hufnagel, K., Hungler, D., & Lundstrom, R.P. (2009). Word study instruction in the K-2 classroom. *The Reading Teacher*, 62(7), 570-578.

Zutell, J. (2009). A student-active learning approach to spelling instruction. Retrieved September 20, 2009 from http://www.zaner-bloser.com/about/newsandresearch.research.detail.aspx?rd=4820

Chapter 4: The Impact of an Independent Reading Program on Students Motivation and Attitudes

Nicole S. Zaremba

Introduction

In an article about adolescent literacy, Wise (2009) wrote that, "Literacy is, in reality, the cornerstone of student achievement, for any student in any grade" (p. 373). United States policymakers, school districts, administrators, and teachers may not be able to agree on much when it comes to education, but few can deny the impact that a student's literacy skills have on the quality of his or her overall education and academic success. Because of that fact, there has been a widespread focus on literacy education in recent years. However, the unique literacy needs of adolescents in the United States are not being met.

Even though adolescent students today acknowledge that reading is important, on average they are reading less than they did in years past. Studies show that most middle grade students do not read for entertainment, and what is worse is that many are even developing negative attitudes toward reading (Ivey & Broaddus, 2000). These are all facts that would not surprise some of the reading teachers who have to deal with the problem on a daily basis, but it is discouraging nevertheless, especially when we consider how important literacy skills are for adolescent students.

When students are adolescents they become experienced and skilled readers ("Supporting," 2002). It is at this time in a student's life, according to the article, that students form the reading habits they will use as adults not only in their personal lives but also in their careers. The field of education is doing a huge disservice to all of the students if we do not find a way to meet the literacy needs of each and every one of them. In order to meet these needs, we must first seek to understand students in the middle grades.

Profile of Middle School Readers

Ivey and Broaddus (2000) researched adolescent readers and found that understanding them is no simple task because they are very complex indeed. As a whole, they do not possess higher level reading comprehension skills. There are exceptions, obviously, which create even more variation in reading abilities in the classroom. Though discrepancies exist between where grade school students should be in reading and where many of them are, those differences are even more evident in junior high age students. As the authors explain, part of this is because the students have had more time to fall behind. Because many of the readers are lacking, it becomes especially important that teachers tailor their instruction to meet the needs of a dynamic group of learners, the main focus of Ivey and Broaddus's research. Additionally, many of the readers who can read have negative attitudes toward and little motivation for reading (Ivey & Broaddus, 2000).

The Strong Reader vs. the Struggling Reader

In the process of studying all different types of readers, experts have found that strong readers exhibit certain traits that struggling readers lack. Santa (2006) describes weak readers as those who are not in control of their own reading, meaning that they don't check for comprehension as they read. When they don't understand a piece of text, they don't reread it but instead keep going. She also describes that when they are not able to comprehend material, they often quit and blame their own inadequacies or lack of intelligence. A proficient reader, on the other hand, will see a difficult passage as a challenge and will try to make meaning of it. What struggling students don't understand is that their struggles do not necessarily relate to intelligence but are more related to having not learned the skills necessary to process the information. Ivey and Broaddus (2000) stress that even though the students are not always the skilled and confident readers we hope to have in our classrooms, educators have the ability to encourage them and push them in a positive direction. The big question is how do we do that?

How Reading Motivation Impacts Reading and Learning

Nearly all research and literature on adolescent literacy stresses the importance of motivation in students' learning (Cassidy, Garrett, & Barrera, 2006). Simply put, if students are not engaged and do not have the will to learn, they won't learn. Tilley (2009) reported similar findings and wrote, "It seems increasingly clear that the chief impediments to literacy are not cognitive in nature. It is not that students cannot learn; it is that they do not wish to" (p. 40). Many teachers attribute reading success or failure to socioeconomic status, but Tilley reported that student engagement and motivation is more important. As a matter of fact, she stated that engaged readers from low-income homes tend to perform higher on standardized tests than do the students who are not engaged readers but are from higher income homes. For educators, this means that that the key to reading success is motivating their students.

One might ask why reading motivation is so crucial to reading success and to learning. Corcoran and Mamalakis (2009) offer a simple explanation. They state that in general, human behaviors are heavily influenced by the pleasure and pain principle, which applies also to adolescent readers. In the school setting, the authors equate pleasure with success and pain with failure. It is in human nature to want to succeed because it brings pleasure, and when reading brings about pleasure, students are more likely to want to do it more. However, as Corcoran and Mamalakis (2009) explain, when reading elicits pain, or in the case of education, failure, students are less likely to want to do it. The implication of this for the classroom is that teachers need to find a way to make reading bring pleasure in order to increase students' motivation and success in reading.

In addition to increasing motivation to read, student engagement also impacts the type of learning that actually takes place. When students are interested and engaged in the text, they are more likely to use higher level thinking skills and truly learn the material. Chances are also greater that learning will become an internal process than they would be if students were reading material that was not engaging for them. When students are not engaged in the material, learning is likely to be temporary and shallow (Corcoran & Mamalakis, 2009). Our goal, as educators, is to strive for learning that is internalized and long-lasting. Tilley (2009) also touts the benefits of student engagement in reading and explains that engaged readers will have more confidence in themselves as readers and will enjoy the learning process even more. The link between student motivation and reading success is emphasized in literacy research, which makes it crucial for teachers to make it a priority in their classrooms.

How Teachers Can Motivate Students to Read and Increase Comprehension

Some teachers think that student motivation is something that is beyond their control. Sadly, I was once one of those teachers who believed that students either wanted to read or didn't, and I didn't believe there was much I could do to foster a genuine love of reading. I figured that some kids just naturally enjoy reading, and others do not. Like many teachers, I considered incentive programs, which are actually considered to be demotivating for students long-term (Lapp & Fisher, 2009). Little by little though, I began to piece together a reading program (with the help of my students) that I hoped would encourage them to be lifelong readers. As it turned out, many of the basic principles of the program were supported by years of research.

Many of those principles are laid out in an article by Santa (2006) where she describes a plan for adolescent literacy instruction. In the plan she focuses on several major components, the first of which is building classroom communities and relationships. She asserts that students must connect with and relate to the teacher. If this doesn't happen, she says that students won't be connected with the course or with the content area. As Santa (2006) states, "The foundation for change always rests with positive human relationships" (p. 467). I knew from my own experiences as a student that I would work more for a teacher whom I respected, so I wanted to be sure that I had a positive relationship with my own students. According to Corcoran and Mamalakis (2009), teachers and students should work cooperatively as partners in the quest for discovery in reading, and that is what I set out to do.

This is not to say that teachers need to try to be the students' friends. Quite to the contrary, Santa (2006) states that these classroom communities and relationships are built through positive classroom management and through structure and routines. Also, teachers should be facilitators for learning who create democratic classrooms where students feel comfortable interacting with the teachers and with other students. They must be engaged in learning and need to feel like they have a voice. This, Santa believes, will create environments conducive to literacy learning. Conley (2007) provides similar insight. He makes it clear that adolescents need to feel valued, and that they need to have a personal incentive to learn. The idea is that before we can focus on literacy, we have to provide an environment for learning.

The second component of Santa's (2006) plan is based around the idea that teachers need to provide instruction on reading strategies and must model them as well. Many teachers simply teach the content of the course, but many students lack the strategies to process the information. By teaching the strategies, Santa believes that students will actually understand how they learn and as a result will have higher self-efficacy, which will in turn increase motivation. This, according to Santa, goes hand in hand with the classroom communities because if students realize that teachers care enough to see to it that the students know *how* to learn, they will feel like that teachers genuinely care about them as people.

The idea of explicitly teaching reading strategies is one that is common in research on adolescent literacy. In 2004, Biancarosa and Snow published the *Reading Next Report* which explained fifteen elements that were essential to a successful adolescent reading program. Explicit instruction of reading comprehension strategies is one of those fifteen elements. The authors describe the importance of teaching students to master such skills as summarizing and monitoring one's own reading. Similarly, Aimonette and Galda (2009) reported the importance of direct instruction on reading strategies and illustrated the value of teaching skills such as making and monitoring predictions and visualizing while reading. They explained that explicit instruction on such skills is a powerful tool for readers that will aid in understanding and engagement of a text. Ivey and Broaddus (2000) believe that although there is a definite need for teaching reading strategies in the middle school classroom, they state that it is rarely utilized at the middle school level. As a result, many readers find failure rather than success because they are not equipped with the skills to succeed.

In teaching the reading strategies, Santa (2006) emphasizes the importance of modeling them for the students. Initially, teachers model their own thought processes as readers so that students can the strategies being used in an authentic way. Deshler and Hock (2007) also write about the importance of teaching the reading strategies and about slowly releasing responsibility to the students. When teaching students how to use a strategy, the teacher should model it first, should then do examples with the students, and finally should let the students do it on their own. Simply put, it should be an "I do, we do, you do" process. This builds confidence in the students and helps them to find success in learning. Tilley (2009) also stresses the importance of modeling and sees it as an opportunity for teachers to demonstrate to the students how reading makes a difference in their lives.

The third area of Santa's (2006) plan is teaching students to internalize the strategies and processes needed to learn. In short, students need to understand how they learn, the reasons why learning takes place, why strategies work, and need to be able to view themselves as learners. Santa mentions the fact that educators know what strategies to use and why, and that students should know this information as well. Doing so will help students to become metacongnitive and will help them to learn how to gain a deeper understanding of material. Conley and Hinchman (2004) also write about the importance of teaching students to be metacognitive. They stress the importance of ensuring that students know how to read and process different kinds of material, that they know which strategies to use and when to use them, and also why different strategies are used for different types of material.

The goal of teaching students to internalize reading processes is so that all students can become strong readers, who are in sharp contrast with struggling readers. A strong reader makes connections to text as they read. They relate it to their own lives and their own experiences and question the material. Also, strong readers will reread any information that they didn't understand upon the first read and have the ability to organize information as they read (Santa, 2006). Teaching students how to internalize the processes may sound complicated, but many of the methods Santa recommends are based around methods many teachers use and consider to be best practice.

One of Santa's (2006) recommendations is for teachers to take the time to build background knowledge. Like Cassidy et al. (2006), Santa recognizes that many students lack the background knowledge necessary for comprehension. Knowing this, teachers need to provide it and can do so by previewing material through questioning or through demonstrations. They need to find information, relate it to something the students have experienced, and build on it in the learning process. Teachers know and understand the importance of relating new information to old knowledge, and as Santa states, students should know the importance as well.

Another thing that teachers can do to help students learn the literacy skills necessary to succeed is to incorporate writing across the curriculum. Not only does writing information down help students to remember information, it also helps students to make connections to and interact with the text. Learning deepens through writing and allows each student the opportunity to make his or her own connections with the information (Santa, 2006). Ivey and Broaddus (2000) support the utilization of the connection between reading writing and even explain that students' writing can benefit from reading because it allows them to learn from great writers. Also, connecting reading and writing gives students the opportunity to practice using the writing skills that will be necessary in high school and beyond (Biancarosa & Snow, 2004).

Teachers should also incorporate discussion into their lessons as a way of teaching students to internalize learning processes. Discussing experiences, questions, and information comes naturally for students because it is a part of their world and also deepens their understanding of information (Santa, 2006). Teachers should provide students with plenty of opportunities to discuss the materials with other students in a capacity that allows everyone the opportunity to talk, not just the instructor ("Supporting," 2002). Doing so makes it so that students take an active role in their own learning and can even start to make their own reading goals and have intrinsic motivation to do it (Santa, 2006). It also gives students practice at problem solving and critical thinking skills and promotes a deeper understanding of the text (Corcoran & Mamalakis, 2009). Students need to have the opportunities to interact with the materials and to interact with one another in order to gain a deeper understanding of what they read (Biancarosa & Snow, 2004).

Aside from integrating reading and writing into every class, there are many steps that each teacher can take to encourage adolescent literacy and motivation toward reading. One way teachers can do this is by differentiating instruction so that it meets the needs of each student. This requires teachers to be knowledgeable as to what each students' needs are and also requires teachers to be well-prepared, but makes it so that instruction is more beneficial and useful for every student ("Supporting," 2002). This idea is a guiding principle in Ivey and Broaddus's (2000) research which emphasizes the importance of teachers getting to know every one of their students as a reader and as an individual. They believe that doing so will increase student motivation and achievement because instruction can be tailored more easily to meet the needs of the individual. Taking the time to find students' strengths and areas for improvements as readers is beneficial for the teacher and for the students. Likewise, using assessments and literacy data, teachers can have a guide for more tailored instruction (Darwin and Fleischman, 2005).

Also, research suggests that teachers should use a variety of materials that the students actually want to read because students learn better when they are engaged ("Adolescent Literacy," 1999). This material should range from fiction to non-fiction, from novels to instruction manuals, from magazines to newspapers. The variety of materials should be used for independent reading and for modeling because it will expose students to a greater range of materials and will make them want to read a wider range of materials (Ivey & Broaddus, 2000). Ivey and Broaddus tell that students are more likely to want to read a genre or a book if they have heard it read aloud to them. This means that teachers can motivate students to want to read something they might not have otherwise picked up simply by sharing it aloud to the class.

Much of the research on adolescent literacy suggests that students need to have a more active role in their own reading and learning. The idea of students having choice is one that is supported by a great deal of research (Corcoran & Mamalakis, 2009; Jenkins, 2009; Tilley, 2009). The research suggests that when students are given a choice as to what they read and the activities that they do, they are more likely to be engaged and motivated to read. It also allows students to find materials that are interesting to them and that are at their reading levels. The ownership gives readers a sense of power and control that is a natural motivator, especially for struggling readers (Ivey & Broaddus, 2000). An added benefit is that students' interests can be taken into consideration which makes it so that they can make connections with the text more naturally (Jenkins, 2009).

Another common theme in adolescent literacy research is the benefits of reading aloud in the classroom. Reading aloud allows teachers to serve as a model for fluency and for comprehension strategies (Tilley, 2009). It gives teachers the opportunity to demonstrate the use of inflection and enthusiasm for reading. Students hear the excitement in their teachers' voices, and the enthusiasm for reading is likely to spread to the students (Ivey & Broaddus, 2009). Reading aloud may sound like a simple thing, but Cunningham (2005) invites readers to explore their pasts and to think about what got them interested in reading. The author states that in surveys, many people responded that their teachers got them interested in reading a specific book or in reading as a whole simply by reading it aloud.

Several authors also emphasize the importance of creating a text-rich environment in the classroom. Teachers need to know their students so they can find books that will be engaging for them so they will actually want to read. Corcoran and Mamalakis (2009) explain that this is especially important for the students who don't have a text-rich environment at home. Simply having an extensive classroom library is not enough, however. Even with the most engaging books, a classroom library will have little impact on the students if they are not encouraged to use the books in it. Teachers need to talk about and promote specific books and generate enthusiasm for them among the students. Equally important is the opportunity to become familiar with a wide variety of books (Tilley, 2009).

Teachers have many tools for increasing student motivation toward reading, and many of them lie in the ways they set up their classrooms and spend class time. In the ideal reading classroom, students are recognized for their reading successes and feel comfortable enough to take risks in the classroom. They are given the opportunity to be creative, and at the same time, they are able to have meaningful conversations with adults about their reading (Tilley, 2009). They also have time to read in class. All too often, we promote independent reading, but we don't actually give students the chance to do it. We tell them it is a priority, but we don't show them that it is enough of a priority for us to use class time for it, even though most students actually do enjoy having time in class to read (Ivey & Broaddus, 2000). Sometimes educators forget that reading is like any other skill; the only way to get better at it is to practice it, and more than anything, students need to practice reading in order to improve (Cunningham, 2005).

Results of Studies

Several studies have been done on different reading programs, each yielding similar results and findings. The results of one study of a group of motivated eleventh grade readers suggested that student engagement can come from many different sources. The particular group of students who was studied would normally have been classified as reluctant and struggling readers. However, the teachers implemented a different type of reading instruction based on student interests, and students believed it made all the difference. They said they were motivated to read because they felt like their voices had been heard in the planning and in discussions. They also enjoyed having the opportunity to work with their peers who also supported them as readers. They believed that having peers who supported them as reader impacted their reading motivation and success. Overall, they attributed much of the success of the program to the ability to have choices (Lapp & Fisher, 2009).

Another study done in 2007 compared SSR (Sustained Silent Reading) to an IR (Independent Reading) program. The teacher had previously used SSR where students read independently and silently during class but were not held accountable for what they read. Teachers also read silently while students were reading. While using SSR, the teacher noticed that a lot of the students' time was spent off-task and that the reluctant readers didn't seem to benefit much. The teacher then decided to use an IR program where students were held accountable for what they read using reading journals, conferences with the students, and small-group lessons. The teacher thought that perhaps the students would not like the change because it meant more work for them, but she found that the students actually found a great deal of success with the program (Trudel, 2007).

After weeks of implementing the IR program, the teacher found that students were responding positively to the changes. They were spending more time on task, and many of the problem behaviors during silent reading have been eliminated. She found that students didn't want to stop reading when the time was up for the day, which was a switch from how things were when she used SSR. Students were even able to pick out appropriate books based on the ability and interest more independently. The students were actively engaged in responding to the texts and participated in discussions with their peers and with the teacher about what they were reading. They were even able to have discussions about the reading strategies they were using. Simply put, the teacher found that when students were asked to respond to what they have read, they were more engaged and motivated to read (Trudel, 2007).

A Closer Look at Two Independent Reading Programs

In my research, I came across information about two independent reading programs that were based on ideas that are similar to what I use in my classroom. The first was done by Trudel (2007) and was described in some detail in the above section. The IR program, as Trudel calls it, is based on several basic principles. The first is the idea that the teacher provides guidance as to what the students read. The students do have some say, but Trudel's program encourages the teacher and student to work together to find appropriate materials for the students. The second key element is that students must keep records of what they read for class. This goes back to the idea that students are more motivated when they are held accountable for what they read. The third basic idea of Trudel's IR program is that students are given the opportunities to reflect on what they've read, which deepens their understanding of the material. Trudel's fourth IR principle is that teachers and students both participate in mini-lessons and discussions. Though Trudel believes student-led discussions are important, she also sees value in teacher-led discussions as well and thinks that both have their place in the classroom. Unlike with SSR, the teacher is not reading independently while the students are. Instead, the teacher is using that time to meet with students to monitor progress and discuss their reading. Trudel believed that a program based on these five key ideas yielded positive results and increased the amount of time spent on-task, increased meaningful connections between students and the text, and helped students with their overall reading and listening comprehension skills.

Another reading program I came across that had guiding principles that were similar to my own reading program was called PIE and was described by Hobbs, Oleynik, and Sacco (2009). The PIE program (or Personalized Independent Enrichment) is designed to meet the needs of readers of every reading level, interest, and ability level. The idea is for students to have the ability to choose their books, find pleasure in reading, and to teach the necessary foundational reading strategies and skills at the same time. Hobbs et al. described the three basic steps involved in the PIE program. The first is for students to choose their own independent reading book so that they have an active role in their own learning, which will help with engagement and motivation. The second step is for students to write about their book. There are specific things they must write about including elements of fiction such as characters, plot, and setting, and the students' writing provides a basis for conversations with the students about the text. The third and final step is for students to share and extend the book. This is accomplished by having students participate in discussions with their peers and with their teachers about the book and by creating and presenting a project to the class. This deepens their understanding and retention of the material and created a learning community at the same time.

Using this program, the authors state that hearing students talk about their books outside of class is nothing out of the ordinary because students are genuinely interested in what they've read. The authors attribute this to the fact that students are allowed to choose their own books and are given the opportunity to read the texts and interact with them in their own ways. It is also based on the idea that students will thrive in reading when given books that they can understand and that they truly enjoy. The authors believe that if reading is not authentic, it will not be enjoyable or beneficial. Most importantly, the authors stress the importance of learning by doing because practice is the only thing that will help students improve their reading abilities (Hobbs et al., 2009).

Summary and how it Relates to My Classroom

When I created an independent reading program in my own classroom, it was sort of haphazard. During the first year, I changed the program often based on feedback from the students and to fit their needs as well as my own. Initially, it was used in only one of my classes and was closer to an SSR program, or Sustained Silent Reading, in that students were not accountable for what they read. The program wasn't necessarily as organized as a true SSR program, but it did allow students to choose their own books, and I did model reading much of the time that we did it. Admittedly, I did not provide much time for independent reading in class, something I would change the next year. Ultimately, the program served its intended purpose of promoting reading for pleasure and seemed to be successful. However, I saw the impact it had on my group of readers, and I thought I could do much more with it.

At the beginning of this school year, I started a program with all of my students that was closer to the PIE program described by Hobbs et al. (2009) and to the IR (Independent Reading) program described by Trudel (2007). Many of its principles were based on feedback from the students in the previous year and on my observations but are supported by the research I've found in the process of doing my literature review.

One of the ideas that became important in my program was the element of student choice. In the first year, I had noticed how much students were motivated by having a voice in what they read, so I decided to utilize that because I could see that it was a natural motivator. I do help my students select their novels, but they have an opinion as well, which is a notion supported by several of the authors and researchers mentioned in this paper (Corcoran & Mamalakis, 2009; Cunningham, 2005; Hobbs et al., 2009: Ivey & Broaddus, 2000; Jenkins, 2009; Lapp & Fisher, 2009; Santa, 2006; Tilley, 2009; Trudel, 2007). I could see that there was no one book that would meet the needs of all students of varied interests and ability levels, and the element of choice allowed them to pick texts they could understand, that they were interested in, and that were relevant to their lives.

There was one aspect of my independent reading program that I wanted to change from the first year to the second, and that was accountability. In the first year, students weren't really accountable for what they read. I figured if students were accountable, they might want to read more and would have a deeper understanding of the text. Some of their accountability comes in the form of a reading journal, and some of it is through discussions with me and with their peers. Having the students conference with me allows me to monitor their progress more closely and gives me the opportunity to have genuine conversations with the students about what they are reading. When they talk to one another, it is clear that their understanding deepens and their engagement increases, both ideas supported by research (Corcoran & Mamalakis, 2009; Cunningham, 2005; Hobbs et al., 2009: Ivey & Broaddus, 2000; Lapp & Fisher, 2009; Santa, 2006; Tilley, 2009; Trudel, 2007). Something else that I have noticed more recently is the peer support in reading that Lapp and Fisher (2009) mention. My students, who used to make fun of each other for reading, now talk about what they are reading and support each other. They constantly encourage each other to read more and recommend novels to one another.

After going to workshops about literacy and doing my own research, I also knew that I wanted to target reading strategies in my instruction. I could see that my struggling readers were not making and monitoring predictions, making connections to the text, making inferences, and could not summarize what they had read on their own. I found ways to explicitly teach reading strategies just as the research suggests is best practice (Biancarosa & Snow, 2004; Ivey & Broaddus, 2000; Santa, 2007; Tilley, 2009). In doing so, I modeled the use of the strategies during read alouds and used a gradual release of responsibility for the students to practice using them on their own. Students demonstrate their use of the strategies with their independent reading books in conjunction with graphic organizers, peer discussions, teacher conferences, and reading journals.

My original purpose in creating an independent reading program was simply to instill a genuine love of reading in my students, but it quickly grew to encompass so much more. I wanted my classroom to be a place that made reading a part of the daily culture among the students and teachers. My hope was that my classroom would be the welcoming and inviting environment that Tilley (2009) describes where students actually want to read and talk about their books, and so far, I feel that I have been successful in that. I've also worked hard to provide the variety of materials Tilley describes so that all students can find engaging, relevant texts, no matter how much they may say they hate to read. Hobbs et al. (2009) wrote that, "Something wonderful happens when children are asked to choose their own books and are given ample time to read and discuss them. They become hungry readers with an appetite for books!" My goal has been to instill that hunger in the students in my classroom in a way that improves their reading comprehension, and hopefully at the end of the year, I will be able to look back and see that I have accomplished that.

Methodology

Participants

The study included several different types of research. To gauge the students' attitudes toward reading, I took both a qualitative and a quantitative approach. I used quantitative data to show how they rate their interests in reading and qualitative to get more in-depth feedback from the using a survey to obtain both.

The participants of this study were the students in my reading classes at Midwestern school district in Illinois during the 2010-2001 school year. They included my two eighth grade classes, which have a total of twenty-seven students and my sixth grade class of twenty-two students.

The school itself is located in a small city Central Illinois and is approximately. It is the only school in the district, and it provides education for approximately 200 students from kindergarten through eighth grade (Interactive Illinois Report Card, 2010). The school population is predominately white (92.9%) and included only a few Hispanic (1.5%), Native American (2%), and Multiracial students (3.6%), in 2009, and 21% of the students were classified as Low Income (Interactive Illinois Report Card, 2010).

The Illinois Interactive Report Card states that the class sizes in 2009 at this school ranged from fifteen to twenty-six students, which is similar to my classes this year. My smallest one this year has twelve students, and my largest has twenty-two. With the exception of the self-contained special education classrooms, the students at Rankin are not grouped by ability. Only a few of my students have had significant discipline issues, and overall, the school has a high level of parental involvement, even though there are a few exceptions.

As for my sixth and eighth grades classes, most of the students perform at or above grade level, though there are a few who do read below grade level. Even though most of them can read, at the beginning of the school year, nearly all of them said that they hated to do it. When asked how many books they read in their free time last year, most of them said none or one. To say the least, my students were reluctant readers.

Instrumentation

In order to assess students' attitudes toward reading, I administered a survey a little over halfway through the school year. The survey used several questions that would show if and how students' attitudes toward reading changed over the course of the year as well as how their motivation changed. The survey asked some quantitative questions to gauge reading interest last year versus this year using a Likert scale and asked how many books students read last school year and how many they read this school year. I asked some more in-depth qualitative type questions to figure out how and why their opinions changed or stayed the same.

Research Questions

Central Question

The purpose of this study was to determine how independent reading impacts students' attitudes and motivation toward reading.

Sub Questions

- What does independent reading look like?
- What are essential comprehension skills for junior high readers?
- How do students' attitudes change throughout the course of the year?

Research Objectives

- To find out what effect(s) an independent reading program has on students' attitudes and motivation toward reading.

Definition of Terms

Independent Reading – Students read novels independently but are held accountable for the material in class.

Results

The data that was used in this study was collected from students who have been in my reading class from the beginning of the school year through February of 2011. It comes from a survey administered in February of 2011 that had seven questions, two of which were Likert-type questions, and included five open-ended questions. It was taken by twenty-six eighth grade students and twenty sixth grade students for a total of forty-six students. Two students did not return the letter of parental consent, and one was absent on the day the survey was administered.

The purpose of the survey was to see how students' attitudes toward reading changed over the course of the year and to see if that impacted the number of books read.

The first question asked students how many books they read independently last school year; it did not include any books that were read as a class. The mean number of books read by eighth grade students last year was 4.35. The mean number for sixth grade students was 3.85 (Figure 1).

Figure 3: Two Year Comparison of the Mean Number of Books Read by Sixth and Eighth Grade Students

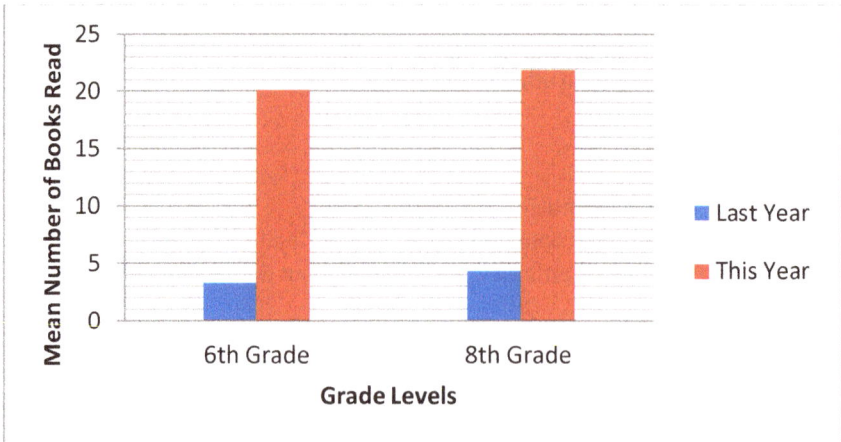

The second question asked students how many books students have read independently this year, again not including any books that were read as a class. The mean number of books read by eighth grade students this year was 21.9. The mean number read by sixth grade students was 20.1 (Figure 1). All but one eighth grade student and one sixth grade student increased the number of books read from last year to this year. The mean increase for books read by eighth grade students from last year to this year was 18.68; the mean increase for sixth grade students was 17.84 (Figure 2).

Figure 4: Mean Increase in the Number of Books Read from Last School Year to This School Year

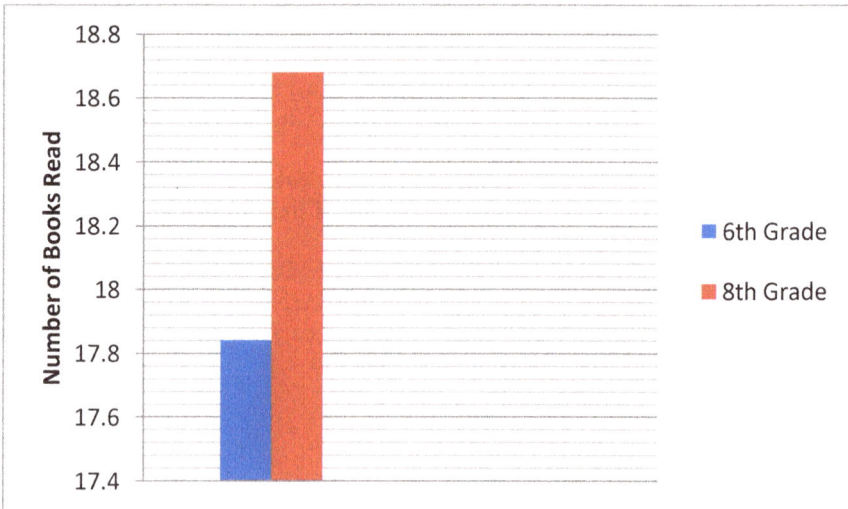

The third question was a Likert-type question asked students how they felt about reading last year on a scale of 1 to 5. Responses were labeled as follows: 1=I hated it, 2=I disliked it, 3=I was neutral to it, 4=I liked it, 5=I really enjoyed it. The mean score for eighth grade students was 1.88, and the mean score for sixth grade students was 2.05.

The fourth question was another Likert-type question, and it asked students how they felt about reading when they took the survey (February 2011). The responses were labeled as they were in the third question: 1=I hate it, 2=I dislike it, 3=I am neutral to it, 4=I like it, 5=I really enjoy it. The mean score for eighth grade students was 3.73, and the mean score for sixth grade students was 4.35.

Out of the twenty-six eighth grade students, twenty-two indicated an improved attitude toward reading. Four students indicated that they felt the same way about reading last year that they did this year. However, three of those students indicated that they already enjoyed reading last year (scoring it as a 4 or 5). Nineteen of the twenty sixth grade students indicated that they has an improved attitude toward reading this year, and one student indicated that he felt the same about reading this year as he did last year. The comparison of questions three and four for both grades can be seen in Figures 3 and 4. The mean increase in scores from question three to four was 2.14 points for eighth grade students and 2.42 points for sixth grade students.

Figure 5: Two Year Comparison of Sixth Grade Students' Attitudes Toward Reading

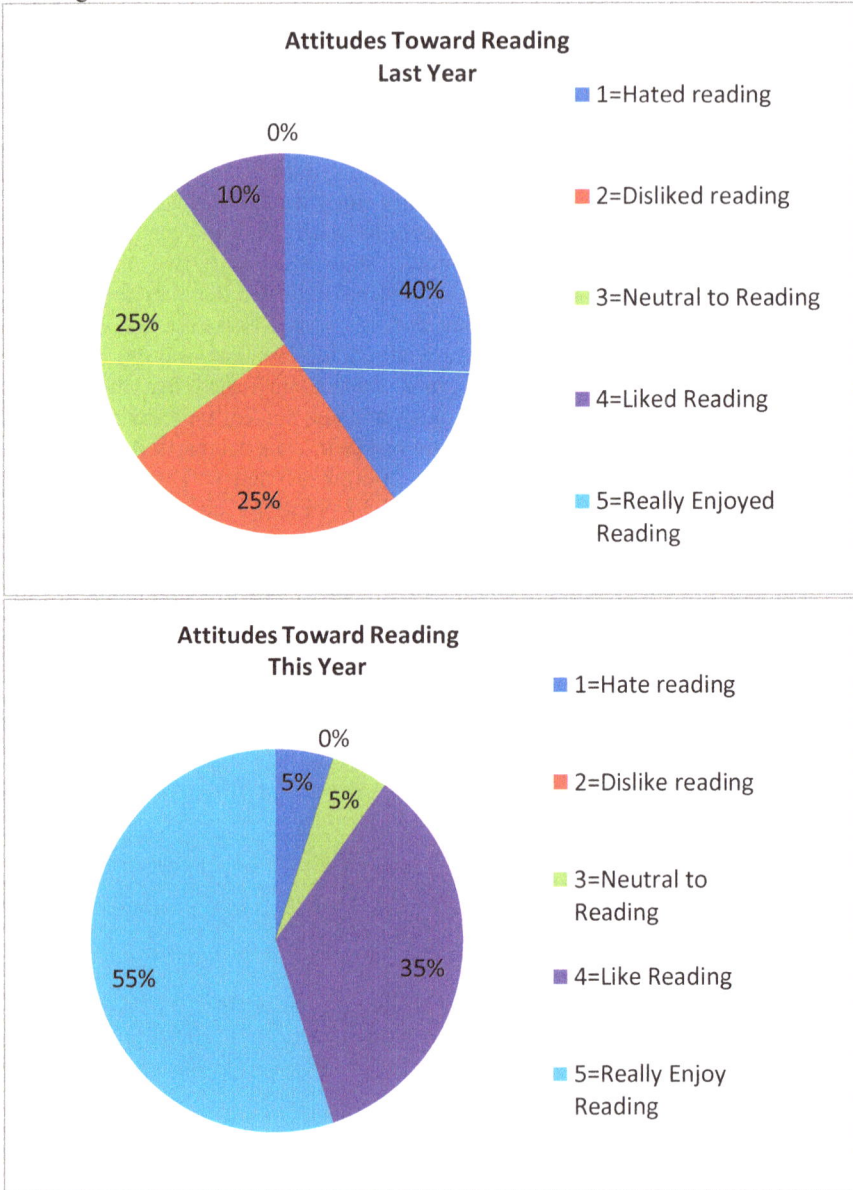

Figure 6: Two Year Comparison of Eighth Grade Students' Attitudes toward Reading

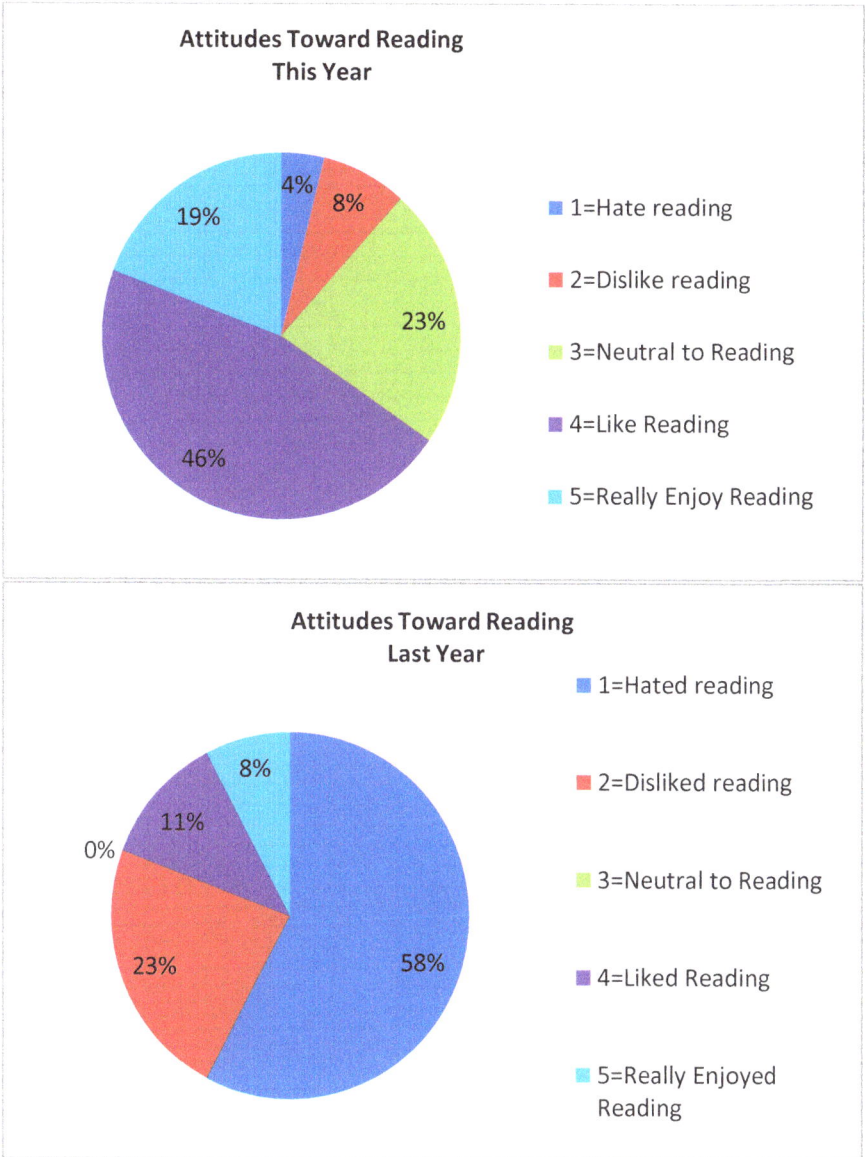

Attitudes Toward Reading This Year

4%
8%
19%
23%
46%

- 1=Hate reading
- 2=Dislike reading
- 3=Neutral to Reading
- 4=Like Reading
- 5=Really Enjoy Reading

Attitudes Toward Reading Last Year

8%
11%
0%
23%
58%

- 1=Hated reading
- 2=Disliked reading
- 3=Neutral to Reading
- 4=Liked Reading
- 5=Really Enjoyed Reading

A detailed breakdown of how each student responded to questions one through four is shown in Figures 5 and 6 below shows

Figure 7: Sixth Grade Students' Responses for Questions 1-4

	Question #1 Number of Books Read Last Year	Question #2 Number of Books Read This Year	Amount of Increase in Number Read Last Year to This Year (Q1 & Q2)	Question #3 Attitude Toward Reading Last Year	Question #4 Attitude Toward Reading This Year	Amount of Increase from Last Year to This Year (Q3 & Q4)
Student 1	7	14	7	3	5	2
Student 2	5	20	15	1	3	2
Student 3	1	26	25	2	5	3
Student 4	2	16	14	2	5	3
Student 5	7	41	34	4	5	1
Student 6	0	20	20	1	5	4
Student 7	1	15	14	1	4	3
Student 8	0	14	14	2	4	2
Student 9	3	24	21	4	5	1
Student 10	2	16	14	3	4	1
Student 11	1	24	23	3	5	2
Student 12	6	19	13	2	4	2
Student 13	1	16	15	1	4	3
Student 14	3	18	15	2	4	2
Student 15	7	15	8	3	4	1
Student 16	10	7	-3	1	1	0
Student 17	0	13	13	1	5	4
Student 18	0	13	13	1	5	4
Student 19	6	36	30	1	5	4
Student 20	4	36	32	3	5	2
Mean	3.3	20.15	16.85	2.05	4.35	2.3

Figure 8: Eighth Grade Students' Responses for Questions 1-4

	Question #1 Number of Books Read Last Year	Question #2 Number of Books Read This Year	Amount of Increase in Number Read Last Year to This Year (Q1 & Q2)	Question #3 Attitude Toward Reading Last Year	Question #4 Attitude Toward Reading This Year	Amount of Increase from Last Year to This Year (Q3 & Q4)
Student 1	1	20	19	2	4	2
Student 2	1	20	19	1	2	1
Student 3	0	13	13	1	4	3
Student 4	0	9	9	1	2	1
Student 5	0	16	16	1	3	2
Student 6	0	17	17	2	4	2
Student 7	1	15	14	1	3	2
Student 8	0	11	11	1	1	0
Student 9	4	21	17	4	5	1
Student 10	5	25	20	2	4	2
Student 11	0	19	19	1	4	3
Student 12	1	7	6	1	3	2
Student 13	0	27	27	2	4	2
Student 14	0	9	9	2	4	2
Student 15	1	9	8	2	4	2
Student 16	37	25	-12	5	5	0
Student 17	0	8	8	1	4	3
Student 18	45	62	17	5	5	0
Student 19	4	10	6	4	4	4
Student 20	2	19	17	1	5	4
Student 21	0	26	26	1	4	3
Student 22	2	37	35	1	3	2
Student 23	1	11	10	1	3	2
Student 24	1	62	61	1	4	3
Student 25	7	58	51	4	5	1
Student 26	0	12	12	1	3	2
Mean	4.35	21.85	17.5	1.88	3.69	1.96

Several different themes emerged from questions five, six, and seven, which were open-ended. Question five asked students if and how their attitudes toward reading changed over the course of this school year. Most of students from both grades wrote that they like reading better this year. Many wrote that they hated it in the past or wouldn't pick up a book before, and now they actually enjoy it. One student even wrote that last year she thought that all books were "pointless and boring" but noted that she would read now. One of my most struggling readers noted that he hated it last year and loves it now because he gets to read easier books. A few students also wrote that they like reading a little better.

Question six asked students what, if anything, changed their opinions toward reading. The most common response related to students having choices as to what they read. Nearly half of the students in both grades wrote that they liked reading more this year because they were able to choose what books they get to read. An additional twenty-five percent of the students responded that the reason they liked it more was because they have been able to find books that they like this year. Another common response was that they liked being able to read when they want to read and at their own pace.

Question seven asked students how they think they will feel about reading next year. There were noticeable differences in the responses from sixth to eighth grade students. About fifteen percent of students said they predict that they will still enjoy reading next year, about fifteen percent said they would enjoy it but wouldn't have time once they started high school, and about thirty percent said that they won't enjoy reading. Several of the students who wrote that they wouldn't enjoy reading in a year noted that it was because they wouldn't get to choose what they read for school next year. For sixth grade, forty percent of the students said they would enjoy reading as much or more in a year. Forty-five percent of the students said they would not enjoy it as much or would hate it because their teacher next year will require a half an hour of reading every night with a nightly summary to fill out.

Other data was collected to see if the reading program had any impact on students' reading abilities. To assess this, I took data from a benchmark assessment program our school uses a few times throughout the year. However, the test increases in difficulty throughout the year, so the test taken at the beginning of the year is not comparable to the test given in January. Thus, the results would not offer any valid or reliable data for comparison, so I opted not to use them in the study.

Discussion

The study was intended to show the effectiveness of a reading program where students read their own novels independently and at their own pace and ability levels while explicitly being taught to use reading strategies. It was also supposed to show how such a program impacted students' motivation and attitudes toward reading. Overall, the study yielded the results that I anticipated in my hypothesis. I expected that when the students were given choices as to what they would read and as to when they would read and were given books at their reading levels, their attitudes toward reading would improve as would their motivation. I expected to see improvement, but I didn't necessarily expect their attitudes to improve as much as they did and was pleasantly surprised with the results. The results of the survey did support my hypothesis and were consistent with the research that I had found on the topic of independent reading programs.

According to question one on the survey and Figures 5 and 6, most students in both sixth and eighth grades read fewer than five books last year. In my opinion, this is because students were not given any choices as to what they read last year. They were told which books they would read, what pages they would read each day, and for the most part, every student read the same novels regardless of reading level or interests. Many of the students didn't like the novels because they didn't find them to be interesting or because they were simply unable to read them. They seemed to assume that all reading and all books were like the ones they were given in class, and they had little to no desire to read independently or for fun because they made the generalization that all reading was boring.

My students had developed the negative attitudes toward reading that Ivey and Broaddus reported most adolescents have (2000). Though Ivey and Broaddus did not explain how many books the average adolescent student reads, they did say that most do not read for entertainment, which was exactly how the majority of my students were before this year. I attribute this to the pain and pleasure principle Corcoran and Mamalakis (2009) detailed. The authors explained that when reading elicits pain or failure, students don't want to do it. When it elicits pleasure, however, students are more likely to be motivated to want to read. I found this to be true with my own students. In the past, reading had brought about a great deal of failure or pain for my students, especially my struggling readers who were unable to find success with grade level texts. Even the students who didn't struggle found pain in reading because it was often followed by daunting assignments. The program I used with my classes improved students' motivation toward reading because it made reading pleasurable for students, and their motivation was evident in the number of books they read.

The responses to question two show that the number of books students read this year increased dramatically (Figures 5 and 6). Last year, most students read fewer than five books; this year, no student read fewer than seven books with nearly all students reading more than ten and a considerable amount who read twenty books or more. I anticipate that the number of books will continue to increase as the survey was administered with fifteen weeks of school still remaining. The students seem to have to motivation to read that they simply lacked last year. Like Tilley (2009) said, "It seems increasingly clear that the chief impediments to literacy are not cognitive in nature. It is not that students cannot learn; it is that they do not want to." (p. 40). My students range in ability levels, and I have both low and high students, but the reason they didn't read last year wasn't because they couldn't. It was because they had no desire to.

Questions three and four of the survey highlighted the huge contrast between students' attitudes toward reading last year and their attitudes toward reading this year. Question three asked students to rate how they felt about reading last year using a Likert-type scale. A score of 1 indicated that the students hated reading; a 5 indicated that the student really enjoyed it. Question four used the same scale but asked students how they feel about reading this year.

In the sixth grade class, 65% of the students indicated a negative attitude toward reading (a response of a 1 or 2) last year, and only 5% indicated a negative attitude this year. Last year, 25% of the sixth grade students were neutral to reading (a score of 3), and this year, 5% were neutral. Only 10% of the students indicated a positive attitude toward reading last year (a score of a 4 or 5), and this year 90% of the sixth grade students indicated a positive attitude toward reading. Of the twenty sixth grade students surveyed in my class, nineteen of them showed an increase in their responses between last year and this year.

The eighth grade students' scores yielded similar results. When asked about their attitudes toward reading last year, 81% indicated a negative attitude; this year, only 12% responded that they had a negative attitude toward it. None of the students indicated that they were neutral toward reading last year, and this year 23% indicated that they were, which was an improvement for all of the students who responded with a score of a 3. 19% of the eighth grade students surveyed indicated that they had a positive attitude toward reading last year, and this year 65% indicated a positive attitude toward it. It is also important to note that twenty-two out of the twenty-six eighth grade students indicated an improved attitude toward reading, one student's negative score stayed the same, and three students' scores who stayed the same had already had indicated a fondness for it before this school year.

When students were asked if, how, and what changed their attitudes toward reading in questions five and six, the responses most frequently related to choice and variety. Many of the students responded that they liked that fact that they were allowed to choose what they read and were able to read at their own pace and liked that the books were matched to their interests. Lapp and Fisher (2009) implemented a similar program and reported that their students were also highly motivated by choice. The students in their study felt engaged because their interests had been taken into consideration, and they liked having a say in what they read. Several other researchers emphasized the importance of choice in reading (Corcoran & Mamalakis, 2009; Jenkins, 2009; Tilley, 2009) and reported that it is a natural motivator for students because it gives students the feeling of power as well as a sense of ownership. Along with having choices in their reading, my students also had access to a variety of texts. I constantly sought out books that covered a wide range of topics and interests, so that no matter what the student was interested in and no matter what they felt like reading, I always had something that they would find appealing. Research also suggests that the variety of text is important in both independent reading and modeling because it exposes students to various types of literature (Ivey & Broaddus, 2000). The link between choices and variety and motivation was clear in both my study and in the current research on the topic.

Though book choice was the most common response listed for why and how students' attitudes have changed for questions five and six, there were other factors that contributed to the reading program's success. One of those is the fact that I spent time getting to know my students and their interests as well as their reading preferences. The students have always been able to choose their books, but I do offer suggestions based on my knowledge of each individual student, and the students trust me because they know that I do know and see each of them as individuals. Ivey and Broaddus (2000) explained in their research that teachers need to take the time to get to know every student as a reader and as an individual in order to increase motivation and achievement, and I found it to be effective with my students.

Along those same lines, another factor that made the reading program successful was the peer relationships that I encouraged in the classroom. At the beginning of the year, the kids jokingly teased the students who were reading many books very quickly, and I strongly discouraged it. Instead, I tried to create a learning community where students encouraged each other to read. It didn't take long before it caught on and I started hearing students talking about the books they were reading and recommending them to their peers. From time to time I would also have some of the classes who were reading more joke about the classes who weren't reading as much. I discouraged this as well and explained to all of my classes that I was proud of them because every class was reading more than they had ever read before. Now I don't hear kids teasing one another for reading too many or too few books; I hear them encouraging one another. Reading has simply become part of the culture in my classroom. I do, however, hear students telling each other, "You have to read this book!" or "This book is awesome! You need to check it out!" Lapp and Fisher (2009) attributed part of the success with their reading program to peer relationships explaining that their students felt that the peer support made them more motivated and more successful readers. Even though my students didn't list it on their surveys, I know that the peer relationships did impact their motivation and their attitudes toward reading.

Questions five and six allowed the students to explain why their attitudes toward reading have changed over the past year. Another factor they didn't list that I know had an impact was in the way that I teach this year, which was a huge change. The changes I made in turn, affected my students' motivation and attitudes toward reading. Instead of teaching novels in a traditional manner, I taught reading strategies explicitly using class novels and independent reading materials as is suggested by a great deal of literacy research (Santa, 2006; Biancarosa & Snow, 2004; Aimonette & Galda, 2009, Ivey & Broaddus, 2000; Deshler & Hock, 2007). The research explains that many students lack the reading strategies to comprehend a text, but it they are taught explicitly and modeled, students learn to use them independently and are able to construct more meaning from a what they read. Like many of the researchers suggest, I start by modeling a skill and gradually release responsibility to the students with each reading strategy and as time went by, the students seemed to have stronger critical thinking skills and did seem to comprehend the material better. Questions five and six on the surveys showed that choice was the biggest motivator for the students, but there have been several other motivators as well.

Question seven of the survey asked students how they thought they would feel about reading a year from now. The responses varied, and big differences were seen between grades six and eight. Many of the eighth grade students wrote that they would still enjoy it but that they didn't think they would have time to read as much once they got to high school. Some students also expressed concern that they might not like it as much because they wouldn't like the material they will have to read. Many of the sixth grade students figure that they will still like reading next year, but several of them expressed concerns about not liking reading it because they will have a different teacher. They know that next year they will have other reading teacher in our building, and they know she requires them to read nightly for thirty minutes, keep a nightly reading log, and write a summary of what they read each night. They speculated that they might not like reading as much because the assignments would take the fun out of it. This goes back to the pleasure and pain principle wherein reading that causes "pain" is no longer motivating but is demotivating (Corcoran & Mamalakis, 2009).

As a whole, the study examined how the independent reading program I created affected students' attitudes and motivations toward reading. What I found was the same thing that researchers have found. Students are more motivated to read when they have a voice in choosing what they read. They are also more motivated when they have access to a variety of texts, have a supportive reading environment, and collaborative relationship with a teachers who sees them as individuals and as readers. Overall, the data I collected suggests that the students' attitudes and motivation definitely increased as a result of the program I had in place.

There are some validity concerns with my research, especially in how the results pertain to other teachers and classes in other schools. While I anticipate similar results with my students next year, I don't think all schools and districts would have the same degree of success. Even though my students were not readers before, most of them are average students with few significant reading problems. I have struggling readers, but they are mild in comparison to the struggles of many students in other districts. I also have the benefit of working in a small district that has a moderate to high level of parental support and has a low mobility rate, few (if any) considerable discipline or behavior concerns, and few major attendance problems. A school that does have these concerns may not have the same success that I had, so the validity is questionable because the results may not apply to other students in other buildings.

There were also some measurement problems with the original research design. Initially, the plan was to study the students' attitudes and motivation toward reading and their reading skills. However, the measurement tool I intended to use proved to be unreliable and invalid. The test is taken at several points throughout the school year, and I came to find out that it increases in difficulty as the year progresses, so it would not give an accurate measure of how the students had improved. As a result, I decided to drop the data from the research plan. Another problem with using the reading skills scores as a measure of success or failure of the reading program was the fact that I didn't have a way to show how the students did with this program compared to how much they would have progressed without it. The surveys showed a significant, inarguable improvement in students' attitudes and motivation in reading, but I was unable to accurately measure any potential change in their reading skills as a direct result of the independent reading program.

The biggest limitation to my study was in the sample size. The independent reading program was implemented for three groups of students in one rural school district. Only forty-six students were surveyed, and there were too few students studied to be considered representative of the population of the area or of the region. The results were significant in my classroom, but the sample size is too small to many any broad generalizations as to how the program would affect other schools.

Even though there were limitations to the study, there are generalizations that could be applied to students in other districts. Though they may not find the exact same degree of success with a different demographic, I am confident that if teachers in other schools used elements from the study, they would find success in increasing their students' motivation and attitudes toward reading.

It is safe to say that nearly all students in nearly all schools will do better and enjoy reading more when they are given choices as to what they read. Research done in various studies done in various places with different demographics all suggests that students like having choices. The research also suggests that it gives students ownership over their learning and allows them to take on more of an active role in their education. Regardless of demographics or location, students need to have access to a variety of materials that are based around their interests and reading level as well. That is not to say that all schools would see the same jump in attitudes and in motivation, but I am confident that they would see improvements over programs that do not incorporate student choice.

Additionally, the generalization can be made that the teacher-student relationship does impact students' motivation and attitudes toward reading. When students feel that the teachers see them as individuals and that the teachers value their interests, they are more likely to be connected with the content area and are more likely to see value in the activities. Seeing each student as an individual also allows teachers to more accurately tailor instruction to meet the needs of everyone rather than trying to find one text that fits the needs of all students. Though the sample size of my study was small, the importance of a positive teacher-student relationship is sure to apply to any group of students.

Finally, the pleasure and pain principle could be generalized for any group of students. If students find pain or failure in reading, most will not want to do it, regardless of reading abilities. If students are given texts they are unable to read and fail or if reading is constantly followed up by daunting, unpleasant assignments, students will not be motivated to read. However, if students are able to find success in reading, find books they genuinely enjoy, and if they are given meaningful assignments and assessments, they will find it to be more pleasurable and are more likely to want to do it. Thus, all reading teachers need to find ways to make reading a pleasurable experience for their students if they want to motivate them and if they want them to have positive attitudes toward reading.

There is definite potential and need for more research into independent reading programs. The biggest area that needs to be researched is how the program impacts actual reading abilities. First, researchers would need to determine what skills they would target, test, and monitor. Then they would need an accurate system and a reliable tool for obtaining baseline data and a precise way to monitor students' reading skills over a progression of time. Also, they would need a control group to see how the use of the program impacts students' reading skills compared to a group who was taught in a more traditional manner. If the study was done right, it would also allow researchers to have an idea as to whether or not students made above average, average, or below average gains compared to other reading programs. Additionally, research needs to be done using a larger sample size so it could be more reliable. The results of the study were undoubtedly important, but more research should be done to determine how it affects students actual reading abilities.

Overall, the research I completed showed that the reading program I implemented this year was effective. The original question asked how the independent reading program impacted students' motivation and attitude toward reading. The data I collected, both formally and informally, strongly suggests that the independent reading program impacted my students' motivation toward reading in a positive way. The surveys indicated that most of my students' attitudes have improved over the course of the year, and they are reading more than they ever have before. I have found success with this program, and though I am sure I will make minor changes to it over the coming years, I am eager to see how it affects future students.

References

Adolescent literacy comes of age. (1999, August). *Reading Today, 162*-8.

Aimonette Liang, L., & Galda, L. (2009, December). Responding and comprehending: Reading with delight and understanding. *The Reading Teacher, 63*, 330-333.

Biancarosa, G, & Snow, C. E. *(2004). Reading next: A vision for action and research in middle and high school literacy. A report front Carnegie Corporation of New York. W*ashington, DC: Alliance for Excellent Education.

Cassidy, J., Garrett, S. D., & Estanislado, S. B. (2006, September). What's hot in adolescent literacy 1997-2006. *Journal of Adolescent & Adult Literacy, 50*, 30-36.

Conley, M.W., & Hinchman, K.A. (2004, September). No Child Left Behind: What it means for U.S. adolescents and what we can do about it. *Journal of Adolescent & Adult Literacy, 48*, 42-50.

Conley, M. W. (2007). Reconsidering adolescent literacy: From competing agendas to shared commitment. In M. Pressley et al. (Ed.), *Shaping Literacy Achievement*. New York: The Guilford Press.

Corcoran, C. A., & Mamalakis, A. (2009). Fifth grade students' perceptions of reading motivation techniques. *Reading Improvement, 46 no 3*, 137-142.

Cunningham, P. (2005). "It they don't read much, how they ever gonna get good?". *International Reading Association, 59*, 88-90.

Darwin, M., & Fleischman, S. (2005, April). Fostering adolescent literacy. *Educational Leadership, 62*, 85-87.

Deshler, D. D., & Hock, M. F. (2007). Adolescent literacy: Where we are, where we need to go. In M. Pressley et al. (Ed.), *Shaping Literacy Achievement*. New York: The Guilford Press.

Hobbs, N., Oleynik, M., & Sacco, K. (2009, November). Reading: Making it personal again - Now serving PIE to hungry readers. *School Library Monthly, 26*, 42-44.

Interactive Illinois Report Card. (2009). Retrieved October 15, 2010, from Northern Illinois University: http://iirc.niu.edu/School.aspx?schoolid=530900980022001

Ivey, G., & Broaddus, K. (2000, September). Tailoring the fit: Reading instruction and middle school readers. *The Reading Teacher, 54*, 68-78. Retrieved November 10, 2010, from EBSCO database.

Jenkins, S. (2009). How to maintain school reading success: Five recommendations from a struggling male reader. *The Reading Teacher, 63*, 159-162.

Lapp, D., & Fisher, D. (2009, April). It's all about the book: Motivating Teens to Read. *Journal of Adolescent and Adult Literacy, 52*, 556-561.

Tilley, C. L. (2009, December). Reading motivation and engagement. *School Library Monthly*, *26 no 4*, 39-42.

Trudel, H. (2007, December). Making data-driven decisions: Silent reading. *The Reading Teacher*, *61*, 308-315.

Santa, C. M. (2006, March). A vision for adolescent literacy: Ours or theirs? *Journal of Adolescent & Adult Literacy*, *49*, 466-476.

Chapter 5: The Impact of Student Choice on Assessment Projects

Julie Horton

Introduction

The link between student choice and motivation as well student choice and effort is an interesting problem. Based on my observations as an eleven-year veteran middle school Spanish teacher, I believe that giving students choices on assignments and projects has the potential to increase their motivation and effort. Although research exists on the connections between motivation and effort (Birdsell, Ream, Seyller & Zobott, 2009), there is limited research that examines the impact that student choice has on these two areas. I hope to extend this research by specifically examining the impact that student choice has on motivation and effort as it relates to assessment projects.

Middle school students desire freedom of choice and opportunities to discover and explore topics of interest (Birdsell et al., 2009). Not offering choices to students will limit their interest and investment in a particular project or activity. Students are more likely to be involved in an activity when they choose it because choice has a powerful motivating effect on them (Cooper, Patall & Robinson, 2008). Students also desire studying their own interests more deeply because they are motivated to do so (Wasserstein, 1995). In the foreign language classroom, it is important to provide students with an authentic context, one that connects to the students' real-life situations and personal interests. Felder and Henriques (1995) agree that foreign language teachers must consider teaching vocabulary and grammar in ways that are relatable to students' personal experiences. In addition, when making content material relatable to students, it is essential that a foreign language teacher provide a wide-range of learning strategies that helps meet the needs and expectations of students who all possess different learning styles, motivations, and preferences (Haskin & Racine, 2003).

Rationale for the Study

Research suggests that the human brain is programmed to make meaning from experience (Met, 1999). Students achieve this by connecting new knowledge to what they already know. As a result, they make meaning out of each new experience. Research shows that learning is enhanced when it is authentically linked to meaning and purpose through real-life tasks and situations that relate to the students' experiences (Met, 1999). One way to provide this context, when dealing with assessment, is by giving students an opportunity to choose a project topic that relates to an area of interest from the unit being assessed. The student is more likely to take the initiative on the project because he/she is already engaged by the topic. In addition to student interest, it is also essential to consider the role that learning styles plays in project development. All students have a particular learning style and may choose a type of product and mode of delivery that lends itself to their learning style (Oxford, 2003).

This study will examine what happens when students combine what they already know, with their personal interests, and create a project using a preferred product and mode of delivery that suits their learning style. The teacher will also be able to assess how well students are able to use what they have learned from the unit in a meaningful and authentic way.

Statement of the Problem

Many students in the middle school setting lack interest in completing teacher choice, assessment projects because the topic, type of product, and delivery mode are all pre-determined by the teacher. This problem is evidenced by students not giving their best effort because they are not invested in the project. It is also characterized by students lacking motivation because they are not engaged in the project. The purpose of this study is to find out what effect student choice or lack of student choice has on student interest, motivation, and investment in a unit assessment project designed for two, level one Spanish classes. This study will examine the following questions: (1) How much more enjoyable was the project to students who had choice of topic, product, and type of delivery versus those who did not? (2) What similarities and differences exist in terms of student interest, motivation, and effort between the teacher choice and student choice assessment groups? (3) Overall, which group of students showed more interest, motivation, and effort in the project?

Review of Literature

Background

A successful middle school is one designed around the unique needs of young adolescents (Van Hoose, Strahan, & L'Esperance, 2006). A middle school is an educational unit with a philosophy, structure, and program which realistically and appropriately deals with eleven to fourteen year olds as they are and behave. Exploratory and enrichment experiences are available to meet the individual interests of young adolescent students (Georgiady, 1974). To ensure that middle schools meet the needs of young adolescents, several reforms in education began to take shape beginning in the late 20th century and continuing through to the 21st century. The first in adolescent education reform included a set of recommendations for transforming middle schools in order to improve the educational experiences of all middle school students called, *Turning Points: Preparing American youth for the 21st century (*Carnegie Council on Adolescent Development, *1989)*. The recommendations included middle schools creating small communities (teams) for learning, teaching a core academic program, and ensuring success for all students. Another leading reform entitled, *This We Believe,* outlines fourteen characteristics of a successful middle school for young adolescents (NMSA, 2003). One of the characteristics mentioned is utilizing constructivist approaches in teaching and learning.

Constructivism is a psychological theory or perspective which argues that humans generate knowledge and meaning from their experiences (Ormrod, 2004). New information is also most easily acquired when people can associate it with things they have already learned. Making that connection to prior knowledge, helps people organize and store the information. Beane (1999) explains that using curriculum integration is one way a middle school can embrace the constructivist perspective. Having students pose questions and concerns about "self" and "world", students are able to identify themes and connect this new information to what they already know which gives them an opportunity to build on that prior knowledge. Murphy (2009) agrees that one way to motivate students to read is by using topics of interest to encourage them. She states, "Making personal and real-world connections to students' prior knowledge about a topic is one way to help them make connections to the text" (p.22). Constructivism also impacts motivation and effort through student engagement as well as influences types of assessment integral to the middle school, such as authentic assessment.

Motivation and Effort

Wigfield, Lutz and Wagner (2005) argue that the transition to middle school can be a difficult time for young adolescents, especially those struggling with changes in other areas of their lives. Many early adolescents' self-esteem and motivation may be particularly vulnerable during this transition. In addition, there is also a specific decline in intrinsic motivation for learning. *Human Learning* defines intrinsic motivation as a source of motivation that lies within the individual and task. The individual finds the task enjoyable or worthwhile without any outside influences (Ormrod, 2004). One way to foster and encourage the intrinsic motivation of a young adolescent is by teachers creating a climate of trust in the classroom. (Strahan (2008) believes this is an essential first step toward increasing students' academic motivation because students are more likely to take the risks that new learning entails when they trust their teachers. Wigfield, Lutz and Wagner (2005) agree teacher support plays a significant role in the amount of academic effort the young adolescent exerts. Davis (2006) examines the student-teacher relationship quality and its effect on student motivation and achievement, and states that "teachers can influence students' social and intellectual experiences via their abilities to instill values in children such as the motivation to learn; by providing classroom contexts that stimulate students' motivation and learning" (p. 193). The results of the study conclude that when a student develops a trusting relationship with a teacher, student motivation for learning in that class will increase. Conversely, when a student has a poor relationship with a teacher, student motivation for learning in that class will decrease.

Once a positive relationship is established between teacher and student, a teacher is able to engage students in ways that connect to their interests and to the curriculum. Strahan (2008) believes that using student-selected topics of interest in the classroom will lead to students making personal connections to the task at hand. This involvement leads to actively engaging students in learning. He states that when teachers develop instructional activities that link inquiry, collaboration, and real-world experiences, student engagement and interest increases which also promotes academic achievement. Teachers can encourage this by developing "skill" and "will" in their students. They need the "will" to want to understand the information and the "skill" to know how best to invest their energies in the learning process so that they are able to learn new concepts in meaningful ways.

Student Choice

Connecting to student interest is one way to engage students; offering choices to students also connects to student interest and motivates them toward academic achievement. Birdsell, Ream, Seyller and Zobott (2009) agree and state that teachers can motivate students by increasing student choice opportunities. In this study, researchers use pre/post interventions such as surveys, a checklist of observable behavior patterns, and student reflections to measure the levels of academic motivation students have both before and after the treatment intervention. The intervention consists of developing a unit that allows for student choice on curricular assignments, group work, and assessment. Results show that when student choice is given in each of these areas, the result is an increase in success and enjoyment of students as well as an increase in feeling like they are able to use their strengths. Therefore, student choice offerings produce more positive behaviors and an increase in academic self-motivation.

House (2009) also examines student choice options by studying the relationship between classroom instructional strategies and interest that students in Korea express for having a career in science. The study investigates how authentic instruction enables students to connect science topics learned in the classroom, with real world context and problems, and whether or not the use of these authentic learning experiences increases student interest in a science career for students in Korea. Results show that students in Korea who more frequently design or plan an original experiment or investigation during their science lessons, and present their work to the class, tend to indicate a high level of interest in a science career.

Van Hoose, Strahan and L'Esperance (2006) explain that by providing options for students to demonstrate their understanding of concepts, successful teachers build movement into their lessons and give students choices about ways to show their comprehension. Teachers can provide options or choices through the topic or type of product being created. Tomlinson and McTighe (2006) explain that "giving students appropriate options for demonstrating knowledge, skill, and understanding and allowing them some choices with a common set of evaluative criteria is beneficial to students" (p. 75).

Assessment

When considering what types of topic or product options to explore, the use of authentic assessment is integral. *Educational Assessment of Students* defines this as, "A type of performance assessment in which students are presented with educational tasks that are directly meaningful instead of indirectly meaningful" (Nitko & Brookhart, 2007, p. 508). By connecting assessment to real life situations, it provides students with opportunities to make the context meaningful. Childre, Sands, & Pope (2009) explain that students personalize learning by creating ways to see how the information relates to what they already know and to their lives- past, present, or future. Projects and performance assessments are most effective as summative or culminating assessments because they allow students to demonstrate an integrated understanding of unit concepts. In addition, incorporating performance and portfolio assessments is one way to push beyond the low level skills commonly found on standardized tests (Beane, 1999). Wiggins and McTighe (2006) explain that quality assessments are those that require explanation, interpretation, application, analysis, synthesis, and self-evaluation. This type of assessment encourages higher level thinking and using the skills learned in the unit. The result is a meaningful experience that engages students and provides teachers with the insight and feedback they need to evaluate what each student knows and has learned from the unit.

Conclusion

Providing student choice options in the classroom will not only appeal to young adolescent students, but also will increase student engagement as well as academic motivation in the classroom. Developing a positive and trusting relationship with the classroom teacher also fosters motivation and self-efficacy, which tends to be low as students transition through their young adolescent years. Understanding key characteristics of a successful middle school, like constructivist approaches to teaching and learning, also help teachers meet the needs of young adolescents better.

Methodology

Participants

The participants in this research study were recruited from a Midwestern Junior High School. The students range in age from 13 to 14 years old. The configuration of the school is sixth through eighth grade. The school considers itself a middle school that is founded on the middle school concept. Total population is 894 students. The ethnic background of the population is: White: 73.4%, Black: 13.6%, Hispanic: 4.9%, Asian: 1.7%, Native American: 0.6%, Multiracial: 5.8%.

The research study consists of 33 eighth grade students enrolled in a level one Spanish class at the Junior High School. Sixteen of these students are in the first hour class. These students will be assigned a teacher choice assessment project. The remaining seventeen students are in the third hour class and will be assigned a student choice assessment project. As their Spanish teacher, these students are available to me on a daily basis and are therefore the foundation for the convenient sample. Students were chosen for this study based on their willingness to participate. Parents and students completed a permission form and assent form, respectively. Since participation was voluntary, students were able to discontinue their involvement in the research study at any time without penalty.

Instrument

Student enjoyment, motivation, and effort serve as the constructs of interest in this research study. One way to operationalize these constructs in a meaningful way is by using a student self-reported survey or reflection survey (Parsons & Brown, 2002). Students from the first hour class will complete the teacher choice survey. Students from the third hour class will complete the student choice survey. Each survey consists of ten questions. Six of the questions have students rate their enjoyment, motivation, or effort based on a scale from 1 (least) to 7 (most). Three of the questions require open-ended responses from the students regarding their enjoyment of the project. One question includes a checklist of items that would have made or did make the project enjoyable.

The project that students will complete is a summative assessment of the information found in unit three; section two of the *¡En Español!* Spanish textbook series. The unit highlights sports and athletes that are popular in Puerto Rico. Sports, sports equipment, locations, and other sports-related words are included as key vocabulary for this textbook section. Students will create a project about a Puerto Rican athlete. The person (athlete), product, and presentation style of this project will either be pre-determined by the teacher or determined by the student depending on which class (first or third hour) each student attends. After the students present their project, they will receive a student reflection survey to complete.

The student reflection surveys being used are an appropriate tool for measuring student enjoyment, motivation, and effort because it involves both qualitative and quantitative methods that result in accurate data collection and interpretation. Qualitative research methods attempt to view the experience holistically, exploring all aspects, including the unique context within which the experience has occurred. In addition, there is an attempt to understand the meaning and patterns of relationship found within the context of the research. Students in the study provide the researcher with their insights, feelings, and observations about the teacher choice assessment project versus the student choice assessment projects. After gathering the data from the surveys, the analysis of the data will include organizing, describing, and interpreting the information in a systematic way in order to facilitate the understanding of the data collected.

In addition to the qualitative methods being used, quantitative methods will also be used to specifically report on the numerical data collected from the reflection surveys. Descriptive statistics such as the mean and standard deviation will also be used as a way of calculating values that represent the overall characteristics of the body of data in order to organize and describe specific groups of data.

Procedure

In this study, two groups of middle school students will participate in a unit assessment project. One group will complete a project in which the topic, product, and presentational delivery of that project is decided by the teacher. The other group will complete a project in which the topic, product, and presentational delivery is decided by the student. After the project is completed, each group of students will participate in a survey that asks them reflection questions about their involvement in the assessment project.

Research Questions

1. How much more enjoyable was the project to students who had choice of topic, product, and type of delivery versus those who did not?
2. What similarities and differences exist in terms of student interest, motivation, and effort between the teacher choice and student choice assessment groups?
3. Overall, which group of students showed more interest, motivation, and effort in the project?

Definition of Terms

Assessment- The evaluation of student development and learning at the end of a unit.

Student choice- The act of choosing or selecting that originates with the student.

Motivation- The incentive to do an activity or task is based on the expected enjoyment of the activity itself.

Effort- The amount of work involved in performing an activity or task.

Data Analysis

The data for this research study was analyzed using a mixed design utilizing qualitative and quantitative methods. The analysis for the qualitative data utilized the concepts of emerging themes and categories. The research then used triangulation as a methodological approach. Tables and graphs was be used to present this data. The analysis for the quantitative data included statistics such as the mean and standard deviation of responses from both the teacher and student choice reflection surveys, as well as a comparison of data between the two. The SPSS data analysis program was used to interpret and organize this information.

Results

The study began with forty six, eighth grade students enrolled in a level one Spanish course at a Junior High School in Midwestern city in Illinois. Twenty one of these students were in the first hour class section and were assigned a teacher choice assessment project. The remaining twenty five students were in the third hour class section and were assigned a student choice assessment project. Out of the twenty one students in the first hour section, five did not return the signed parent permission form. Out of the twenty five students in the third hour section, six did not return the signed parent permission form and two were absent on the day that the survey was administered. A total of thirty three students completed the assessment project reflection survey. The survey contained a total of ten questions. Six of the questions used a seven point Likert-type scale while three of the remaining questions were open ended. The last question was a preference question in which students marked all the choices that applied.

For each of the questions on the survey using the Likert-type scale (questions 1, 6-10), the mean score and standard deviation are given in Table 1 for the first hour class that completed the teacher choice assessment project survey and Table 2 for the third hour class that completed the student choice assessment project survey. Responses to questions one and six through eight on the teacher choice assessment project survey and the student choice assessment project survey were rated on a scale that consisted of: 7=very much enjoyed, 6=enjoyed, 5= mainly enjoyed, 4= neutral, 3= somewhat enjoyed, 2= barely enjoyed, 1= least (not very much) enjoyed. Responses to question nine on the teacher choice assessment survey were rated on a scale that consisted of: 7=very much, 6=more than average, 5=average, 4= neutral, 3= somewhat, 2= barely, 1= not much. Responses to question nine on the student choice assessment survey were rated on a scale that consisted of: 7=very difficult, 6=more difficult, 5=slightly more difficult, 4= difficult, 3= somewhat difficult, 2= barely difficult, 1=not very difficult. Reponses to question ten on both the teacher and student choice assessment project surveys were rated on a scale that consisted of: 7= best effort, 6=more than average effort, 5=average effort, 4=some effort, 3= minimal effort, 2=little to no effort, 1=no effort.

Question one on the survey inquired about how much students enjoyed the assessment project. The mean score for those who completed the teacher choice assessment was 4.5 and a mean score of 4.5 for those who completed the student choice assessment project.

Question six on the teacher choice assessment survey asked students how much more they would have enjoyed the project if choice of topic had been an option. A mean score of 5.7 was produced. Question six on the student choice assessment asked students how much more they would have enjoyed the project had choice of topic not been an option. The mean score for this question was 3.4.

Question seven on the teacher choice assessment survey asked students how much more they would have enjoyed the project if the product choice had been an option. This produced a mean score of 5.4. Question seven on the student choice assessment inquired about how much more the students would have enjoyed the project, had choice of product not been an option. A mean score of 3.3 was produced.

Question eight on the teacher choice assessment survey asked students how much more they would have enjoyed the project had delivery (presentation) style been an option. The mean score was 5.0. Question eight on the student choice assessment asked students how much more they would have enjoyed the project had delivery (presentation) style not been an option. A mean score of 3.4 was recorded.

Question nine on the teacher choice assessment survey asked students if having choice of topic, product, or delivery style had been an option, would it have motivated them that much more to work harder on the project. This question produced a mean score of 5.4. Question nine on the student choice assessment survey inquired about the opposite, how difficult would it have been to do the project if choice of topic, product, and delivery style had been taken away. The mean score for this question was 4.0.

Question ten was the same for both the teacher and student choice assessment project surveys and inquired about student effort and what level of effort students put into the project. The mean for the teacher choice assessment project surveys was 6.6 and 6.4 for the student choice project assessment surveys.

Table 1: Teacher Choice Assessment Project Likert-Survey Results

Question	N.	M.	S.D.
1. How much did you enjoy the project?	16	4.5	1.5
6. If topic of choice had been an option, how much more would you have enjoyed the project?	16	5.7	1.2
7. If product choice had been an option, how much more would you have enjoyed the project?	16	5.4	1.5
8. If delivery (presentation) style had been an option, how much more would you have enjoyed the project?	16	5.0	1.7
9. If the factor(s) indicated had been an option, how much more would it have motivated you to work harder on the project?	16	5.4	2.0
10. What level of effort did you put into the project?	16	6.6	.63

Table 2: Student Choice Assessment Project Likert-Survey Results

Question	N.	M.	S.D.
1. How much did you enjoy the project?	17	4.5	1.9
6. If topic of choice had not been an option, how much more would you have enjoyed the project?	17	3.4	1.4
7. If product choice had not been an option, how much more would you have enjoyed the project?	17	3.3	1.2
8. If delivery (presentation) style had not been an option, how much more would you have enjoyed the project?	17	3.4	1.8
9. If the factor(s) indicated were taken away, how difficult would it be to do the project?	17	4.0	1.8
10. What level of effort did you put into the project?	17	6.4	.71

Question 5 on the teacher choice assessment project survey asked students to put a check mark next to the factor(s) that would have made the project more enjoyable. The factors included: (5a) Topic of choice, (5b) Product of choice, (5c) Delivery (presentation) style of choice, and (5d) Other factor(s) not mentioned. Students checked all of the factors that applied. Table 3 shows how often students in the class selected each factor. There are a total of sixteen students who completed the teacher choice assessment project. In question 5a, fifteen students indicated that having topic of choice would have made the project more enjoyable while one person did not think it made a difference. Question 5b showed that eleven students would have enjoyed choosing a product of their choice while five students indicated that it did not matter. Seven students said that having a delivery or presentation style of their choice would have made this project more enjoyable while nine students indicated that it did not make a difference. Only one of the sixteen total students indicated another factor not already mentioned that would have made the project more enjoyable. The student stated that having choice over the gender of the athlete would have made the project more enjoyable.

Table 3: Teacher Choice Assessment Project Frequency Results

Put a check mark next to the factor(s) that would have made this project more enjoyable.		
5a. Topic of Choice	Frequency	Percent
Checked by student	15	93.8
Not checked by student	1	6.3
Total amount of students	16	100.0
5b. Product of Choice	Frequency	Percent
Checked by student	11	68.8
Not checked by student	5	31.3
Total amount of students	16	100.0
5c. Delivery (presentation) style of Choice	Frequency	Percent
Checked by student	7	43.8
Not checked by student	9	56.3
Total amount of students	16	100.0
5d. Other factor(s) not mentioned	Frequency	Percent
Checked by student	1	6.3
Not checked by student	15	93.8
Total amount of students	16	100.0

Question 5 on the student choice assessment project survey asked students to put a check mark next to the factor(s) that made the project enjoyable. The factors included: (5a) Topic of choice, (5b) Product of choice, (5c) Delivery (presentation) style of choice, and (5d) Other factor(s) not mentioned. Table 4 shows how often students in the class selected each factor. There are a total of seventeen students who completed the student choice assessment project. In question 5a, sixteen of the seventeen students stated that having topic of choice made the project more enjoyable. Fourteen students indicated that product of choice made the project more enjoyable while three students did not think that it did in question 5b. In question 5c, ten students stated that having choice of delivery (presentation) style made the project more enjoyable while seven students disagreed. Five of the seventeen students indicated that other factors besides the others mentioned also made the project more enjoyable. These factors included (1) working with friends, (2) choosing groups, and (3) costumes and dressing up.

Table 4: Student Choice Assessment Project Frequency Results

Put a check mark next to the factor(s) that made this project enjoyable.		
5a. Topic of Choice	Frequency	Percent
Checked by student	16	94.1
Not checked by student	1	5.9
Total amount of students	17	100.0
5b. Product of Choice	Frequency	Percent
Checked by student	14	82.4
Not checked by student	3	17.6
Total amount of students	17	100.0
5c. Delivery (Presentation) style of Choice	Frequency	Percent
Checked by student	10	58.8
Not checked by student	7	41.2
Total amount of students	17	100.0
5d. Other factor(s) not mentioned	Frequency	Percent
Checked by student	5	29.4
Not checked by student	12	70.6
Total amount of students	17	100.0

The open ended questions revealed emerging themes for both the teacher and student choice assessment project student reflection surveys. The same three open ended questions appeared on each of the surveys. Question two asked students what they enjoyed about the project and why. Several students who completed the teacher choice assessment project said that they liked researching the athlete. One student responded, "Getting to learn about famous athletes from different countries was enjoyable because I never heard of most of them." Being able to work with a partner and doing something other than just a regular pencil/paper test were also given as responses to this question. "Being able to work with a partner was fun because I like having someone double check my work." Another student stated, "It was fun doing something different (a skit) and working with a partner made it easier and helped me when being in front of people.

Students who completed the student choice assessment project also shared their opinions about question two on the survey. Many of them enjoyed having a chance to choose an athlete to research as well as choosing a partner to work with. One student commented, "I liked how we got to choose our own athlete and not had one assigned. It was fun to research our own person." Another student added, "I got to pick my partner and work with someone that I like to work with." Several students in this class already have an interest in sports. One student stated, "I like that it was about sports because I'm interested in sports." Several students also enjoyed the costuming and acting portions of the project. Some student comments include: "I like getting to wear costumes and act out a skit. I really like acting and I get excited when I get the chance." Another student remarked, "I liked getting to dress up like your person (athlete) because it really added to the project."

Question three on the survey asked students what they did not enjoy about the project and why. The students who completed the teacher choice assessment explained that they did not enjoy memorizing a skit and presenting it in front of the class. "I didn't like having to do the skit because I don't like having to memorize things and then say them to the class." "I don't like performing in front of everyone. I get nervous and forget the words and then my grade isn't good." One student explained that doing acting is just not her product of choice. She states, "I didn't like having to present in front of the class because I do not like presenting skits to the class." Several students also shared that having more time to practice would have helped. One student said, "I did not enjoy not having more time because finding the information and writing the script and memorizing it in only four days was not enough time for most people."

Many students who completed the student choice assessment project had some of the same concerns about the project like not having enough time to complete it. Some remarks to question three include, "I did not enjoy that we had such little time to prepare. I think we could have accomplished more and made the project better with more time." Another student added, "I did not like that we only had a few days to write and perfect it. I felt very rushed to learn it." Memorizing and presenting in front of the class was another area of concern. "I did not like how we had to speak in front of the whole class because I get nervous to talk in front of large groups of people." Another student added, "Presenting in front of the class is hard because I forget my lines or stutter because I'm nervous."

Question four asked students what they would change about the project to make it more enjoyable and why. The majority of students who completed the teacher choice assessment project agreed that being able to choose their own athlete, what type of product to create, and having more control over their delivery style would have made the project more enjoyable. One student was not interested in sports and explained, "What would have made the project more enjoyable was making it on a different topic other than sports, because to me, sports aren't the most interesting thing to learn about." Other students liked the topic, but did not like not being able to choose their own athlete to research and said, "I would have let us pick our athletes".

Other students disliked having to create a skit which was the teacher's product of choice. Many students were resistant because they do not like presenting in front of the class. One particular student stated, "I wish we wouldn't have had to present because I HATE talking in front of people in Spanish." Another student commented, "I wish I could have chosen my presentation. Making a poster would be better for me because I could draw and not have to try to memorize a skit when I forget it anyway because I'm nervous. In addition to wanting more product selections, some students suggested having "… a video or power point instead of a skit."

When answering question four, students who completed the student choice assessment project appreciated having control of the topic, product, and delivery choice, but commented on broadening the choices even more. "I would have let there be more options for projects because some people don't like to get up and do skits in front of the group." The most frequent request was the need for more time. One student stated, "I could have used just one more day to practice." Another said, "Having more time on the product because more time to memorize the lines."

Discussion

This study examined the effects that choice had on student assessment projects and whether or not there was a connection between student choice and motivation or effort. According to the results from question one on Table 1 and 2, the students that completed the teacher choice assessment project enjoyed the project as much as the students who completed the student choice assessment project. The mean score for both was 4.5. The factor of choice did not have as much of an impact on enjoyment as was predicted. Even though overall student enjoyment of the project seemed average for both groups, there were specific aspects of the project students enjoyed that related to student choice.

According to question two on both surveys, students who did the student choice assessment cited that they enjoyed choosing their topic and their partner for the project. They also liked the acting and the costuming. This result was consistent with Strahan (2008), who believes that using student-selected topics of interest in the classroom will lead to students making personal connections to the task at hand. These connections will help students become more actively engaged in learning. The majority of the student choice group was interested in sports, and chose an athlete they admire from the sport they play. Their high interest increased their interest in the project. In addition, many of these students also enjoyed role playing and were able to take this enjoyment and choose a product and delivery style that suited their interests. As a result, students made personal connections to their projects which lead to active engagement throughout the project process.

Students who completed the teacher choice assessment said that they enjoyed the project because it was unique and different from a traditional pencil/paper test that they are used to taking. This study predicted that student enjoyment for the teacher choice assessment group would be much lower. However, despite not having topic, product, or delivery choice, students found enjoyment in the nature of the project. House (2009) supports this notion that providing students with authentic instruction that connects to the topics learned in the classroom with real world context, increases student interest and engagement with the task at hand. Students who participated in the teacher choice assessment were still given an authentic situation in which students did original research about an athlete they received from the teacher and then reported on this topic within the context of an interview/skit.

Question three from each survey asked both groups of students why they did not enjoy the project. Interestingly, similar concerns were cited for each group. Not having enough time to prepare and memorize the information was a hindrance to both groups. Also, presenting in front of the class generated a lot of fear for students in each group. The teacher choice assessment group had to present a skit as their product and delivery style. The student choice assessment group was given more product choices and delivery options, but all of the options still integrated an oral component to the presentation. As a result, many students were resistant because they felt inadequate about their Spanish-speaking abilities and were concerned about failing or sounding foolish in front of their classmates. This reaction was surprising because several of the same students who were excited about acting also were insecure about being in front of the class. Wigfield, Lutz and Wagner (2005) attribute this to early adolescents' self-esteem, being vulnerable during this developmental and emotional transition of their life. They explain that students struggle with the changes occurring in their lives at this pivotal time. Student self-esteem and motivation are directly related. When self-esteem is low, so is the motivation to complete the task.

Question four on the survey gave both groups an opportunity to express what they would have changed to make the project more enjoyable. The student choice assessment group stated that having more time to practice and memorize the script would have made them feel better about the project and more confident in presenting it to their classmates. Van Hoose, Strahan and L'Esperance (2006) explain that young adolescents experience what psychologists' term as the "big lie" during young adolescence. Students believe that others are better than themselves and that they are not good enough. Believing this lie affects them academically and damages their sense of competence when completing their work. Van Hoose, Strahan and L'Esperance (2006) also state that students are able to think about thinking as a result of developmental changes that occur intellectually during young adolescents. Because students are more aware of this and are able to negotiate their self-concept, they tend to make conclusions about whether or not they are able or unable to complete a task even before attempting it. This occurred in the choice study. Both groups of students mentioned a concern for presenting in front of the class and having enough time to prepare and memorize the skit, which caused some hesitance when completing the task.

The student choice assessment group also mentioned the need to broaden the choices even more. Previous research by Strahan (2008), indicates the importance of offering student-selected topics, but there is little or no research that examines the effects that choice has on product or delivery style. Students appreciated having control of the topic, product, and delivery style, but wanted even more choices. Comments from students, who completed the teacher choice assessment project, were consistent with Strahan (2008) and said that having choice of topic and control over the athlete they reported on would have made the project more enjoyable.

Table 1 and 2 also showed the mean results for the Likert-scale questions on both surveys. Questions six through eight on the teacher choice assessment project survey (Table 1) asked students how much more they would have enjoyed the project if choice of topic, product, and delivery style had been an option. The results showed an increase in the average mean for each question six through eight respectively (M=5.7, 5.4, 5.0) as compared to overall student enjoyment of the project (M=4.5). Therefore, the results showed that student enjoyment would have increased from a more neutral opinion of the project, to mainly enjoying the project if student choices had been an option.

The students who completed the student choice assessment project did have options and their survey questions were stated slightly different. Questions six through eight (Table 2) asked students how much more they would have enjoyed the project if choice of topic, product, and delivery style had not been an option. The results indicated a decrease in the average mean for question six through eight respectively (M=3.4, 3.3., 3.4) as compared to the overall student enjoyment of the project (M=4.5). The results from this survey showed that student enjoyment would have decreased from a more neutral opinion of the project, to enjoying the project somewhat less. Murphy (2009), Ormrod (2004), and Strahan (2008) suggested that this would be the case. Although an increase in enjoyment was noted for students who preferred having choice options and a decrease was noted for student who would have had the choice options taken away, the differences for both groups were minimal. Unlike the previous research mentioned, the lack of dramatic increase or decrease questions the amount of impact that student choice options really do have on a project.

Question nine on Table 1 inquired about the level of motivation students would have exercised if choice of topic, product, and delivery style had been an option. Would adding student choices lead to an increase in motivation to work harder on the project? Results indicated that an increase in choices would not substantially motivate these students to work harder on the project. A mean of 5.4 showed that students would have been motivated to give an average amount of additional effort to complete the project with the addition of choice options. Although additional motivation and effort was noted, it is not a dramatic increase. Ormrod (2004) explained that when students find the task enjoyable or worthwhile, the effort and motivation they bring to the task lies within them-intrinsic motivation. He proposed that an enjoyable task results in an increase of motivation. The students who participated in the teacher choice assessment project for this study were predicted to not enjoy the project and for their motivation to be low. Even though this is the reverse of what Ormrod (2004) stated, it is still consistent with his definition of intrinsic motivation. The results showed that students who completed the teacher choice assessment project had a neutral opinion about their overall enjoyment for the project (M=4.5 from question one Table 1). Therefore, including choices would have only made an average increase in their motivation to do the project (M=5.4).

The connection to effort is also important. In question ten (Table 1), students from the teacher choice assessment group reported that they gave a more than average effort (M=6.6 out of 7.0) and almost best effort on the teacher choice assessment they completed despite their neutral opinion of the project. Therefore, despite not having any choice options, students gave nearly their best effort which is contrary to what Birdsell, Ream, Seyller and Zobott (2009) proposed. They stated in their research that teachers can motivate students by increasing their student choice opportunities in the areas of curricular assignments, group work, and assessments. In their study, the choices substantially motivated the students to work harder. The same was not true for the groups who participated in this study.

Question nine on Table 2 asked students who completed the choice assessment about how difficult it would have been for them to do the project had the choice options of topic, product, and delivery style been taken away. The students indicated that it would be neither difficult nor easy, and instead, had a neutral opinion (M=4.0). Therefore, losing choice options would not have increased or decreased the difficulty of the project for the students. These results were consistent with student response from question 10 (Table 2). Students indicated that they provided nearly their best effort on the project (M=6.4 out of 7.0). Much like the teacher choice assessment group, effort was mainly unaffected by the choices (or lack of choices) that the project offered.

Although choice options only marginally impacted motivation and effort they did, however, influence enjoyment of the project. Results for question five on both surveys are shown in Table 3 (Teacher choice assessment project frequency results) and Table 4 (Student choice assessment project frequency results). Students who completed the teacher choice assessment survey put a check mark next to the factor(s) that would have made the project more enjoyable. Table 3 reported the frequency of students who would have enjoyed the project more if it had included the following factors: (5a.) Topic of choice: 93.8%, (5b.) Product of choice: 68.8%, (5c.) Delivery (presentation style) of choice: 43.8%, and (5d.) Other factor(s) not mentioned: 6.3%. Based on these results, topic of choice is the factor that mattered most to students. Murphy (2009) and Strahan (2008) agreed that using student-selected topics of interest will more actively engage students and impact their enjoyment level.

Students who completed the student choice assessment survey put a check mark next to the factor(s) that made the project enjoyable. Table 4 outlined the frequency of students that enjoyed the project because of the following specific factors it included: 5a.) Topic of choice: 94.1%, (5b.) Product of choice: 82.4%, (5c.) Delivery (presentation style) of choice: 58.8%, and (5d.) Other factor(s) not mentioned: 29.4%. The results confirmed that topic of choice also mattered most for this group as well. Interestingly, the percentages were almost the same for both groups (Teacher choice group: 93.8% Student choice group: 94.1%). It appears that topic of choice was the most impactful. Results from both groups reinforced the importance of student-selected topics highlighted in Murphy (2009) and Strahan (2008). Childre, Sands and Pope (2009) added that students are able to personalize learning by creating ways to see how information relates to what they already know and to their lives- past, present, or future. By personalizing learning and connecting to their prior knowledge, students are better able to organize and store the information and are more engaged in the process (Beane, 1999).

Although topic of choice had a clear impact on both groups, the other factors did not have the same impact, except for product choice in the student choice assessment group. Question 5b in Table 4 showed that 82.4% of students indicated that having a choice of product made the project more enjoyable. Students were able to choose from a variety of products (i.e. skit, interview, video, etc.). The product options did not make the project as enjoyable as the topic options, but still had an impact on their level of enjoyment. Interestingly, question 5b in Table 3 showed that 68.8% of students who completed the teacher choice assessment believed that having product options would have made the project more enjoyable. There is a considerable difference between the two groups with a definitive decrease in the teacher choice assessment group. Perhaps this group did not have as much prior knowledge or prior experience (Beane, 1999) with choosing product options. However, a list of examples was given to them on the survey.

Clearly, delivery (presentation) style of choice (Table 3: 43.8% and Table 4: 58.8%) and other factor(s) not mentioned (Table 3: 6.3% and Table 4: 29.4%) were less impactful on project enjoyment than topic of choice and product of choice. Perhaps is it because students did not prefer the oral component and disliked presenting in front of the class or acting. Results also show a slight increase in the amount of students who had choice of delivery style (Table 4: 58.8%), as compared to the students who only hypothesized about having it (Table 4: 43.8%). The slight decrease may connect to the teacher assessment group not having as much experience or prior knowledge of choosing specific delivery styles.

Overall, this study examined the effects that choice had on this student assessment project and whether or not there was a connection between student choice and motivation or effort. The results showed that students from both the teacher choice assessment group and the student choice assessment group shared an equal amount of enjoyment from the project. When taking a closer look at each choice factor available, students agreed that having topic of choice was most preferred. Choice of product and delivery style did not have the same impact as topic of choice and were less preferred. Finally, no major increases in motivation or effort were found from these results.

Conclusion

Two groups of students participated in this study. Both groups completed a summative assessment project at the end of the sports vocabulary unit in a level one Spanish class. The teacher provided student choice options including topic of choice, product, and delivery (presentation) style to one group (student choice assessment group) and assigned a topic, product, and delivery (presentation) style to the other group (teacher choice assessment group). After completing the project, students reported their opinions about the project to the teacher on the student reflection survey. Each group completed their own version of the survey. Previous research shows that providing students' choice options in the classroom appeals to students and will increase their motivation to succeed academically, and also their engagement in the task.

The research done in this study indicated that the assessment project was equally enjoyable to students that had choice of topic, product, and delivery, and those who did not. This was a surprising result because it is contrary to what previous research shows. Students without any choice options still found it reasonably appealing, while those without choice options only found it reasonably appealing.

Having choice of topic was the most essential factor that impacted student enjoyment of the project for both groups. Those who did not have it, would have preferred this type of choice option more than the other two-product or delivery style. The students who did have choice options said that this choice option was the most impactful. Students without choice would have been slightly more motivated to do the project had they been given choice options. However, motivation did not increase or decrease for those who already had choices. Effort was unaffected by the choices for both groups. Both groups reported that they gave nearly their best effort whether they had choices or not.

Students who had topic of choice showed more interest in the project. However, both groups gave an excellent effort. I believe that outside factors like fear of not speaking the language well, fear of being in front of classmates, and time to prepare, neutralized some of the positive effects that choice options offered. In the end, this affected student motivation and some of their intrinsic motivation to create a quality product was eliminated.

Implications for Future Research

Although this study focused on the effects that student choice had on assessment projects, other factors and conditions impacted student enjoyment of the project. The novelty of the project, inexperience with having product and delivery style choice options, and insecurity about their ability to perform well are examples of these unforeseen factors.

This study provided one example of a student choice project assessment. Although authentic and alternative assessments occur several times a year, this was the first summative assessment conducted for the school year and was viewed as a novelty by both groups. This made the assignment unique and may have skewed the results. In order to make the data more reliable, a series of projects needs to be conducted regularly throughout the year and a collection of the data over time to identify patterns and trends.

Students' lack of experience with product and delivery style choice options also contributed to skewed results. Students related well to the topic of choice options, but had a more difficult time self-assessing their preferences in terms of product and/or delivery style choices. Students embraced the topic of choice option in both groups perhaps because they already had a reasonable amount of prior experience with choosing topics and were comfortable in doing so. However, the percentages for choice of product and delivery style were much lower for the teacher choice group. Students in this group were unable to see a detailed list of possible choice options for the project, unlike the student choice assessment group. Therefore, they relied on their personal experiences or limited background knowledge to help them understand what product and delivery choices would have been available to them. The product and delivery style percentages for the student choice group were substantially higher than the students who completed the teacher choice assessment. Providing all participants (students) with choice option definitions for topic, product, and delivery style factors, as well as discussing these terms with them, while citing examples of each type of option, is something that would be beneficial to do upon future study of topic.

Fear of presenting in front of the class and student insecurity about their ability to perform in Spanish were also factors not taken into consideration upon the completion of this study. Although students liked or would have preferred choice options for their assessment, many students were resistant to presenting in front of their peers because they did not want to sound foolish by mispronouncing words in Spanish or forgetting their lines. Perhaps this fear neutralized some of the positive effects that having choice options provided and thus decreased students' overall enjoyment. In order to minimize student insecurities, future researchers must consider offering students ample time to work on their presentation and practice. Giving students a chance to run through the presentation privately in the location where they will be presenting may minimize the fear and doubt they are experiencing about the project.

Although a variety of research exists on choice of topic, there is minimal research available on the effects that product or delivery style of choice has on assessment projects. Continuing this line of research would be beneficial students and educators alike. Motivating students to do their best, and having them receive enjoyment from the learning process along the way, will encourage student success and accomplishment.

References

Beane, J. A. (1999). Middle schools under siege: Points of attack. Middle School Journal, 30(4), 3-9.

Beane, J. A. (1999). Middle schools under siege: Responding to the attack. Middle School Journal, 30(5), 3-6.

Birdsell, B.S., Ream, S.M., Seyller, A.M. & Zobott, P.L. (2009). Motivating by Increasing Student Choice. Unpublished thesis, St. Xavier University, Chicago, IL.

Carnegie Council on Adolescent Development. (1989). Turning Points: Preparing American youth for the 21st century. Washington, DC: Carnegie Council.

Childre, A., Sands, J. R., & Pope, S. T. (2009). Backward design: Targeting depth of understanding for all learners. TEACHING Exceptional Children, 41(5), 6-14.

Cooper, H., Patall, E. A., & Robinson, C. (2008). The effects of choice on intrinsic motivation and related outcomes: a meta-analysis of research findings. Psychological Bulletin, 134(2), 270-300.

Davis, H. A. (2006). Exploring the contexts of relationship quality between middle school students and teachers. Elementary School Journal, 106(3)

Felder, R. M. and Henriques, E. (1995). Learning and Teaching Styles in Foreign and Second Language Education. Foreign Language Annals, 28, No. 1: 21-31.

Georgiady, N. P. (1974). What are the characteristics of the middle school? NASSP Bulletin, 58, 381, 72-77.

Haskin, J. Smith, M., & Racine, M. (2003). Decreasing Anxiety and Frustration in the Spanish Language Classroom. Dissertation. St. Xavier University, Chicago, IL.

House, J. D. (2009). Classroom instructional strategies and science career interest for adolescent students in Korea: Results from the TIMSS 2003 assessment. Journal of Instructional Psychology, 36(1), 13-19.

Illinois State Board of Education (2009, October 30). Interactive Illinois Report Card.   Retrieved fromhttp://iirc.niu.edu/School.aspx?source=School_Profile&schoolID=1 70640050261003&level=S

Met, M. (1999). Making Connections. In J.K. Phillips (Ed.), Foreign language standards: Linking research, theories, and practices (pp. 137-164). Lincolnwood, IL: National textbook.

Murphy, P. (2009). Using picture books to engage middle school students. Middle School Journal, 40(4), 20-24. National Middle School Association. (2003). This We Believe Successful Schools for Young Adolescents. Westerville: NMSA.

Nitko, A. J., & Brookhart, S. M. (2007). Educational Assessment of Students. Upper Saddle River: Pearson Education, Inc.

Ormrod, J. E. (2004). Human Learning. Upper Saddle River: Pearson Education, Inc.

Oxford, R. L. (2001). Language learning styles and strategies. In M. Celce-Murcia, Teaching English as a second or foreign language (3rd ed.) (pp. 359-388). Boston: Heinle & Heinle.

Parsons, R.D., & Brown, K.S. (2002). Teacher as Reflective Practitioner and Action Researcher. Belmont, CA: Wadsworth.

Patall, E. A., Cooper, H., & Robinson, J. C. (2008). The effects of choice on intrinsic motivation and related outcomes: A meta-analysis of research findings. Psychological Bulletin, 134(2), 270-300.

Strahan, D. (2008). Successful teachers develop academic momentum with reluctant students. Middle School Journal, 39(5), 4-12.

Tomlinson, C. A., & McTighe, J. (2006). Integrating Differentiated Instruction. Alexandria: Association for Supervision and Curriculum Development.

Van Hoose, J., Strahan, D., & L'Esperance, M. (2006). Promoting Harmony: Young Adolescent Development and School Practices. Westerville: National Middle School Association.

Wasserstein, P. (1995). What middle schoolers say about their schoolwork. Educational Leadership, 53(1), 41-43.

Wigfield, A., Lutz, S. L., & Wagner, A. L. (2005). Early adolescents development across the middle school years: Implications for school counselors. Professional School Counseling, 9(2), 112-119.

Wiggins, G. & McTighe, J. (2006). Understanding by Design. Upper Saddle River: Prentice Hall.

Chapter 6: Raiders 101: The Implementation and Effectiveness of 9th Grade Transition Programs

Casey Kelly & Amber McGee

Background of the Study

Illinois high schools have been backed into a precarious corner. Since the dawn of No Child Left Behind, and in the advent of its heir, Race to the Top, the federal government has expected results. As a State, Illinois is currently 39th in terms of test scores—meaning, only 11 States are testing lower. However, Illinois is the only State that requires testing for *all* students. (Massachusetts is #1 in scores, but #43 in number of students tested.) According to the data, Bloomington High School is actually ahead of the curve when it comes to the abysmal State data. Since 2005, BHS has had meets/exceeds scores of at least 5% above the State average. What is more, Bloomington also represents more racial and socioeconomic diversity than the average of Illinois, contradicting the stereotypes associated with the Achievement Gap. Nevertheless, all of these positives are obscured by the pervasive problem that Bloomington High School has not met AYP in over half a decade (Bloomington High School Report Card, 2008). Principals, in an effort to close the Achievement Gap, make AYP, and, ultimately, save their schools, have begun to look to commonalities amongst the problems. One of the most indicative symptoms of a struggling school is the Freshman Failure Rate. Educators, rightly, so, see the freshman year as a watershed moment in a high school student's career; all that comes after may be determined by its success. Offering supplemental programs to help students assimilate to the secondary education culture serves as a way for principals to progressively treat the symptoms of freshman failure, rather than retroactively diagnosing them.

The purpose of this study was to quantitatively compare the rate of success of two groups of 9th grade students: Raiders 101 veterans vs. non Raiders 101 veterans, in the hopes that the data would help prove the effectiveness and benefits of this program's existence and implementation.

Significance of the Study

This study provides Bloomington District 87 with quantitative data proving a grant-funded program's validity and worth; this will go a long way during tough economic times to ensure that Raiders 101 will continue. Educators and taxpayers will recognize that schools are taking proactive steps in helping all students succeed—even those who typically fall through the cracks.

BHS, as stated before, is not unique. High schools across the State have programs very similar to Raiders 101. Charting a specific program's effect in these areas benefits not only the school, but all involved: teachers, students, parents, not to mention the community at large.

Review of Related Literature

Problems facing American High Schools

American public secondary education is largely a 20th century construct, and the problem-of rising dropout rates, freshman failures, and a gradual decline in standards-is hardly an emerging one. "...the U.S. high school graduation rate peaked at around 80 percent in the late 1960's and declined by 4-5 percentage points; the actual high school graduation rate is substantially lower than the 88 percent estimate" (Heckman & LaFontaine, 2008, p.3).

Students decrease in their levels of achievement as they move from the early grades through high school. The percentage of students meeting or exceeding the state standards in mathematics decreases from 79% in 3rd grade to 53% in 11th grade. In science, the decreases are similar-from 71% meeting or exceeding the standards in 4th grade to only 53% meeting or exceeding the standards in 11th grade (Sandel & Bindu, 2009).

"Compared with past years, an increasing number of 9th graders are failing to be promoted to the 10th grade" (Barton, 2006, p.15). While many factors-low socioeconomic status, the rise of single-parent homes, and an increasingly apathetic view towards education-can be subjectively attributed as symptoms of this malady, the obvious-albeit superficial-truth is in the age group.

Freshman year is one of the most awkward, self-conscious time periods in *any* student's life. Making the jump from middle to high school is turbulent at best; students often find themselves searching, literally and figuratively, for their place in the world which they will occupy for the next four years. "Students described the transition to high school as including new academic challenges, a more complex environment, new social demands, and new interactions with teachers" (Newman, Lohman, Newman, Myers, & Smith, 2000, p.390).

With a new school, and with it new teachers, lockers, schedules, extracurricular activities, relationships, cliques, temptations, freedom, responsibilities, and pressure, it is inevitable that one of these elements will suffer. "In fact, the transition to high school has never been more treacherous nor the consequences more personally disastrous for so many. All over America, thousands and thousands of ninth graders are and have been painfully failing.

Many drop out, often shortly after they enter high school, or they fall behind and fail to graduate on time" (Mizelle & Irvin, 2005, p.1).

Unfortunately, academics typically suffer from the culture shock of assimilating to the new environment and its expectations. "While they liked being able to choose their classes and extracurricular activities, they were concerned about how difficult the classes were and how to manage their time when they got involved in extracurricular activities. School seemed a lot more difficult and demanding than it had in middle school. How to study and how to manage their time were major concerns once these young adolescents made the transition into high school" (Mizelle et al., 2005, p.2).

Bloomington High School is a fairly "typical" Central Illinois institution: 1,600 students, higher diversity than the State average, SES rates across the board from affluent to impoverished, and an annual influx of 9th grade students from the Bloomington Junior High School. BJHS, until 2009, practiced Social Promotion, a process by which all students-including those failing core classes-advance to the next grade level. For many BHS incoming freshmen, 9th grade is the first time that "failing" a class means retaking the class, which entails a forfeiture of credit, which entails remaining a freshman for one-and-a-half-to-two years, which eventually may entail a late graduation date, or an overall dropout. And though the high school completion rates appear to be increasing in Illinois; however, only 70-75% of all of the 9th grade students will complete high school (Illinois School Report Card).

Causes

To explore this ongoing problem more thoroughly, special attention must be paid to its potential causation. Attendance is one of the fundamental factors used to determine scholastic success. According to Wilkins (2008), there has been documentation on the link between absenteeism and dropping out; dropping out is related to the increased possibility of unemployment, dependency on welfare, and imprisonment. There is evidence in research suggesting that high school dropouts are more likely than graduates to have chronic absences as early as first grade (Jacobson, 2008). Studies have shown that secondary schools tend to have an increased percentage of chronically absent students when compared to elementary schools (Sheldon & Epstein, 2004).

One of the things that Henry (2007) discovered through her analysis was that having large amounts of unsupervised time after school, poor grades, low educational aspirations and drug use were among the most significant predictors of truancy. "Furthermore, several school-related variables (including academic performance, commitment to a rigorous academic program, future aspirations, and perception of safety at school) are also associated with truancy" (p. 33). Other studies have shown that low attendance and completion rates are connected to coming from low-income or single-parent families, getting low grades in school, and changing schools (Barton, 2006).

Truancy is predictive of maladjustment, poor academic performance and school dropout, substance abuse, delinquency, teenage pregnancy, poor adult outcomes, violence, marital instability, job instability, adult criminality, and incarceration (Henry, 2007). Also, the achievement goals are directly affected by attendance because studies have shown that students with better attendance than their classmates have superior performance on standardized achievement tests

(Moonie, Sterling, Figgs & Castro, 2008; Sheldon, 2007). Moonie et al. (2008) proposed in their research that attendance is very strongly related to assessment instruments and was the strongest predictor of percent passing the Graduation Exit Exam.

"In the U.S, consistent absence during the first 30 days of 9th grade is the strongest predictor of which students will drop out of school" (Richards, 2009, p.10). "Ninth grade also has been noted for having the highest enrollment. The Ninth Grade Bulge is a term characterizing the high volume of students in 9th grade, varied from transitioning 8th graders to those held back from the tenth grade" (Richards, 2009, p.10). What is most shocking about this statement is that many see 9th grade as a time to "weed out" students almost destined to fall through the cracks. The Ninth Grade Bulge is distinct because many students do not make it to 10th grade; instead, other options-alternative school, GED, dropping out-are pursued. If the Bulge ends, where do these students go?

Attendance is linked to both grades and discipline. Typically erratic attendance can lead to delayed/prolonged administrative disciplinary action, student frustration over the abyss of makeup work, and the self-fulfilling prophecy of defeat. With all of this knowledge of how important student attendance is, schools have begun to examine how to get students in the building on a consistent basis, in their classrooms enough to learn the material, and out of the office enough to become an active citizen of the high school community. The solution is getting-and keeping-students in the school from the beginning of 9th grade.

Innovative Solution

For a long time, schools have provided a reactive approach to this problem, citing student apathy and a lack of parental involvement as the causes of the dwindling Ninth Grade Bulge. The advent of No Child Left Behind, and its subsequent measures of holding schools accountable for test scores and graduation rates, has led to a more proactive approach of trying to fix the problem before it truly becomes a problem—metaphorically, treating the disease before the symptoms begin showing. Several studies have shown that some schools are implementing prevention and intervention programs aimed directly at attendance issues (Balfanz, Herzog, & Mac Iver, 2007). "Data further confirm that dropouts in 9th grade occur more often than any other grade. Although multiple solutions are needed to eradicate this problem, implementing a transition period from middle school to high school has been shown to reduce dropout rates for at-risk students" (Richards, 2009, p.8).

On paper, BHS has not met AYP in testing in over five years. It is currently in its 4th year of Academic Watch Status. Any school not meeting AYP must form a restructuring plan if progress is not made. Raiders 101 is exactly that—a restructuring plan. Raiders 101 began in the Summer of 2007 with 25 hand-picked students from the Junior High; these students were selected strategically based on their disciplinary/attendance/academic histories, with the intent of starting high school off on the right note.

Raiders 101 has evolved into a 2-week program for over one hundred students (in the Summer of 2010) with sixteen high school teachers utilizing character education, community service and immersion into the mindset and expectations of high school. Today it serves all kinds of students, rather than singling out certain demographics who "need" help socially, academically, and/or behaviorally. Staff lobbied at BJHS in the Spring of 2010 to recommend students from all across the 8th grade board.

Here is the general layout of the program: Two weeks in July, Monday through Friday, from 8:30-12:30. Students are given a mid-morning snack and ample lunch (often donated from area businesses). Bussing is provided for all students participating in the program. Students are broken into teams, aiming to gain points through a mixture of competitions, classroom behavior, and service to the school. 101 students are given early access to the school, their locker combinations, their class schedules, and relationships with teachers. A study completed by Wilkins (2008) illustrated that all-school functions that enabled students to get to know other students and teachers resulted in a close-knit school that provided a feeling of comfort and safety.

When schools make quality family and community involvement part of their intervention plan, students will succeed academically because they will be more likely to attend school regularly (Sheldon, 2007). Raiders 101 reaches out to parents in an effort to establish positive relationships early on, through a graduation ceremony for the attendees. Students, families, teachers and administrators work together to foster a strong foundation on which to build during the upcoming school year.

"...it is clear that the most effective programs pay attention to activities that increase academic skills, work to improve student behavior, and focus on student's promotion from grade to grade" (Richards, 2009, p.8). Raiders 101 teaches character education development, with an emphasis in treating the school as a *community*, and not simply a place where students go for 7-9 hours a day. Community service is also stressed; this past summer, the 101-ers helped stuff backpacks for the Salvation Army. In addition, each morning a different extracurricular group—cheerleaders, football team, film club, speech team, French club, book club, band—from the high school presents to the students, promoting the myriad options available to them in the Fall.

In a nutshell, the aim of Raiders 101 is to provide all students with the most positive first impression of high school possible. When these veterans come for the real thing in late August, they should have a jump over the general population of ninth graders. This program is built upon the claim that students who participate will do better than those who do not. The idea is that if a student spends time meeting teachers, becoming acclimated to the environment, and is presented with opportunities and expectations, and, moreover, school is presented as a positive place to be—and not just an eternal detention—then the failure rate will drop, the graduation rate will rise, the test scores will improve, and Bloomington High School will meet AYP and distinguish itself as a progressive asset to public secondary education. The purpose of this study was to determine the legitimacy of this claim.

Methods

Research Design & Variables

For this study an observational design approach was used. In an observational study, the researchers do not do an experiment on the participants, but rather observe what has already taken place without altering it in any way. To analyze the data, a statistical inference for proportions was used. Using an observational design approach, this study sought to answer the following research questions:

1. Is there a significant difference in academic achievement between the experimental (Raiders 101 veterans) and control (entire 9th grade class) groups?
2. Is there a significant difference in attendance between the experimental (Raiders 101 veterans) and control (entire 9th grade class) groups?
3. Is there a significant difference in discipline between the experimental (Raiders 101 veterans) and control (entire 9th grade class) groups?

Variables included in the study were student attendance, academic achievement, and discipline. Data was collected from the 2009-2010 school year to show the number of absences and disciplinary incidents of each student over the course of the year. Student academic achievement was measured by student Explore and SAT-10 test scores.

Participants of the Study

The participants for this study included Bloomington High School's Class of 2013. The control group consisted of all students who began and completed the 2009-2010 school year as freshman. Of this group of 381 students, 222 were white, 91 were black, 28 were Latino, 10 were Asian and 30 were Multiracial. Of the students in this group, 315 were in regular education and 66 were in special education. The experimental group consisted of only the students that participated in Raiders 101 during the summer of 2009. Eighth grade teachers were asked to recommend students by answering the question: which students would benefit socially, academically, and/or behaviorally from a two-week introduction to the high school? Of this group of 69 students, 35 were white, 20 were black, 4 were Latino, 0 were Asian and 10 were Multiracial. Of the students in this group, 48 were in regular education and 21 were in special education.

Ethical Issues

This study used secondary data and therefore did not involve direct interactions with human subjects. Even so, great lengths were taken to ensure anonymity. Students' identities were coded using their school ID numbers, assuring that no one's privacy was violated. Once assigned a number, the anonymous participants' information was used.

Study Procedure

Students from Bloomington High School were used in this study. All participants in Raiders 101's 2009 Program were used for the experimental group and students that started and finished the 2009-2010 school year as freshman were used for the control group. Data collected included student absences for the 2009-2010 school year. The term absence referred to any day the student was not in class. The researchers distinguished between excused and unexcused absences.

Academic achievement was measured in terms of each student's Explore and SAT-10 test scores. An overall score of meets or exceeds according to state benchmarks represented excellent achievement and an overall score of below or academic warning according to state benchmarks represented little to no achievement. Data was collected using the IlliniData collection software, with the help of specialists working with this program. The Data was online and password protected. Only the researchers had access to this data.

Discipline was measured in terms of the number of office visits the student received throughout the 2009-2010 school year. A total of zero to ten office visits represented excellent behavior and anything above ten visits represented poor behavior. After collecting records of attendance, test scores, and discipline, researchers examined the relationship between the results of the control group versus the experimental group.

Threats to Validity

The expected threats to the study's internal validity included the degree of parental involvement, student involvement in extracurricular activities, socioeconomic status, and student's intrinsic motivation and behavior. Other expected threats included threats to the study's external validity. While the study population consisted of several students, the generalization of the study remained low. The student sample remained localized to Bloomington High School and the study participants were selected by means of convenience.

Data Analysis Procedures

Descriptive analysis was conducted after study data was collected. The analysis examined the means and standard deviations of the group data for attendance and office visits, and the proportion of the group that met or exceeded state benchmarks for academic achievement. The data was analyzed both descriptively and inferentially. It was the aim of the study to explore the implications that can be made about the implied success of transitional programs such as Raiders 101. The researchers' goal was to find a significant relationship between participation in Raiders 101 and grades, discipline and attendance.

Limitations of the Study

The obvious limitation of this study was that the data disregarded the individual—by randomizing a subgroup, the data inevitably did not contain all the information needed to understand each student case, and the extraneous factors which can often contribute to student absence, discipline, and/or academic struggles. Another limitation of this study was the subjective definition of discipline. In an effort to remain objective, the researchers decided to consider an office visit as a disciplinary action. This neglected to take into account the severity of the incident leading to said office visit. One more limitation was that the data itself could not explicate the individual success stories experienced by veterans—students and teachers—of the program. However, with test scores more and more becoming the way in which a school is gauged, it seemed natural to use the same means to evaluate a program designed to raise said means.

Results

Analyses comparing participation in Raiders 101 to academic achievement, attendance, and discipline indicated that the program had a significant impact on the number of unexcused absences and office visits, but did not significantly impact academic achievement.

Our first research question compared the difference in academic achievement between the Raiders 101 students and the entire freshman class. When looking at test scores, the State divides the scores into Academic Warning, Below Average, Meets, and Exceeds. We divided these four categories into two categories, Academic Warning/Below Average and Meets/Exceeds. We used a 2-sample proportion z-test to measure the proportions of the groups falling in the Meets/Exceeds category for the Explore Math Test, Explore Reading Test, SAT-10 Math Test, and SAT-10 Reading Test. The analysis showed that the percentage of students that Met/Exceeded was 32 for the Raiders 101 students and 41 for the entire freshman class for the Explore Math Test, 30 for the Raiders 101 students and 52 for the entire freshman class for the Explore Reading Test, 43 for the Raiders 101 students and 67 for the entire freshman class for the SAT-10 Math Test, and 41 for the Raiders 101 students and 57 for the entire freshman class for the SAT-10 Reading Test (see Table 1).

Table 1: Percentage of Raiders 101 Students and the Entire Freshman Class that Met or Exceeded on the Explore Math Test, Explore Reading Test, SAT-10 Math Test, and SAT-10 Reading Test.

	Percent Meets/Exceeds Explore Math	Percent Meets/Exceeds Explore Reading	Percent Meets/Exceeds SAT-10 Math	Percent Meets/Exceeds SAT-10 Reading
Raiders 101 Students	32	30	43	41
Entire Freshman Class	41	52	67	57

Upon analysis of the p-value of the two groups, the results showed that the proportion of Raiders 101 students who Met or Exceeded was not significantly different ($p<0.05$) than the entire freshman class, was significantly lower ($p<0.05$) than the entire freshman class, was significantly lower ($p<0.05$) than the entire freshman class, and was significantly lower ($p<0.05$) than the entire freshman class, for the Explore Math Test, the Explore Reading Test, the SAT-10 Math

Test, and the SAT-10 Reading Test, respectively (see Table 2). Therefore, these results suggest that participating in Raiders 101 does not significantly impact academic achievement.

Table 2: P-Values for the Proportion of Students that Met or Exceeded on the Explore Math Test, Explore Reading Test, SAT-10 Math Test, and SAT-10 Reading Test for the Raiders 101 Students and the Entire Freshman Class.

Test Type	P-Value
Explore Math Test	0.1711
Explore Reading Test	<0.0001
SAT-10 Math Test	<0.0001
SAT-10 Reading Test	0.0076

Our second research question compared the difference in absence rates (both excused and unexcused) between the Raiders 101 students and the entire freshman class. We used a 2-sample z-test to measure the central tendency of the two groups. The analysis showed that the average unexcused absence was 1.2 (s.d. = 3.38), 2.35 (s.d. = 6.70), for the Raiders 101 students and the entire freshman class, respectively. Regarding excused absences, the analysis showed that the average was 8.83 (s.d. = 7.43), 10.03 (s.d. = 6.70), for the Raiders 101 students and the entire freshman class, respectively (see Table 3).

Table 3: Averages and Standard Deviations for the Number of Unexcused Absences and Excused Absences.

	Average Number of Unexcused Absences	Standard Deviation for Number of Unexcused Absences	Average Number of Excused Absences	Standard Deviation for Number of Excused Absences
Raiders 101 Students	1.2	3.38	8.83	7.43
Entire Freshman Class	2.35	6.70	10.03	6.70

Table 4 provides information on the p-values of the two groups for unexcused and excused absences. The results showed that the number of unexcused absences was significantly lower ($p<0.05$) for the students in Raiders 101 when compared to the entire freshman class, but that there was no significant difference ($p<0.05$) when comparing the number of excused absences between the two groups. Therefore, these results suggest that participating in Raiders 101 does significantly impact unexcused absence rates.

Table 4: P-Values for the Number of Unexcused Absences and Excused Absences for the Raiders 101 Students and the Entire Freshman Class.

	P-Value
Unexcused Absences	0.0221
Excused Absences	0.1182

Our third research question compared the difference in the number of office visits between the Raiders 101 students and the entire freshman class. We used a 2-sample z-test to measure the central tendency of the two groups. The analysis showed that the average number of office visits was 6.03 (s.d. = 10.48), 10.03 (s.d. = N/A), for the Raiders 101 students and the entire freshman class, respectively (see Table 5).

Table 5: Averages and Standard Deviations for the Number of Office Visits.

	Average Number of Office Visits	Standard Deviation for Number of Office Visits
Raiders 101 Students	6.03	10.48
Entire Freshman Class	10.03	N/A

When analyzing the p-value of the two groups for the number of office visits, the results showed that the number of office visits was significantly lower (p–0.0023, p<0.05) for the students in Raiders 101 when compared to the entire freshman class. Therefore, these results suggest that participating in Raiders 101 does significantly impact the number of office visits.

Discussion

The results of this study showed that participation in Raiders 101 has a significant impact on office visits and unexcused absences, though not on academic achievement. The results did effectively answer the research questions, and the hypotheses were supported the way the researchers had expected, though not in quite the way the researchers had initially hoped.

Our first research question compared the 101 group with the freshman at large with regards to academic achievement. The results show that the percentage of Raiders 101 veterans Meeting/Exceeding state standards in the Explore and SAT-10 tests is significantly lower than the percentage of the entire 2009 BHS freshman class. It would be a mistake to assume that this data is an attack on the Raiders 101 Program in general. For one thing, Raiders 101 recruitment is fairly open-ended. The 2009 group was enrolled for the summer program solely based on Bloomington Junior High School teacher recommendations. 8th grade teachers were asked to identify any student on their class rosters who might benefit from a two-week pre-orientation to high school. The benefit(s) could be academic, social, and/or behavioral. With such open parameters, 101 instructors found that in its infancy, the Program was not representative of the greater student population. There are many factors—race, gender, socioeconomic status—which help make up the demographic of a school, but low grades were a large impetus in a prospective student's recommendation for Raiders 101. Simply put, many students were sent to 101 because of their underperformance in Junior High, with the hopes that the Program itself might act as a pre-emptive strike against future academic problems. Most educators know that it takes much more than two weeks of half days in the summer to turn a negative primary academic experience into a positive secondary one. Raiders 101 was not founded upon the idea that it could act as Miracle Worker with regards to scholastic achievement. "In fact, the transition to high school has never been more treacherous nor the consequences more personally disastrous for so many. All over America, thousands and thousands of ninth graders are and have been painfully failing. Many drop out, often shortly after they enter high school, or they fall behind and fail to graduate on time" (Mizelle & Irvin, 2005, p.1). Standardized testing has long been criticized for being the sole indicator of a student's, and school's, worth; a one- or two-day testing experience is not indicative of all the other factors—building relationships, accountability, socialization, and effort—which go into the semester- or year-long process of a high school class. If students were handpicked due to their anticipated struggles in high school, then it is worth noting that they would indeed struggle. The data, and previous research, show the struggle. "Students described the transition to high school as including new academic challenges, a more complex environment, new social demands, and new interactions with teachers" (Newman, Lohman, Newman, Myers, & Smith, 2000, p.390).The program's aim was and is to help relieve some of the burden of that struggle.

Our second research question compared the 101 group with the freshman class at large with regards to excused and unexcused absence rates. The quantitative data show that while the number of excused-8.83 for 101 vets, 10.03 for general population—absences were not significantly lower for Raiders 101 participants, the number of unexcused-1.2 for 101 vets, 2.35 for general population—were significantly lower. One of the fundamental objectives of this program is to give students a positive first impression of high school, in the hopes that students will see school as a place not to be feared or dreaded. The Literature Review referenced Wilkins's 2008 study over the relationship between poor attendance and problems-such as unemployment, low income, time in prison-later on in life. "Furthermore, several school-related variables (including academic performance, commitment to a rigorous academic program, future aspirations, and perception of safety at school) are also associated with truancy" (Henry, 2007, p. 33). Much of the research indicated a strong link between attendance and performance on standardized tests and graduation exams. An obvious limitation of this study was the quantitative approach to absences. Teachers work in a controlled environment: for 50 minutes a day, students come to a safe classroom and structured atmosphere. The school is in constant combat with the chaotic life many students face outside the building. There are myriad factors-work, transportation, family obligations, deaths in a family, illnesses, to name a few-inhibiting a student from coming to school. And these are all excused absences, as long as a parent calls in on behalf of the student. (This is mentioned because the attendance office of any school is imperfect, relying on an honor system of parents calling in honestly for a student.) Unexcused absences are more of a focused concern of the program, because Bloomington High School, not unlike many other Illinois schools, uses discipline to retroactively treat truancy. Unexcused absences are a slippery slope for all students, but the freshman year is crucial in establishing a healthy pattern of attendance. "In the U.S, consistent absence during the first 30 days of 9th grade is the strongest predictor of which students will drop out of school" (Richards, 2009, p.10). Ideally, excused absences account for extenuating circumstances beyond the student's control, from which he can bounce back to school with ease. Truancy, on the other hand, can keep a student, when he *does* show up, in his administrator's office or the in-school suspension room during class time, thereby missing *more* school to account for the unexcused time he has already missed. Raiders 101 students, on average, had a total of 1.2 unexcused absences. This is almost half of the 2.35 unexcused absences the entire freshman class averaged. It would be speculative to assume that Raiders 101 alone compelled its participants to want to come to school (much in the same way it would be problematic in assuming that the program should have raised students' grades). That said, given the population of participants and the typical positive correlation between truancy and academic warning, these students are going against the grain of the normal population. Preemptively establishing a positive high school environment does help in retaining students throughout the school year.

Our third research question compared the 101 group with the freshman class at large with regards to number of office visits. This was the most significant impact we found, with 101 vets averaging 6.03 office visits, and the general population averaging 10.03 office visits. Participants averaged a full four office visits less than the non-participants. It seems too good to be true! Well, because in a way, it is. Unfortunately, to be fair, the limitations to the study affect this favorable conclusion. There are many variables to consider, especially when looking at a blanket term such as an "office visit." Not all office visits are bad. Visits to the nurse and the guidance office are included. Sometimes a student actually desires to speak to her dean, because of a positive relationship she shares with her administrator. This study looked at office visits holistically, not individually. An even *finer* print issue to address is that one office visit can mean many different things, including: Bringing a weapon to school, cheating in class, inappropriate bus behavior, showing defiance, drugs/alcohol, fighting in school, fighting on school grounds, inappropriate behavior in class, inappropriate behavior in the cafeteria, inappropriate behavior in the hallways, inciting others to fight, leaving class without permission, leaving the building without permission, not dressing for PE, not serving an after-school detention, threatening a teacher, threatening a student, possession of banned electronics (such as cellular phones and iPods), tardy detention (3 tardies in any individual class results in a 2-hour detention), truancy, and sexual harassment. For the class of 2013, the Top Two most common offenses among students were Class Tardies (904 instances) and Missed Detentions (542). Detentions based on tardiness and truancy to previously given detentions are hardly in the same disciplinary ballpark as verbal/physical threats and violence. Many students rack up a healthy "permanent record" due to an inability to get to a certain class on time; others may only see their dean once their entire high school career, but for an offense warranting in- or out-of-school suspension, or, in some extreme cases, expulsion. This data neglects the reason for each office visit, as well as the action taken for each visit. BHS's 2009-'10 discipline records show that sophomores average 10.7 office visits, juniors average 17.5, and seniors average 15.3. Across the board, BHS students in general visited the office 13.37 times throughout the school year. This is brought up to further show the significant difference between Raiders 101 participants and the rest of the freshman class, and the student body in general. "...it is clear that the most effective programs pay attention to activities that increase academic skills, work to improve student behavior, and focus on student's promotion from grade to grade" (Richards, 2009, p.8).Once again, Raiders 101 does not claim direct causality for less office visits, but coming to high school armed with strong teacher relationships, clear expectations and guidelines, can certainly help curtail the number of times a student is called down.

All in all, the results were close to what the researchers expected, mostly because of the narrow demographic of the students involved this particular year. The program has grown significantly since the period which was studied. The researchers are planning to continue tracking the academic, disciplinary and attendance progress of Raiders 101 participants. The program is growing roughly 25% each consecutive year, the overall goal being 100% attendance by incoming freshman classes. Future research will be best conducted on a qualitative level; the limitations of this study inhibited the definition of "Success" applicable to freshman.

Fortunately, the results showed that while the program itself may not significantly impact student achievement, it did show a correlation between participation in the program and attendance and office visits. The researchers are optimistic in believing that Raiders 101 is a major factor, if not a singular catalyst, in helping a freshman successfully transition to high school.

Conclusions and Implications

To reduce the freshman failure rate and the significant number of students dropping out or not receiving a diploma, it is important for schools and universities to begin implementing programs and strategies to ensure student success. The aim of this study was to explore the implementation of Raiders 101, a freshman transition program, and to chart its overall effectiveness with regards to student attendance, academic achievement, and disciplinary action. The following is a summary of our findings:

- Raiders 101 does not significantly impact academic achievement,
- Raiders 101 does significantly impact the number of unexcused absences,
- Raiders 101 does significantly impact the number of office visits.

According to our results, Raiders 101 does not significantly impact academic achievement. However, there are several expected threats that influence the research's validity. Students' academic achievement is an integrated production. Besides attendance, there are many other internal and external factors which could have affected the students' achievement. For instance, parental involvement is a significant ingredient in academic achievement; parents' attitudes towards education can motivate or demoralize their children's learning. Several other factors include but are not limited to: familial support, intrinsic motivation, peer influence, teaching styles, extracurricular activities, and/or socioeconomic status. Due to the many threats, it is difficult to pinpoint what hindered or produced the results of this study. It is not rational or considerate to conclude that Raiders 101 had no positive impact on academic achievement.

When examining the significant relationship between Raiders 101 and the number of unexcused absences and office visits, other factors such as intrinsic motivation, familial influence, or socioeconomic status may have been attributes of the results. However, the results imply that the program had a positive influence on the students and created a safe and comfortable environment that encouraged them to continue coming to school and stay out of the office.

For those interested in researching this topic, there are implications that should be considered. Further studies should focus on a variety of students being involved in the program and not just the hand-picked group we had. The results may be more accurate if academic achievement were expanded to include the students' GPA or class grades. Other suggestions for further studies would be to find a way to account for other factors that affect academic achievement, absences and office visits. Also, studies should be conducted over a longer period of time to obtain more reliable results.

References

Balfanz, R., Herzog, L., & Mac Iver, D. J. (2007). Preventing student disengagement and keeping students on the graduation path in urban middle-grades schools: Early identification and effective interventions. *Educational Psychologist, 42*(4), 223-235.

Barton, P. E. (2006). The dropout problem: Losing ground. *Educational Leadership, 63*(5), 14 18.

Bloomington High School Report Card (2008-2009). *www.district87.org*. http://iirc.niu.edu/School.aspx?source=Test_Results&schoolID=170640 870250001&level=S&source2=PSAE

Heckman, J. J., & LaFontaine, P. A. (2008). The declining American high school graduation rate: Evidence, sources, and consequences. *National Bureau of Economic Research Reporter, 1,* 3-5.

Henry, K. L. (2007). Who's skipping school: Characteristics of truants in 8th and 10th grade. *Journal of School Health, 77*(1), 29-35.

Jacobson, L. (2008). Absences in early grades tied to learning lags (cover story). *Education Week, 28*(6), 1-12.

Mizelle, N., & Irvin, J. (2005). Transition from middle school into high school. *National Middle School Association,* 1-12. http://www.temescalassociates.com/documents/resources/transition/Tran sitionfromMiddleSchoolintoHighSchool.pdf

Moonie, S., Sterling, D. A., Figgs, L. W., & Castro, M. (2008). The relationship between school absence, academic performance, and asthma status. *Journal of School Health, 78*(3), 140-148.

Newman, B., Lohman, B., Newman, P., Myers, M., & Smith, V. (2000). Experience of urban youth navigating the transition to ninth grade. *Youth Society, 31*(4), 387-416.

Richards, C. (2009). Transition programs used to bridge incoming ninth grade at-risk students. *Chapel Hill,* 1-12.

Sandel, K., & Bindu, B. (2009). The gap persists: Closing Illinois' achievement divide. http://www.keepingillinoiscompetitive.niu.edu/ilstem/pdfs/STEM_ed_re port.pdf

Sheldon, S. B. (2007). Improving student attendance with school, family, and community partnerships. *The Journal of Educational Research, 100*(5), 267-275.

Sheldon S. B., & Epstein, J. L. (2004). Getting students to school: Using family and community involvement to reduce chronic absenteeism. *The School Community Journal, 14*(2), 39-56.

Wilkins, J. (2008). School characteristics that influence student attendance: Experiences of students in a school avoidance program. *The High School Journal,* 12-24.

Chapter 7: Inquiry versus Traditional Science Instruction

Wanda Severtson & Stacy Snoble

The Problem and Its Background

On January 8, 2002, President George W. Bush signed the No Child Left Behind (NCLB) Act of 2001 into law. Each year the law requires an increasing percentage of students to perform at proficient levels on state assessments. By the 2013-2014 school year all students must perform at passing levels. Failure to reach the yearly goals results in penalties and restructuring requirements for schools. Based on 2008 testing information, 63.5% of Illinois high schools did not meet adequate yearly progress as required by NCLB (Interactive Illinois Report Card, 2009). Schools statewide are researching and implementing various programs to improve student achievement in all areas. One possible method of improving science achievement is by instructing through scientific inquiry.

Traditional techniques of conveying material to students have been used for many years even though they are not necessarily the best methods to teach students today. As stated by Doris Morgan (1999), the use of traditional methods fails to expand student's critical thinking and problem-solving skills while repressing natural ingenuity and inquisitiveness. The use of lecture, notes, worksheets, and tests that have students memorize information do not allow the students to adapt the information and skills to their needs. The traditional techniques were acceptable with students in the past since their family life and work ethic were different from the ideals of today's youth. To stimulate the minds of students in the twenty-first century and allow them the opportunity to incorporate the material into their repertoire of skills requires using new methods of delivery. This, coupled with the release of the National Science Education Standards in 1996, has caused science education to undergo a pedagogical shift. While science has always lent itself well to hands-on instruction, the Standards emphasize the importance of scientific inquiry at all levels of education. Inquiry is defined by the Standards as "the diverse ways in which scientists study the natural world and propose explanations based on the evidence derived from their work.   Scientific inquiry also refers to the activities through which students develop knowledge and understanding of scientific ideas, as well as an understanding of how scientists study the natural world" (National Research Council, 1996, p. 23).   The significance of this instructional method was underscored in a position statement adopted in 2004 by the Board of Directors of the National Science Teachers Association (NSTA). In that statement, the Board "recommends that all K-16 teachers embrace scientific inquiry" and commits to "helping educators make it [scientific inquiry] the centerpiece of the science classroom" (NSTA, 2005).

While traditional hands-on science lessons are beneficial, these activities are largely expository in nature. They require students to follow specific detailed instructions provided by the teacher in order to arrive at a predetermined outcome. The students have little to no control of the process and generally do not gain substantial, meaningful conceptual knowledge from the activity (Gaddis & Schoffstall, 2007). Inquiry lessons are designed to mimic the manner in which real-life scientists go about their work – designing then implementing their own processes to answer their own questions. As students develop their critical thinking skills through inquiry, they also develop a better understanding of science by using questioning and evidence to solve problems.   By doing experiments they extend their thinking, increase their comprehension, and engage themselves as active scientists instead of passive learners (Hohloch, Grove, & Bretz, 2007).

Inquiry-based learning has its roots in constructivism. The constructivism theory explains how students build their own understandings and knowledge through experiences and activities (Bruning, Schraw, Norby & Ronning, 2004). Inquiry and constructivism are similar in that both approaches to learning are student centered and allow students to discover relationships with minimal input from the teacher. Students must have some foundation knowledge on which to build upon, but new knowledge is added to their existing framework based on their past experiences and the connections they make to the new information.

There are different levels or degrees of inquiry-based activities and each has its own purpose and attributes.   Open-ended inquiry activities have no predetermined outcome. Students completely develop their own hypotheses and procedures. Open-ended inquiry experiments lead to increased critical thinking and planning skills. However, this level of inquiry has a high degree of student independence and may be harder to implement at K-12 levels due to time constraints and inadequate student-knowledge base. Having many groups of students performing different procedures may also result in organizational problems for the teacher (Gaddis & Schoffstall, 2007).

Problem-based experiments, like open-ended inquiry, require student-developed design but are more structured because all students are working towards answering a teacher-proposed question or solving a teacher-proposed problem.   Problem-based activities require students to have a fundamental knowledge base and are, therefore, more applicable to upper-level grades and ability levels. Critical thinking skills and increased interest in subject matter are advantages of this type of inquiry (Gaddis & Schoffstall, 2007).

Guided-inquiry activities are perhaps the most applicable across many grades and ability levels. They combine characteristics from both open-ended inquiry and expository experiments, making them easier to implement and manage. Guided-inquiry lessons are also known as discovery-based and provide students with a prescribed procedure to arrive at a predetermined, but unknown outcome. Increased interest and critical thinking, as well as higher cognitive achievement, are all outcomes of guided-inquiry (Gaddis & Schoffstall, 2007). This type of learning is not restricted to laboratory experiments alone. The National Science Foundation partially funds a program called Process Oriented Guided Inquiry Learning (POGIL) which is a research based learning environment where students are actively engaged in mastering course content and in developing essential skills by working in self-managed teams on guided inquiry activities. Apart from the laboratory component of the program, students examine common, familiar concepts then apply them to chemistry-related topics in order to learn the fundamental principles of chemistry (The POGIL Project, 2007).

Lessons designed to be inquiry in nature have the potential to produce more in-depth learning experiences because students are actively engaged in the learning process. The increased control also provides students a sense of ownership and can increase their motivation for learning science. Research shows this is especially true for lower ability, general science students (Pickens & Eick, 2009). Inquiry-based learning has also been shown to improve students' abilities to ask a greater number of questions that are better and more relevant due to their deeper understanding of concepts (Hofstein, Navon, Kipnis, & Mamlock-Naaman, 2005).

Disadvantages exist for inquiry-based learning, as well. Even though the National Science Education Standards have been in existence for over ten years, many teachers are reluctant to incorporate inquiry into their curriculum on a regular basis. One reason for this is the lack of inquiry-based instruction and learning in science education programs. Pre-service teachers are often taught science in a traditional, expository manner which they then repeat with their own students (Hohloch, Grove, & Bretz, 2007). Inquiry activities tend to be more time consuming than expository activities. With the increasing accountability of NCLB, many teachers feel they have more content to teach and, therefore, opt for more traditional, time efficient activities. Another drawback is the reluctance of students who, not being accustomed to inquiry learning, become easily frustrated when goals and outcomes are ambiguous. The majority of students' educational experiences have been about getting "right" answers and when this changes, they feel uncomfortable (Pickens & Eick, 2009).

Teaching science today requires instructors to use new methods to present the information since many students do not handle traditional methods of conveying the material. The use of inquiry-based learning assists the students with the development of necessary skills to solve problems they will face in their lives. The interest in the use of inquiry-based learning versus traditional methods is related to the importance of developing these critical thinking skills in the students. If the students do not feel confident enough to attempt a task, then they will struggle to develop these skills. Although some drawbacks also exist, inquiry learning may lead to increased achievement which, in turn, may help schools meet the challenges of NCLB.

Problem and Significance of Study

For many years science has been taught using traditional methods which have fallen short when assisting students in developing the necessary thinking skills for solving life's issues and for succeeding on standardized tests, such as the ACT, which are used to determine adequate yearly progress for NCLB. Inquiry-based instruction requires the students to question what they observe, collect data, and analyze the information to reach a conclusion. The purpose of this study is to compare the development of problem-solving skills using traditional methods and inquiry-based methods of instruction.

Literature Review

Educators are constantly searching for ways to improve student learning and increase achievement. The implementation of state learning standards and federal legislation have increased accountability and made improved learning an even greater priority. To accomplish this, numerous options are available. Inquiry-based instructional strategies hold promise, not only to increase student achievement in science, but also to improve students' questioning abilities, reasoning skills, and attitudes toward science. Incorporating inquiry into science instruction is of particular interest because it allows students to assume the role of a scientist and many believe learning by doing is the best method to learn science.

Effect on Achievement

Numerous examples of research studies linking inquiry-based instruction to improved science achievement exist. One such study conducted by Mao, Chang, and Barufaldi (1998) generated data indicating improved comprehension of earth science concepts by a group of ninth-grade Taiwanese students. The experimental group consisted of three classes which received inquiry-based instruction for a period of two weeks. These students collected information and data about the apparent motion of the sun in the sky by performing hands-on activities. Group discussions, teacher-student discussions, and class presentations were used to interpret the findings. The teacher's explanation of the earth-sun system concluded the unit. The control group also consisted of three classes but received traditional, teacher-centered instructional methods. The teacher provided all the information through lectures and demonstrations. Student achievement was measured by comparing pre- and post-test scores on selected items taken from Taiwan's two most widely used achievement-related and science process skills tests. Analysis showed the inquiry group demonstrated significantly improved learning "especially at the comprehensive and integrated levels. However, there were no significant gains in student achievement at the factual level" (p. 365). These findings indicate that inquiry-based instruction better develops students' process skills and higher-order reasoning abilities but does not affect retention of lower-level factual knowledge. The Science Reasoning portion of the ACT does, as the name implies, test the scientific reasoning abilities of students. Therefore, it would seem inquiry-based instruction might lead to improved performance on this test.

A similar investigation by Chang and Mao (1999) also supported the hypothesis that inquiry instruction produces higher achievement scores than traditional instruction. This study centered on ninth-grade Taiwanese earth science students, as well. The sample was larger than in the first study discussed and consisted of sixteen classes at five public junior high schools. For four weeks, eight of the classes followed an inquiry approach and collected information through hands-on experiences carried out in research teams of their own choosing. The other eight classes received lectures, explanations, and demonstrations from the teacher. The researchers found, once again, that the experimental inquiry group significantly outperformed the control group on a topic-related achievement test. The researchers attribute the difference to the ability of the treatment group to "plan their own investigations, gather and interpret data, analyze results, and share findings with their classmates" (p. 344).

Both of the studies described thus far were conducted in Taiwan and the researchers point out that cultural differences must be considered. Chang and Mao (1999) state, "Students in Taiwan are generally quiet and passive learners and usually are not able to enjoy cooperative learning. In addition, the conventional teaching method has prevailed in the science classrooms for many years" (p. 345). In spite of these factors, inquiry instruction resulted in improved science achievement suggesting students can adapt to new and different instructional techniques at any time.

Inquiry instruction was also shown to be more productive than traditional instruction in the field of biology in a study conducted by Johnson & Lawson (1998). This investigation assessed achievement in inquiry versus traditional classrooms after measuring the reasoning abilities and prior biology knowledge of students enrolled in a community college. They found reasoning ability to be a bigger contributor to achievement than prior knowledge in both the inquiry and traditional settings. The results also suggested students in the inquiry classes actually improved their reasoning abilities over the course of the semester than did the students in the traditional classes. These finding are consistent with others and indicate an inquiry approach to science instruction leads to higher achievement and improved reasoning ability.

Questioning is a common occurrence in science classrooms. However, in many instances, the teacher poses questions for students to answer. Often any student-initiated questions are informative and lower level in nature. Deeper comprehension of scientific concepts results in and enables students to ask higher cognitive level questions. A study conducted in Israel by Hofstein, Navon, Kipnis, and Mamlok-Naaman (2005) presents evidence that inquiry-based laboratory activities aid students in developing higher-level questioning abilities. During the two-year study, fifty-five twelfth-grade chemistry students carried out fifteen inquiry-type laboratory experiments, while fifty-six students performed traditional-type experiments. To assess the students' ability to ask high-level, scientific questions, they were asked to propose questions about a simple chemical reaction they performed as a lab practical test. They were also asked to write questions about a scientific article they were given to read. The results showed that students in the inquiry group asked more high-level questions and more questions in general concerning both the chemical reaction and the article than the students in the control group. Additionally, students in the inquiry group appeared to take the assignments more seriously by devoting more time and attention to the task. Several students in the control group did not complete the assignment. As a result, the researchers felt that "through the involvement in inquiry experiments, the students developed scientific skills and habits that are applicable to other learning situations" (p. 801).

Peer-Led Guided Inquiry (PLGI) is the topic of a study conducted by Lewis and Lewis (2008) which investigates the effectiveness of this teaching practice in a college chemistry course. PLGI is structured so students work in small groups to perform inquiry activities under the guidance of a peer leader which is an undergraduate student who has previously earned an A or B in general chemistry. The large-scale study spanned three years and used data collected from sixteen sections of general chemistry. During the fall semester of each year, PLGI was implemented in one section while the other sections were taught in a traditional manner primarily with lectures. Achievement was assessed through four midterm exams and a final exam produced by the American Chemical Society. Analysis showed PGLI improved performance on the final exam and on this basis the researchers "recommend that other entry-level college science courses employ inquiry activities as the shared goal of cooperative learning groups, with PLGI as an option for a large class" (p. 806).

The afore mentioned studies focused on three different disciplines within the field of science and have investigated learners ranging from junior high school age to college age. However, the results of all five studies are consistent and provide evidence supporting the use of inquiry methods in science classrooms. Inquiry-based instructional methods elicit deeper understandings, improved reasoning abilities, and better questioning skills in learners leading to overall increased science achievement.

Effect on Standardized Testing

The implementation of No Child Left Behind (NCLB) has resulted in states requiring students to pass a standardized test to demonstrate their proficiency in several areas including science. Illinois uses the ACT exam as part of the Prairie State Achievement Exam to determine whether students are making adequate yearly progress. Some research reveals a connection between students exposed to inquiry instruction and better performance on standardized testing.

One study by Schneider, Krajcik, Marx, and Soloway (2002) analyzed the effect of a project-based science program on the achievement of students on the National Assessment of Educational Progress (NAEP) test, which is a national measurement tool. The researchers conducted the experiment at a small alternative public high school in an urban university town in the Midwest. The teachers and educational researchers from the University of Michigan designed and implemented a 3-year program called Foundations of Science (FOS) which involved projects ranging from 7 – 8 weeks to 15 – 16 weeks in length. Project based units that integrated science content including biology, chemistry, and earth science concepts were developed since earth science, physical science, and life science were the major fields covered on the national test. The projects were completed mainly by groups of two to four students using computers to acquire information, analyze and graph data, generate models, and write reports.

The demographics of the students represented in the study corresponded to that of the district which included two other high schools. The students involved in the FOS program, in general, were not necessarily interested in science since many of the students interested in science attended the other two schools in the district that offered a more traditional science program including advanced placement science courses. A comparison of the test scores by Schneider, Krajcik, Marx, and Soloway (2002) showed the FOS students scoring marginally higher in science (66% to 65% and 54%) and higher in reading (73% to 60% and 51%) than the other two district high schools while their scores in math (72% to 70% and 70%) and writing (47% to 57% and 44%) were basically similar to the other district high schools. The FOS students' scores were also compared to the scores reported by NAEP for the national sample, and overall the FOS students scored higher than comparable students from the national sample.

The use of inquiry-based instruction could possibly allow students an advantage on standardized testing (Schneider, Krajcik, Marx, & Soloway, 2002). As the type of instruction used for the FOS students caused them to extend their thinking, it also resulted in better performance on tests with increased response length questions. The researchers agree that the number of science classes taken by the FOS students and when they were taken in relation to the administration of the test could have affected the results. Another reason for the FOS students' performance could be related to the block schedule of 90-minutes periods meeting four days a week, which could allow them to be more attentive to a topic for an extended time.

A study conducted by Geier, Blumenfeld, Marx, Krajcik, Fishman, Soloway, and Clay-Chambers (2008) involved analyzing data from the Schneider, Krajcik, Marx, & Soloway (2002) study. Geier et al. compared 7th and 8th grade students who participated in the project-based program created by the Center for Learning Technologies in Urban Schools, or LeTUS, to 7th and 8th grade students who did not participate. They analyzed the pre-test and post-test data to determine if the project-based lessons affected both test scores and participation based on gender.

Students involved in the LeTUS project groups demonstrated higher achievement in several performance areas. Overall performance on the Michigan Educational Assessment Program standardized testing by the LeTUS project-based groups was higher (13% and 14%) than the group that did not participate, while passing rates for the LeTUS groups increased by 19% and 14 % respectively over the group not participating. Both LeTUS groups saw an increase in test scores based on gender with a noticeable reduction in the achievement differences between girls and boys.

Geier et al. (2008) noticed a positive impact on standardized achievement test scores with the use of well-aligned standards-based reform efforts. They also realized that inquiry-based units alone will not increase achievement; they need to be used in conjunction with professional development and learning technology. Repeated exposure to standard-based learning and inquiry instruction will result in continued growth in achievement. The true effects of inquiry-based investigations might not be seen for several years.

Another study by Turner and Rios (2008) examined whether inquiry-based activities would increase students' ability to develop investigations similar to items presented on Washington State's standardized testing. The Washington Assessment of Student Learning in Science (Science WASL) necessitates that students use skills such as critical thinking, problem solving, applying reasoning skills, and designing laboratory investigations, which are commonly learned in an inquiry-based science class. The participants for this study were sophomore students in biology classes taught by Mr. Turner. He lectured, led small group discussions, demonstrated experiments, supervised laboratory activities, collected assignments, and analyzed student work. A pre-test and post-test were used along with student assignments to determine the effects of inquiry-based learning on student standardized testing performance.

Turner and Rios (2008) discovered that average pre-test and post-test scores for comprehension of all scientific components analyzed remained the same or improved. The data supported an increased knowledge of the scientific method, but not a gain in experimental development competence. They also found a more significant change in the general biology classes than in the honors biology classes, which the researchers believe may have resulted from the students in the honors classes having more prior experience with the skills being assessed. Attendance appeared to have a negative impact on test scores especially if the absences occurred on days involving critical lab design and discussion. The researchers also found that several students while having performed interesting experiments did not appear to understand the importance of completing the lab reports.

Results from their research led Turner and Rios (2008) to conclude that inquiry-based instruction while requiring more time and teacher facilitation, as well as being less predictable, should be implemented. Inquiry-based lessons allow students to develop the necessary skills to solve problems, analyze data, and develop their own investigations. Since success on standardized tests requires students to achieve knowledge in the content area, acquire reasoning skills, and develop a better understanding of the nature of science, it is imperative that students be instructed in a manner that promotes the acquisition of these skills.

Effect on Students of Different Abilities

Inquiry-based instruction's impact on the achievement of students with differing abilities is less decisive. While some research indicates significantly higher gains in the achievement of lower ability students when compared to students of average or high ability, other research shows no real difference between the benefits experienced by the two groups.

By the time they reach high school, some students have a long history of underachievement and academic failure. The science curriculum provided to these low achieving students is usually comprised of watered-down facts and explanations of phenomena that bear no relationship to their lives. Yerrick (2000) conducted an investigation to study the effects of open inquiry instruction on low achieving high school students enrolled in a general science class of a suburban high school near East Lansing, Michigan. The researcher developed a curriculum centered around everyday events such as how batteries make appliances work. For twenty weeks, students were encouraged to present hypotheses, gather supporting evidence, conduct experiments, and discuss their results. Interviews were conducted before and after the twenty week instructional period. Initially students focused on finding one, "correct" answer and often responded they did not know the answer. However, the exit interviews showed these lower ability students presenting explanations based on evidence. Yerrick concluded, "This study suggests that students' responses show a fundamental shift in the ways in which they approach science and real-world problems in lower track contexts" (p. 830). Interview data was only taken from five students and there was no comparison with an average to high ability control group, however the results do suggest that lower ability students can develop science reasoning skills through inquiry-based instruction.

A larger-scale study conducted in Nigeria with physics students yielded similar results. Folashade and Akinbobola (2009) report a "significant difference between the academic achievements of low ability physics students taught with problem based learning technique and those taught with conventional methods" (p. 49). One hundred and five students from forty secondary schools in Taraba state Nigeria were administered a physics achievement test. Additionally, the fifty-one member treatment group was administered a physics ability level test and the results were used to classify students into three ability groups - high, average, and low. Heterogeneous groups were formed and received problem-based learning instruction on the topic of waves. Likewise, the control group used the same content outline but received conventional instruction. After four weeks all students completed a physics achievement post-test. Data analysis indicated students in the treatment group performed better than those of the control group. Further, the difference in achievement levels was more pronounced for the low ability students. Based on these findings, the researchers conclude that problem based learning improves the achievement of low ability students and, therefore, should be integrated into science instruction. They even contend this instruction method "will improve the performance of students in public exams" (p. 50).

Inquiry-based instructional methods are most commonly thought of in terms of laboratory activities and group discussions. It is also possible to incorporate this instructional method into textbooks. This is the topic of a research study conducted by Mucheno and Lawson (1999) using one hundred twenty-three ninth and tenth graders in the southwestern United States. As the Nigerian study previously described, the students were tested for reasoning ability and classified as empirical-inductive, meaning their thinking is limited to direct observation, transitional, or hypothetical-deductive, meaning they use higher order reasoning patterns effectively. The students were then arbitrarily chosen to receive either an inquiry-based or a traditional text passage describing symbiosis, mutualism, commensalism, and parasitism. A post-test was completed immediately after the reading and again one week later. The results showed students using the inquiry-based passage scored higher on both post-tests. However, no significant differences appear among the students of different reasoning abilities. In other words, students with lower-level reasoning abilities benefited equally as students with higher-level reasoning abilities when using inquiry-based texts.

Similar results were illustrated in a study of thirty-eight secondary school students in Singapore. Ng (2004) reported "inquiry based learning lessons do have an impact on students' acquisition of scientific reasoning skills. However, there was no significant difference when comparing the impact on students in the 3 different levels of General Ability" (p. 5). All thirty-eight students were assigned to one of three ability level groups, low, intermediate, or high, based on scores from a general ability test. Students were also given a scientific reasoning test. Students in the test group then received a series of one inquiry lesson per week for eight weeks. After the test period, all students were administered another scientific reasoning test. Ng attributes the success of the test group to their "opportunities to learn independently, pose questions, make assumptions, plan detailed procedures, and draw conclusions" (p. 1). Ng further states, "The involvement in such learning opportunities over a sustained period of time will help students to better internalize the scientific concepts and acquire the habits of reasoning and problem-solving" (p.1). Even though this study showed no significant difference between the benefits of inquiry-based instruction to students of low and high ability, its findings are consistent with other studies in citing benefits to all students.

Conclusive evidence suggesting the inquiry approach to science instruction is more advantageous to low ability students than high ability students is scarce. However, evidence suggesting inquiry-based instruction benefits students of all ability levels is plentiful. Motivation and attitude toward learning also play key roles in academic success. Students of higher ability may be intrinsically motivated naturally and experience success regardless of instructional method. Lower ability students, on the other hand, may find the active, hands-on approach of inquiry to be more motivating leading to increased achievement.

Effect on Student Motivation and Interest

Motivation can have an enormous impact on science achievement due to the importance of the skills a student requires to evaluate the information presented in a science course. To ensure success for all students, schools need to determine what items affect students' motivation and adjust the lessons accordingly. Singh, Granville, and Dika (2002) identified some items as affecting motivation which included missing school, skipping classes, being tardy, and coming to class without necessary supplies. Some research conducted at an alternative school found a correlation between the relationship students perceive to have with school personnel and the positive environment of the school (Poyrazli, et al., 2008). A positive school environment could affect the students' motivation by increasing attendance as a result of decreasing the amount of tardies, skipped classes, and missed school. While a positive school environment can help, using goal setting with students might be another technique to increase motivation.

Two academic goals that have been identified as being connected to motivation are learning goals and performance goals. The extent to which students pursue these two goals is related to their achievement in math and science (DeBacker & Nelson, 2000). Allowing students to be in command of their own learning and recognize the importance of science in their future can be achieved by assisting them with setting their own goals. When students are more involved in their learning, they are more likely to have greater achievement in school and life. Several patterns emerged from research by DeBacker and Nelson (2000) including students being more likely to pursue learning goals in science classes when they also (1) valued science, (2) perceived having a high ability in science, and (3) did not hold a gender stereotype about the science domain. Setting learning goals might be a valuable tool to assist unmotivated students with understanding the significance of learning, especially with students who are unable to distinguish the importance of science in their life.

Many students feel that science is not a required subject for success in life, nor do they understand how science connects to the problems they will need to solve as adults. These individuals fail to see that student achievement and motivation to learn in any subject area are closely related. Constructivist theory states that students must be motivated for meaningful learning to happen (Palmer, 2008). For this reason, using strategies that increase student motivation would be to the benefit of the students and teachers.

A study by Palmer (2009) was conducted to identify classroom strategies that would best enhance student motivation. In a previous study he discovered that multiple experiences of situational interest in science had positive effects on the students' concept, anxiety, enjoyment, and motivation (Palmer, 2004). The college students in this previous study detailed that their curiosity was sparked by several factors including learning science concepts, hands-on activities, group work, and the uniqueness of the situation. The current study (Palmer, 2009) involved ninth grade students (52% male and 48% female) from five high schools in a town in Australia. The student groups, each with about eight students, participated in a 40-minute inquiry-based lesson consisting of four phases: demonstration, proposal, experiment, and report. The researcher varied the topic being studied to alleviate the chance of topic generated interest rather than task generated interest. He also had the students copy notes before and after the lesson to use for comparison. The students were asked to rate their level of interest at the end of each part followed by an interview session after the lesson.

Results of the study showed that while the students were engaged in using inquiry skills they appeared to lack experience, so their skills were not of a high standard. The researcher also noted that interest levels fluctuated during the lesson based on the task being performed. An unexpected outcome was the students identifying learning as a source of situational interest especially since previous research had supported the opposite outcome. Physical activity was a main source of interest in the experimental phase of the lesson while uniqueness was also identified in the demonstration and experiment phases.

Most of the inquiry-based strategies emphasize developing scientific understanding rather than motivation or interest of the students. Consequently, students' interest and motivation need to be considered since these could increase the participation level leading to increased development of scientific skills. Palmer (2009) states that one limitation was using small groups of students rather than entire classes since it could have affected the outcome of the experiment. Developing inquiry-based lessons that also increase motivation could possibly have a tremendous impact on student achievement.

A paper by Morgan (1999) discusses the impact of cooperative learning on student success in a college biology class. If a student is a motivated and active participant, then traditional methods of presenting material can be successful. However, the less motivated student is often excluded from lectures and discussions in class since they are too shy or less confident, so they do not participate often leading to further isolation. Using cooperative learning groups has numerous benefits for all individuals involved.

Cooperative learning for small groups allows students to develop a relationship with other students and encourages them to communicate with each other while learning. The small groups also allow individuals to feel less intimidated which could affect interest levels. Morgan (1999) discovered that being in small groups encourages students to participate which leads to better development of scientific skills. She also relates the advantages of cooperative learning, which includes students feeling less overwhelmed, clarifying their goals and interests, thinking critically, and appreciating other's viewpoints.

There are numerous ways to use cooperative learning in the science classroom to increase student interest and motivation. Even though instructors will need to invest more time and effort into the development of the lessons, the benefits for the students are great (Morgan, 1999). Student motivation and interest in science is usually affected by how they perceive the knowledge and skills being learned, but can also be affected by their instructor's attitude towards the material.

Another study by Pickens and Eick (2009) examined the perceptions of teachers and high school students related to the students' motivation in differently tracked science classes. The manner in which material is presented has been shown to have an impact on the performance and motivation of students. The lowering of course expectations causes the students to lower their own standards resulting in a downward spiral leading to decreased motivation. As Pickens and Eick state, "Too many students enter the science classroom with preconceived ideas that the subject is boring and irrelevant to their world (p. 350). They agree with Singh, Granville, and Dika (2002) and other researchers who believe connecting with the students' natural inquisitiveness by using scientific inquiry could and should lead to students being more motivated and develop skills to solve their problems.

The study involved two motivated teachers and their students in tenth through twelfth grades at a large suburban high school in the southeastern United States with a conventional 4 x 4 block schedule. Both teachers had several years of experience, a higher degree, and a desire for stressing student achievement even though they taught students of different ability levels. The students ranged from the college bound, highly motivated, and meticulous students in an AP class to the low achievers who lacked self-confidence to learn science in a general science class. While the AP classes were less structured and student directed, the general science classes were more structured and organized involving follow-up discussions to demonstrate the importance of the relevance of the material being covered.

After interviewing the teachers, observations of seven or eight class periods involving lessons perceived to be especially motivating were made to determine the impact of their teaching strategies. The researchers recorded descriptive and reflective notes on the lessons in order to evaluate the effectiveness of the strategies after conducting the debriefing interview with the teachers (Pickens & Eick, 2009). Students were also given a Likert-type anonymous survey to assess their views on motivation as it related to learning, science, and strategies. The data was arranged into the following categories: dialogue in the classroom, relevant lessons, classroom environment, inquiry learning, lesson presentation, building rapport, and teacher enthusiasm (p. 353). The researchers also analyzed the student surveys to determine the strategies' effects on student motivation. Four major themes identified for each teacher allowed them to increase the motivation level of their classes. The four themes used by the AP Biology teacher included teacher enthusiasm to excite students, promotion of a nonthreatening environment, storytelling, and utilization of popular media connections to concepts, while the Physical Science teacher encouraged student-to-student dialogue, made lessons relevant through practical applications, built student confidence, and used hands-on scientific inquiry. Even though the two teachers used different strategies with their students they both were able to achieve some degree of success.

Data analysis resulted in five strategies apparently affecting student motivation including enthusiasm, positive classroom climate/high expectations, relevancy of content to students' lives, student dialogue/voice, and inquiry activities. The enthusiasm exhibited by the two teachers in the study was different, but both teachers were able to motivate at least some of their students. A positive classroom climate and high expectations were used in the Physical Science classes to build student self-confidence by supporting them, while the AP Biology classes had a nonthreatening environment which allowed the students to become part of the learning process motivating them even more (Pickens & Eick, 2009). Both teachers connected the material being covered in class to the students' lives to increase motivation, but the manner used was slightly different. The AP Biology teacher used anecdotes to make the connection while the Physical Science teacher provided practical applications for the concepts. The use of cooperative groups and inquiry learning in the Physical Science classes was encouraged and led to improved student motivation as observed when the students questioned each other and were more involved in the lessons. The hands-on activities in an inquiry-based lesson with the proper structure can be used to learn concepts and scientific principles while assisting the students to understand the importance of cooperation and teamwork.

Summary

Historically, teachers have been at the center of classrooms presenting content material for their students to learn. This instructional method, while efficient, may not be the most effective in eliciting reasoning ability and higher-level thought processes in science students. Research consistently shows inquiry-based instruction encourages students to develop deeper understandings of content material because they are more actively involved in the learning process. Inquiry-based activities are student-centered and focus as much on process skills as actual content knowledge. Students learn to question, think, and analyze like scientists. Using inquiry-based instruction has been shown to improve the achievement of learners of all ages and ability levels and is effective across all science disciplines. Students appear to perform better on content area assessments as well as state and national standardized exams. Students exposed to inquiry-based instruction also display higher levels of motivation which leads to increased achievement. Evidence supports the conclusion that inquiry-based instruction has many advantages over traditional instruction and therefore, should be integrated into all science classrooms.

Methodology

Participants

This study was conducted at Midwestern High School in Illinois. The district consists of approximately 2,200 students in ninth through twelfth grades with an average class size of about 19 students (Illinois Interactive Report Card, 2010).

The ethnicity of the student body of the school is 96.2% Caucasian, 0.8% Black, 1.3 % Hispanic, 0.8% Asian, 0.4% Native American, and 0.6% Multiracial/ethnicity as reported for 2009 on the Illinois Interactive Report Card website (2010). The socioeconomic status of the students in the district is reported as 29 % living at or below poverty (Illinois Interactive Report Card, 2010). The diversity of the students at the High School is representative of the community in which it serves.

The subjects of this study consisted of 147 fourteen to nineteen year old high school students assigned to one of eight science classes at the High School. The selection of the students for the study was based on their enrollment of the students in researchers' classes for the spring semester of 2010. The classes involved in the study were two classes in each of the following subjects: Biology II, Chemistry II, AP Chemistry IV, and Integrated Science IV. Biology II, which is predominately freshmen, and Chemistry II, which is predominately sophomores, are the second semester of a first year course consisting of students of average to higher learning ability. AP Chemistry IV is predominately juniors of higher learning ability, while Integrated Science IV is predominately sophomores of lower learning ability.

Research Instrumentation

This study had both a quantitative and a qualitative component. Quantitative data was collected from two different sample ACT Science and Reasoning tests. One test was administered as a pre-test at the beginning of the study before instruction for the two sets of classes had been differentiated. The second test was administered as a post-test at the end of the study after one set of classes had received traditional instruction and the other set had received inquiry-based instruction. The test scores were then compared. A similar research design was used by Geier, Blumenfeld, Marx, Krajcik, Fishman, Soloway, and Clay-Chambers (2008) while investigating the effects of inquiry-based science lessons on standardized test scores in Detroit Public Schools. The qualitative aspect of this study was an attitude survey which was also administered both before and after two different instructional methods were used to teach the two sets of classes. The survey statements were designed to assess the students' feelings toward science. A similar survey was used by Palmer (2009) to assess student interest during inquiry skills lessons.

The sample ACT Science and Reasoning tests consisted of forty multiple choice questions which were answered within thirty-five minutes and tested a student's ability to apply scientific reasoning based on information given in passages that addressed various subject areas in science such as chemistry, biology, and physics. The ACT was chosen because it requires students to answer questions based on information presented in three styles: data representation, research summaries, and conflicting viewpoints. Answering the questions correctly required students to read for meaning, interpret, and think on a higher level than the simpler recall questions. Scientific inquiry has been shown to improve all of these skills (Gaddis & Schoffstal, 2007). The ACT is also a component of the Prairie State Achievement Examination which is the tool by which NCLB's Adequate Yearly Progress is determined for high schools in Illinois. The tests were taken from *Amsco's Preparing for the ACT Mathematics and Science Reasoning: All you need to ace the ACT* (2000). The attitude survey was a Likert-scale survey of fifty statements pertaining to the students' feelings about science. Students selected a number from one to five expressing the extent to which they strongly agreed or strongly disagreed with each statement. The survey was adapted from a survey by Gibson and Van Strat (2000).

The ACT Science and Reasoning sample tests and the attitude surveys were administered by the researchers during regular class sessions. The multiple choice, paper and pencil based ACT test component was taken in the students' regular classrooms and scored by machine. The attitude survey, however, was taken online and, therefore, required the use of one of the computer labs at the High School. The survey results were tabulated by the online survey tool website www.zoomerang.com.

The use of multiple choice sample tests published by a reputable source limits the possibility of bias and subjectivity. Likewise, the survey's format was selected response and used unbiased language.

Procedure/Analysis

The analysis of the data consisted of the use of the online analysis tools BrightStat (www.brightstat.com) and the online survey site www.zoomerang.com. BrightStat was used to compare both group and individual pre-test and post-test scores. A comparison of group and individual scores for the data representation, research summaries, and conflicting viewpoints sections of the two different sample ACT Science and Reasoning tests was also conducted. The before-instruction and after-instruction attitude surveys will be analyzed at a later time. The results from the pre-test and post-test were compared in both table and graph formats.

Research Questions

1. Does using inquiry-based learning versus traditional methods affect student performance on a sample ACT Science Reasoning Test?
2. Does using inquiry-based learning versus traditional methods affect student performance on the different types of questions (Data Representation, Research Summary, and Conflicting Viewpoints) on a sample ACT Science Reasoning Test?
3. What effect does inquiry-based learning have on performance of students with different abilities on a sample ACT Science Reasoning Test?

Definition of Terms

1. Traditional methods – use of lecture format with practice worksheets to study class material
2. Inquiry-based Learning – use of situations where students take the role of scientists to study class material; requires the use of problem-solving skills
3. Data Representation – questions involving the use and interpretation of graphs, tables, and other schematic forms
4. Research Summary – questions involving the use of descriptions of one or more related experiments
5. Conflicting Viewpoints – questions using expressions of several related hypotheses or views that are inconsistent with one another

Limitations of the Study

The limitations of the study include the validity of the responses of the students to the test questions, the motivation of the students to complete their responses to the best of their abilities, and the validity of the test questions.

Results

Two sections each of Biology II, Chemistry II, Integrated Science IV, and AP Chemistry IV were instructed using either traditional methods or inquiry-based methods for a period of eight weeks during the spring of 2010. Prior to the instructional period, the classes were administered a sample ACT Science Reasoning Test as a pre-test. An alternate second sample ACT Science Reasoning Test was administered after the instructional period as a post-test. The results of the pre-test were compared to the results of the post-test to determine the effect the type of instruction had on test performance.

Research Question #1: Does using inquiry-based versus traditional methods of instruction affect student performance on a sample ACT Science Reasoning Test?

Table 1 summarizes the descriptive statistics on the pre-test and post-test scores, as well as the difference between the two scores for all students taking the tests. It is evident that the post-test scores of both groups decreased; however, the decrease was slightly less for the inquiry group. Table 2 shows the same information using the trimmed mean of each group. Again, the inquiry taught group experienced a smaller decrease in post-test scores than did the traditionally taught group.

Table One: A summary of the means and standard deviations of the pre and post tests and the difference between the two groups

Groups	Pre-test Means	SD	Post-test Means	SD	Differences in Means	SD
Inquiry	20.24	7.74	19.1	8.15	-1.14	4.73
Traditional	20.82	7.3	18.56	7.22	-2.26	5.3

Table Two: A summary of the means and standard deviations of the pre and post tests and the difference between the two groups using the trimmed means for each group

Groups	Pre-test Means	SD	Post-test Means	SD	Differences in Means	SD
Inquiry	19.08	6.4	18.55	6.62	-0.53	4.71
Traditional	20.65	7.42	18.82	5.64	-1.82	5.14

Table 3 summarizes the Paired Sample t-Test analyses using all students' test scores. The results indicate that post-test scores of both groups were significantly different than the pre-test scores ($p < 0.05$). Table 4 summarizes the Paired Sample t-Test analyses using the trimmed mean of each group. These results show a significant difference in post-test scores for the traditionally taught group ($p < 0.05$).

Table Three: A summary of the paired sample *t*-test for the two groups

Groups	t	df	p (2-tailed)
Inquiry	2.14	78	0.035
Traditional	3.53	67	0.001

Table Four: A summary of the paired sample *t*-test for the two groups using the trimmed mean

Groups	t	df	p (2-tailed)
Inquiry	0.07	39	0.485
Traditional	2.07	33	0.047

Graphical representations of the differences in students' pre- and post-test scores show the number of post-test scores decreasing to the left of the vertical line at 0 and the number of post-test scores increasing to the right of the vertical line at 0. The independent variable is the difference between the post- and pre-test scores, and the dependent variable is the number of students exhibiting that difference.

Chart 1 shows all seventy-nine students experiencing inquiry-based instruction. Thirty-three students experienced a score increase while the scores of forty-four students decreased. Two students scored the same on the post-test as they did on the pre-test.

Chart 1: Differences in ACT Science Scores of Inquiry Based Students

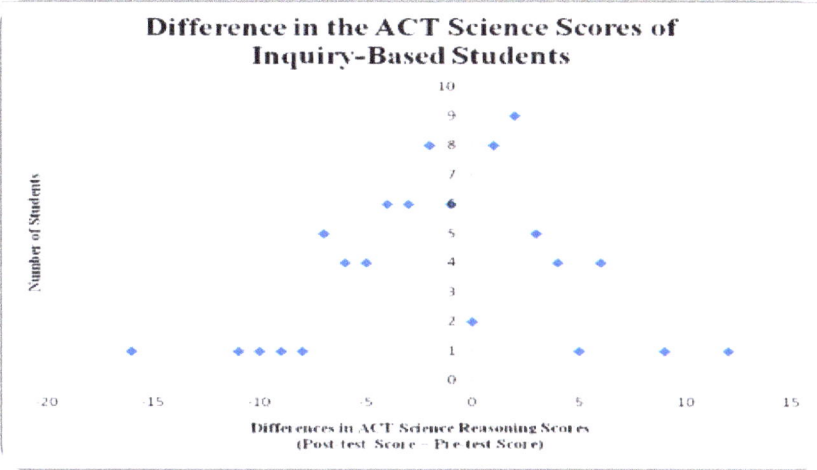

Chart 2 shows the trimmed mean (forty students) experiencing inquiry-based instruction. Sixteen students experienced a score increase while the scores of twenty-two students decreased. Two students scored the same on the post-test as they did on the pre-test.

Chart 2: Differences in ACT Science Scores of the Trimmed Mean of Inquiry Based Students

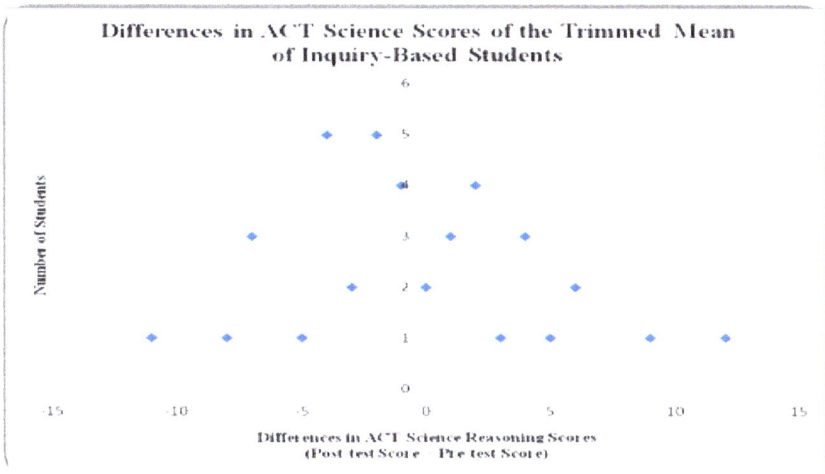

Chart 3 shows all sixty-eight students experiencing traditional instruction. Nineteen students experienced a score increase while the scores of forty-four students decreased. Five students scored the same on the post-test as they did on the pre-test.

Chart 3: Differences in the ACT Science Scores of Traditional Students

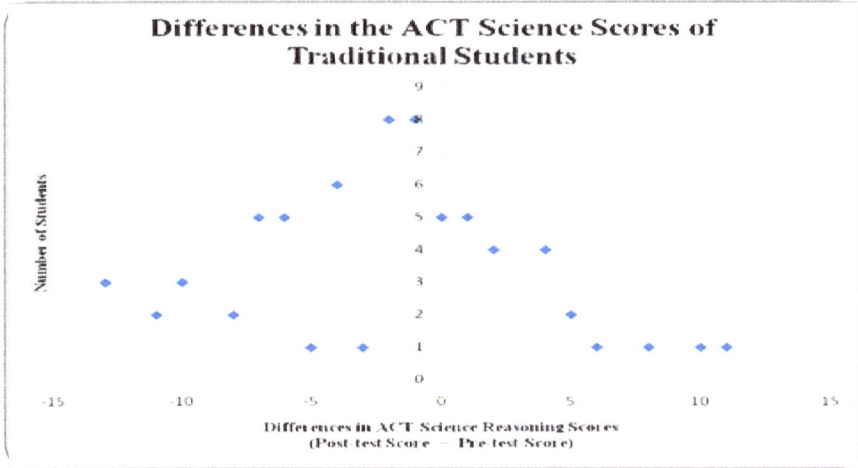

Chart 4 shows the trimmed mean (thirty-four students) experiencing traditional instruction. Nine students experienced a score increase while the scores of twenty-one students decreased. Four students scored the same on the post-test as they did on the pre-test.

Chart 4: Differences in the ACT Science Scores of the Trimmed Means of Traditional Students

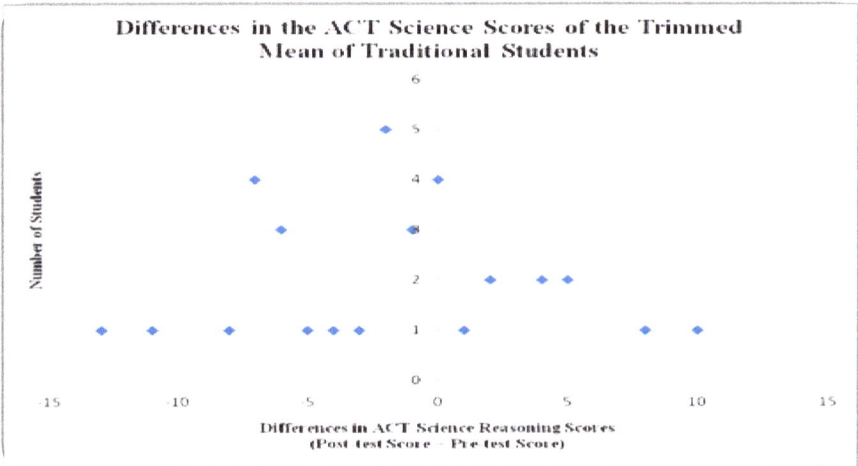

Chart 5 is a graph showing the post-test scores plotted against the pre-test scores for the trimmed mean of both the inquiry group and the traditional group with lines of best fit for both. The equation of the trend line for the inquiry group shows a slightly steeper slope than that of the traditional group suggesting the ratio of post-test to pre-test score for this group is larger.

Chart 5: A summary of the post-test scores plotted against the pre-test scores for the trimmed mean of both the inquiry group and the traditional group with lines of best fit for both

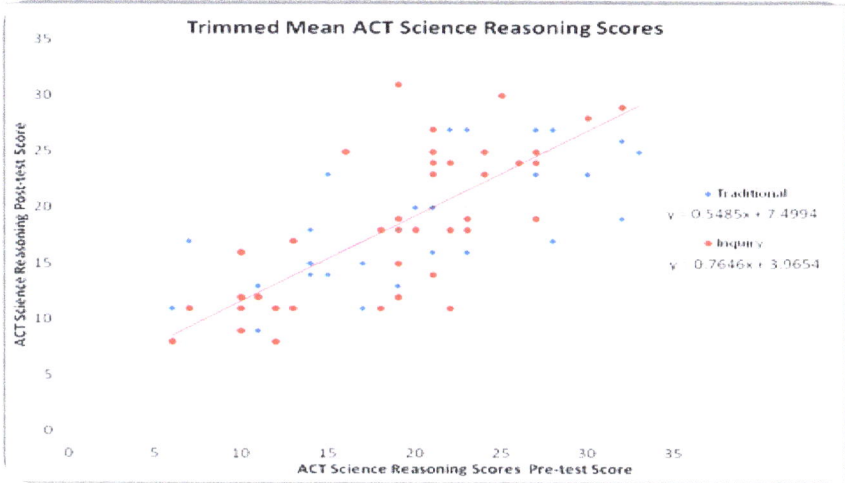

Research Question #2: Does using inquiry-based methods versus traditional methods affect student performance on the different types of questions (Data Representation, Research Summary, and Conflicting Viewpoints) on a sample ACT Science Reasoning Test?

Overall, using inquiry-based methods of instruction resulted in greater improvement in test scores than did instruction using traditional methods. The inquiry-based classes performed better on Data Representation, Research Summary, and Conflicting Viewpoints portions of the sample ACT Science Reasoning Test than the traditional classes.

On the Data Representation portion, the results for the inquiry-based classes compared to the traditional classes are represented in Table 5. The average difference for the inquiry-based classes was 4.28 percentage points higher, while the average difference for the traditional classes was 1.42 percentage points lower for the number of incorrect responses as compared to the total number of responses. The greatest increase for the inquiry classes occurred in the Biology class, while the Integrated Science class scored lower on this section of the post-test. The greatest increase for the traditional classes occurred in the Biology class, while the greatest decrease occurred in the Integrated Science class followed closely by the AP Chemistry class.

Table 5: A comparison of the average difference of incorrect responses between the two groups on the data representation questions

Data Representation	Pre-test % missed	Post-test %missed	Pre-test % minus Post-test %	Average Difference
Inquiry Classes				4.28
Biology	63.33	53	10.33	
AP Chemistry	32.73	26.97	5.76	
Chemistry	45.83	41.94	3.89	
Integrated Science	70.48	73.33	-2.85	
Traditional Classes				-1.42
Biology	56.67	53.33	3.34	
AP Chemistry	52.5	50.56	1.94	
Chemistry	25	30.42	-5.42	
Integrated Science	70.56	76.11	-5.55	

On the Research Summary portion of the sample ACT Science Reasoning Test both sets of classes scored lower on the post-test than on the pre-test. For the inquiry-based classes the average difference of the number of incorrect responses as compared to the total number of responses decreased 10.76 percentage points, whereas the average difference for the traditional classes decreased 13.89 percentage points as shown in Table 6. The Traditional Integrated Science class showed the most improvement overall while only slightly more than the Inquiry Integrated Science class. The Traditional Biology showed the greatest decrease of all the classes.

Table 6: A comparison of the average difference of incorrect responses between the two groups on the research summary questions

Research Summary	Pre-test % missed	Post-test %missed	Pre-test % minus Post-test %	Average Difference
Inquiry Classes				-10.76
Integrated Science	76.19	78.97	-2.78	
AP Chemistry	30.3	43.18	-12.88	
Chemistry	40.97	54.17	-13.2	
Biology	52.78	66.94	-14.16	
Traditional Classes				-13.89
Integrated Science	66.67	69.44	-2.77	
AP Chemistry	26.39	44.79	-18.4	
Chemistry	46.76	56.48	-9.72	
Biology	40.97	65.63	-24.66	

The number of missed questions compared to the total responses for the Conflicting Viewpoints portion of the sample ACT Science Reasoning Test resulted in the inquiry-based classes' average improvement being 9.33 percentage points while the traditional classes' average improvement was 6.03 percentage points as shown in Table 7. The Inquiry AP Chemistry class showed the most improvement on this section of the test followed by the Traditional Biology which demonstrated the greatest improvement of the traditional classes. The two chemistry classes both performed worse on this section with Traditional Chemistry doing better than the Inquiry Chemistry. Both Integrated Science classes performed better with the inquiry-based class showing greater improvement.

Table 7: A comparison of the average difference of incorrect responses between the two groups on the conflicting view point questions

Conflicting Viewpoints	Pre-test % missed	Post-test %missed	Pre-test % minus Post-test %	Average Difference
Inquiry Classes				9.33
AP Chemistry	46.1	26.62	19.48	
Integrated Science	74.49	64.29	10.2	
Biology	57.14	47.14	10	
Chemistry	47.02	49.4	-2.38	
Traditional Classes				6.03
Biology	62.5	45.54	16.96	
AP Chemistry	37.5	32.14	5.36	
Integrated Science	48.21	67.86	2.38	
Chemistry	70.24	48.81	-0.6	

The percent differences using the total responses for the three sections of the ACT Science Reasoning Test for the two groups are represented below in Tables 8 and 9. The inquiry-based classes performed higher on the Data Representation and Conflicting Viewpoints sections while scoring lower on the Research Summary section. The traditional classes only showed improved scores for the Conflicting Viewpoints section while decreasing on the Data Representation and Research Summary sections.

Table 8: The percent difference of the total responses on the three sections of the ACT Science Reasoning for the inquiry classes

Inquiry classes totals	# of Responses	Pretest # missed	Posttest # missed	% Difference
Data Representation	1200	611	553	4.83
Research Summary	1440	679	845	-11.53
Conflicting Viewpoints	560	303	253	8.93

Table 9: The percent difference of the total responses on the three sections of the ACT Science Reasoning for the traditional classes

Inquiry classes totals	# of Responses	Pretest # missed	Posttest # missed	% Difference
Data Representation	1020	512	520	-0.78
Research Summary	1224	540	712	-14.05
Conflicting Viewpoints	476	252	226	5.46

Research Question #3: What effect does inquiry-based learning have on performance of students with different abilities on a sample ACT Science Reasoning Test?

A comparison was made between the students enrolled in Chemistry and Integrated Science classes because both courses consisted predominantly of sophomores. However, students enrolled in Chemistry are primarily college-bound and higher ability while students enrolled in Integrated Science are primarily not college-bound and lower ability.

Table 10 summarizes the descriptive statistics on the pre-test and post-test scores, as well the difference between the scores for all students taking the tests. Overall the mean scores decreased for each group on the post-test. Both groups of the lower ability Integrated Science students experienced smaller decreases in post-test scores. Table 11 shows the same information using the trimmed mean of each group. The same trend is seen in the trimmed mean. The inquiry-based Integrated Science class showed the same mean score on the pre-test and post-test, while the traditional Integrated Science class showed a slight improvement in mean post-test score.

Table 10: A summary of the descriptive statistics on the pre-test and post-test scores, and the difference between the scores for all students

Type of Science Class	Pretest Score Mean	SD	Posttest Score Mean	SD	Difference Mean	SD
Inquiry Integrated Science	10.5	3.11	10.29	2.73	-0.21	3.47
Traditional Integrated Science	12.5	3.66	11.33	2.99	-1.17	4.57
Traditional Chemistry	20.33	6.07	18.83	6.72	-1.5	6.16
Inquiry Chemistry	22.45	5.99	20.5	5.72	-1.95	3.43

Table 11: A summary of the descriptive statistics on the pre-test and post-test scores, and the difference between the scores for all students using trimmed means

Type of Science Class	Mean pre-test Score	SD	Mean post-test Score	SD	Mean Difference	SD
Traditional Integrated Science	11.5	3.73	11.67	1.75	0.17	3.82
Inquiry Integrated Science	10.13	2.47	10.13	1.56	0	2.51
Traditional Chemistry	19.83	6.53	18.83	3.79	-1	6.15
Inquiry Chemistry	22.58	2.61	20.83	3.04	-1.75	3.39

Table 12 summarizes the Paired Sample t-Test analyses using all students' test scores. The results indicate that post-test scores of the inquiry-based Chemistry class were significantly different than the pre-test scores ($p < 0.05$). Table 13 summarizes the Paired Sample t-Test analyses using the trimmed mean of each group. These results show no significant difference in post-test scores for any group ($p > 0.05$).

Table 12: A summary of the Paired Sample *t*-test results using all students' test scores

Type of Science Classes	*t*	df	p (2-tailed)
Inquiry Integrated Science	0.23	13	0.821
Traditional Integrated Science	0.88	11	0.395
Traditional Chemistry	1.19	23	0.245
Inquiry Chemistry	2.8	23	0.01

Table 13: A summary of the Paired Sample *t*-test results using trimmed means

Type of Science Classes	*t*	df	p (2-tailed)
Inquiry Integrated Science	0	7	1
Traditional Integrated Science	-0.107	5	0.919
Traditional Chemistry	0.56	11	0.585
Inquiry Chemistry	2.8	11	0.101

The sections instructed using traditional methods versus inquiry-based methods showed some slight variation in their scores after the instructional period. Overall, the scores on the post-test improved for both teaching methods from the scores obtained on the pre-test. The improvement for the inquiry-based group appears to be greater than those for the traditional methods group.

Analysis and Discussion

Prior research shows inquiry-based instruction improves student achievement in specific areas of science content (Chang & Mao, 1999). Additionally, research by Mao, Chang, and Barufaldi (1998) on the effects of inquiry-based instruction on science achievement test scores has demonstrated an improvement in the development of students' process skills and higher-order analysis of science information. The purpose of this study was to determine the impact of inquiry-based instruction on student performance on the science reasoning portion of the ACT exam. The slightly better performance on this section of the test by the inquiry-based instruction group in this study could be attributed to the inquiry-based lessons assisting the students with developing their processing skills. The inquiry-based lessons used in the study were designed to challenge the students and support the development of their science processing skills. Evidence supporting the development of extended thinking and higher-level questioning was reported by Schneider, Krajcik, Marx, and Soloway (2002) and Hofstein, Navon, Kipnis, and Mamlik-Naaman (2005) respectively, as well. According to a previous study done by Turner and Rios (2008), the average pre-test and post-test scores for scientific components remained the same or increased by exposing students to items similar to those on the standardized tests. While the results of this study showed marginal improvements in the experimental group. The researchers do not believe the results are conclusive.

In examining the pre-test and post-test score differences of the seventy-nine participants receiving inquiry-based instruction and the sixty-eight students receiving traditional instruction, it appeared several students did not put forth their best efforts on the post-test because those scores were substantially lower than the pre-test scores. This phenomenon was most prevalent among the freshmen, sophomores, and seniors because the ACT exam is not as important to them as it is for the juniors. Because the ACT exam is administered to students in the spring of their junior year, freshmen and sophomores have one or two more years to ready themselves, and therefore, might have approached the test more casually since they did not see the immediate value and relevance of taking practice tests. Seniors on the other hand, seemed to demonstrate an apathetic attitude towards the test since they had already received their official ACT test scores, and therefore, had little interest in taking additional practice exams. In an effort to eliminate the outliers, the researchers opted to examine the results of the trimmed mean of both groups in addition to the overall means. Scores were sorted from highest to lowest based first on post-test score then based on pre-test score. The top and bottom twenty-five percent of the score differences were then disregarded, leaving forty students in the inquiry group and thirty-four in the traditional group. The study by Chang and Mao (1999) utilized six hundred twelve students. A similar study conducted by Mao, Chang, and Barufaldi (1998) was based on two-hundred thirty-two students, while another by Johnson and Lawson (1998) studied three hundred sixty-six students. All three of the cited studies involved significantly larger sample sizes than this current investigation.

Comparing the differences in scores for both the entire group and the trimmed mean of each group indicates the inquiry group had a higher mean difference than did the traditional group, even though both groups, on average, scored lower on the post-test than on the pre-test. To see if this difference was statistically significant, a paired sample t-test was conducted. For all groups except the trimmed mean of the inquiry group, $p < 0.05$ indicating the variation in score difference was statistically significant. Some concern exists because the paired sample t-test was two-tailed meaning it included differences where the post-test score was higher and lower than the pre-test score even though the focus of this study was score improvement from inquiry-based instruction. The scatter plots of the score differences shown in Charts 1-4 of the results section show in both the inquiry and traditional groups and for both the total sample and the trimmed mean more scores decreased than increased. Previous research conducted on this topic has used analysis of variance, analysis of covariance, and multivariate analysis of covariance for data analysis (Chang & Mao, 1999; Johnson & Lawson, 1998; Mao, Chang & Barufaldi, 1998).

One of the several factors that could have influenced the results included the duration of the study. Students in this study experienced differentiated instruction for eight weeks. Other research concerning the effects of inquiry-based instruction has spanned comparable lengths of time ranging from two to eight weeks. However, they focused on specific science content and utilized chapter test-like, content-based tests as evaluation tools (Chang & Mao 1999; Mao, Chang & Barufaldi, 1998; Ng, 2004). Studies such as those of Hofstein, Navon, Kipnis, and Mamlok-Naaman (2005) and Johnson and Lawson (1998) concentrated on students' reasoning abilities instead of specific content and spanned longer periods of time ranging from fifteen weeks to two years. The researchers of this study believe an eight-week instructional period is not long enough to significantly impact ACT Science Reasoning test scores.

Familiarity with the topic of the questions could be another factor influencing the results of this study. Even though the students of this study were tested on science reasoning ability, the topic of the test questions may also have influenced the students' confidence, and therefore, their ability to perform to their fullest potential on certain questions. The students may not have applied themselves to the same extent on material with which they did not feel as familiar. The following table summarizes the number of questions pertaining to each science topic on the pre-test and post-test:

Table 14: A summary of the number of questions pertaining to each science topic on the pre-test and post-test

Science topics	Number of Questions on pre-test	Number of Questions on post-test
Biology	5	7
Chemistry	10	11
Earth Science	7	6
Ecology	0	6
Environmental Science	12	5
Physics	6	5

Each test contained two passages relating to chemistry, so the Biology and Integrated Science students may have been intimidated by these questions since they had not taken a high school chemistry class. An examination of the information presented in Tables 5, 6, and 7 of the results section reveals the AP Chemistry and Chemistry classes of both instructional groups exhibited the lowest percentage of missed questions on all three types of questions except in two instances in which the inquiry-based Biology class missed the fewest and one instance in which the traditional Biology class missed the fewest.

ACT test prep courses and retaking the ACT test appear to impact studen performance on the ACT test and are two more factors affecting this study. According to ACT (The ACT, 2009-2010), a student who retakes the test has a 55 percent chance of improving his or her score, a 22 percent chance of scoring the same, and a 23 percent chance of scoring lower. Having previously taken the pre-test could have resulted in students being more relaxed when taking the post-test which could result in increased scores for some students. Some of the juniors also may have performed better on the test due to their participation in a review course for the ACT since these courses teach the participants what to expect. Based on this, post-test scores would be expected to improve slightly independent of any differences in instruction. Seven of the AP Chemistry students were enrolled in an ACT preparation course during the last four weeks of the eight week differentiated instructional period and were receiving information about

ACT test-taking strategies in addition to other sample questions and/or explanations putting them at an advantage over the other participants in the study.

Another variable influencing exam scores included the time of day the test was taken. Of the eight classes included in the study, Traditional and Inquiry Biology, Traditional and Inquiry AP Chemistry, and Traditional Chemistry were morning classes scheduled before lunch. Traditional and Inquiry Integrated Science and Inquiry Chemistry were afternoon classes. Research indicates many adolescents get less sleep than they need due to "early school starting times and the role of various biological and social influences on adolescents' self-selected bed times" (Dahl, 1999, p. 354). This leads to sleepy students who may experience brief mental lapses and have difficulty focusing on tasks with abstract goals (Dahl, 1999). The scores of the students in the earlier morning classes may have been affected by decreased student alertness.

There are several limitations of this study. The small sample size was addressed previously and can be considered a limitation of this investigation. The short duration of this study is also a limitation because most students are not accustomed to the inquiry-style of learning. A period of adjustment may be necessary and the effectiveness of inquiry-based instruction may not reach its full potential in such a short period of time. As described in the literature review section of this research, inquiry-based instruction takes on many forms depending on the degree of student independence. Guided inquiry was the primary form used in this investigation which is considered midway in the inquiry spectrum. Giving students even more responsibility for their own learning may result in more significant differences.

Conclusion

Research has shown that inquiry-based instruction allows students to develop critical thinking skills and a better understanding of science by questioning and using evidence to solve problems. Students who are involved in their own learning are more apt to ask in-depth questions as they are exploring the topics being studied. Science instruction lends itself very easily to inquiry-based lessons due to the investigative nature of the subject. During the last decade, the trend in science education has been to develop students' higher order thinking skills and reasoning abilities through inquiry-based instruction. This method of instruction places students at the center of their own learning and leads them to discover concepts and relationships for themselves in much the same way actual scientists solve problems and answer questions. If inquiry-based methods were used more in science classes, then, besides developing life-long problem solving skills, student performance on standardized tests might be positively impacted.

The effects of inquiry-based learning on the development of scientific processing skills that students use to solve problems in their daily lives are slightly harder to quantify. These are the same skills students need to successfully answer questions on the science reasoning portion of the ACT exam which is administered to juniors in the state of Illinois each spring to gauge whether or not high schools are meeting AYP according to NCLB. Correctly answering the exam questions depends more on students' abilities to read and interpret information from graphs and charts and less on their actual science content knowledge. Exposure to inquiry-based lessons has the potential to provide students with experience in reasoning and drawing conclusions from presented material; whereas traditional instruction directly supplies students with facts and explanations without any of their own thinking required. Over time, the incorporation of inquiry-based methods into all science classes could result in increased test scores.

After experiencing eight weeks of inquiry-based instruction, the experimental group of this study showed marginally improved scores on the science reasoning portion of a practice ACT exam. Even though the mean post-test score was lower than the mean pre-test score for both the traditional and the inquiry groups, the inquiry group experienced a smaller decline. This trend is also seen when comparing the percentage of missed questions. For two of the three question types, the inquiry group had fewer incorrect responses on the post-test than they did on the pre-test. The outcome was less clear when a comparison was made between mean scores of only the Integrated Science and Chemistry classes. This suggests the difference the effects of inquiry-based instruction had on the lower and higher ability students of this study was not significant.

Implications

The results of this study point to a link between improved ACT science reasoning scores and inquiry-based instruction. Additional research in this area should investigate how inquiry-based instruction affects students' confidence in their ability to answer higher level, reasoning-type questions. After completing a pre-test, students could complete a short Likert-style survey evaluating their feelings of self-efficacy toward the exam questions. The same survey could be administered after the post-test to see if a link exists between confidence and actual performance. The results might also show if students felt more confident and prepared after experiencing inquiry-based instruction. The survey responses could reveal that many students may resent having to spend time taking the practice tests and/or do not relate to the subject matter on the test. For example, if a student prefers biology they might not perform as well on chemistry questions.

Additionally, further investigations should span a longer period of time. Ideally, inquiry-based science instruction should begin at the early elementary level and continue through all grades in an attempt to increase the development of the higher level processing skills. Reasoning ability and divergent thinking are skills that must develop over many years in order to be integrated and used effectively by students. A long-term study tracking students' progress over at least five to seven years is suggested to yield more definitive results.

Finally, future studies should integrate multiple levels of inquiry. At the introductory level, students should be given primarily guided-inquiry activities and receive extensive scaffolding. As mastery occurs with those skills, and a broader content base is acquired, students could gradually be given more independence and responsibility through problem-based activities. Ultimately, students should have the knowledge and skills to embark upon open-ended inquiry-based activities. This format would require several years to implement and reach full potential but would hopefully show that ACT science reasoning scores can be improved through the use of inquiry-based instruction.

References

The ACT (2010). Retrieved April 24, 2010 from http://www.actstudent.org/.

Bruning, R. H., Schraw, G. J., Norby, M. M., & Ronning, R. R. (2004) Cognitive psychology and instruction. 4th Ed. Upper Saddle River, NJ: Pearson.

Chang, C. Y., & Mao, S. L. (1999). Comparison of Taiwan science students' outcomes with inquiry-group versus traditional instruction. *The Journal of Educational Research, 92*(6), 340-346.

Dahl, R. E. (1999). The consequences of insufficient sleep for adolescents: Links between sleep and emotional regulation. *Phi Delta Kappan, 80*(5), 354-359.

DeBacker, T., & Nelson, R. (2000, March). Motivation to learn science: Differences related to gender, class type, and ability. *Journal of Educational Research, 93*(4), 245. Retrieved June 22, 2009, from Professional Development Collection database.

Folashade, A., & Akinbobola A. O. (2009). Constructivist problem based learning technique and the academic achievement of physics students with low ability level in Nigerian secondary schools. *Eurasian Journal of Physics and Chemistry Education, 1*(1), 45-51.

Gaddis, B. A., & Schoffstall, A. M. (2007). Incorporating guided-inquiry learning into the organic chemistry laboratory. *Journal of Chemical Education, 84*(5), 848-851.

Geier, R., Blumenfeld, P. C., Marx, R. W., Krajcik, J. S., Fishman, B., Soloway, E., & Clay-Chambers, J. (2008). Standardized test outcomes for students engaged in inquiry-based science curricula in the context of urban reform. *Journal of Research in Science Teaching, 45*(8) 922-939.

Gibson, H. L. & Van Strat, G. A. (2000, April). The impact of instructional methods on preservice teachers' attitudes toward teaching and learning. Paper presented at the annual meeting of the American Educational Research Association, New Orleans, LA. Retrieved fromhttp://www.eric.ed.gov/ERICDocs/data/ericdocs2sql/content_storag e_01/0000019b/ 80/16/48/1f.pdf.

Hofstein, A., Navon, O. Kipnis, M., & Mamlok-Naaman, R. (2005). Developing students' ability to ask more and better questions resulting from inquiry-type chemistry laboratories. *Journal of research in science teaching, 42*(7), 791-806.

Hohloch, J. M., Grove, N., & Bretz, S. L. (2007). Pre-service teacher as researcher: The value of inquiry in learning science. *Journal of Chemical Education, 84*(9), 1530-1534.

Interactive Illinois Report Card. (2010). Retrieved April 24, 2010 from http://iirc.niu.edu/compare.aspx?level=s.

Johnson, M. A., & Lawson, A. E. (1998). What are the relative effects of reasoning ability and prior knowledge on biology achievement in expository and inquiry classes? *Journal of Research in Science Teaching, 35*(1), 89-103.

Lewis, S. E., & Lewis, J. E. (2008). Seeking effectiveness and equity in a large college chemistry course: An HLM investigation of peer-led guided inquiry. *Journal of Research in Science Teaching, 45*(7), 794-811.

Mao, S. L., Chang, C. Y., & Barufaldi, J. P. (1998). Inquiry teaching and its effects on secondary-school students' learning of earth science concepts. *Journal of Geoscience Education, 46*(4), 363- 368.

Morgan, D. C. (1999, July 1). Cooperative learning in the community college biology classroom.   (ERIC Document Reproduction Service No. ED437115) Retrieved September 26, 2009, from OVID database.

Musheno, B. V., & Lawson, A. E. (1999). Effects of learning cycle and traditional text on comprehension of science concepts by students at differing reasoning levels. *Journal of   Research in Science Teaching, 36*(1), 23-37.

National Research Council. (1996). *National Science Education Standards.* Washington, DC: National Academy Press.

Ng, B. E. (2004). The effects of general ability and inquiry based learning on acquisition of scientific reasoning (Master's thesis, National Institute of Education, Nanyang Technological University, 2004). Retrieved November 17, 2009 from http://conference.nie.edu.sg/paper/Converted%20Pdf/ab00584.pdf

NSTA Board of Directors. (2005, October). Scientific inquiry. In *NSTA position statement.* Retrieved September 19, 2009, from National Science Teachers Association website: http://www.nsta.org/positionstatement%pisd=43

Palmer, D. H. (2009). Student interest generated during an inquiry skills lesson. *Journal of research in science teaching, 46*(2), 147-165.

Pickens, M. & Eick, C. J. (2009). Studying motivational strategies used by two teachers in differently tracked science courses. *The Journal of Educational Research, 102*(5), 349-362.

Poyrazli, S., Ferrer-Wreder, L., Meister, D., Forthun, L., Coatsworth, J., & Grahame, K. (2008, September). Academic achievement, employment, age, and gender and students' experience of alternative school. *Adolescence, 43*(171), 547-556. Retrieved June 22, 2009, from Professional Development Collection database.

Postman, R. D. (2000). Amsco's preparing for the ACT mathematics and science reasoning: All you need to ace the ACT. New York, NY: Amsco School Publications, Inc. The POGIL Project. (2007). Retrieved from http://new.pogil.org.

Schneider, R.M., Krajcik, J., Marx, R.W., & Soloway, E. (2002). Performance of students in project-based science classrooms on a national measure of science achievement. *Journal of Research in Science Teaching, 39*(5), 410-422.

Singh, K., Granville, M., & Dika, S. (2002, July). Mathematics and science achievement: Effects of motivation, interest, and academic engagement. *Journal of Educational Research,   95*(6), 323. Retrieved June 22, 2009, from Professional Development Collection database.

Turner, M.J. & Rios, J.M. (2008). Determining paths to success: Preparing students for experimental design questions on standardized tests. *The American Biology Teacher, 70*(3), 140-152.

Yerrick, R. K. (2000). Lower track science students' argumentation and open inquiry instruction. *Journal of Research in Science Teaching, 37*(8), 807-838.

Chapter 8: Students' Perceptions of the Impact of Instructional Strategies on the Motivation to Achieve in Science

Shanda Beard-Corry & Britta Maddox

Introduction

"Reform of our educational system will take time and unwavering commitment. It will require equally widespread, energetic, and dedicated action. For example, we call upon the National Academy of Sciences, National Academy of Engineering, Institute of Medicine, Science Service, National Science Foundation, Social Science Research Council, American Council of Learned Societies, National Endowment for the Humanities, National Endowment for the Arts, and other scholarly, scientific, and learned societies for their help in this effort." (National Commission on Excellence in Education, 1983 Nation at Risk Report)

These closing words from "A Nation at Risk" by the National Commission on Excellence in Education in 1983, served as notice to the nation as a whole; stating that true educational reform would require not only the efforts of parents, students, and teachers, but also of scholarly societies to provide empirical evidence as to what quality education is. Eighteen years later these recommendations became required when the No Child Left Behind Act of 2001 established that federal funding be provided to education programs which are evidence based. Recommendations, reports, and eventually laws have resulted in researchers and scholarly societies developing goals and standards for education, including science education, based on empirical evidence.

Within science education, a number of documents have been produced, such as Benchmarks for Science Literacy (American Association for the Advancement of Science, 1993) and National Science Education Standards (National Research Council, 1996), which provide research-based evidence for what goals and standards should be part of science education. In addition, researchers have identified what science content is essential to scientific literacy (Osbourne, 2003).

These efforts to identify what science content should be taught in our schools should be applauded yet the vital component of understanding how this science content is most effectively taught has not received as much research attention.

This one-sided approach to what should be taught has resulted in marginal gains in science achievement. This is evident in the National Assessment of Educational Progress 2005 report showing that most states showed no improvement in science achievement in 4th & 8th grade and a decline since 1996 in science achievement (National Center for Education Statistics, 2005).

According to the Nation's Report Card in 2005 there were no significant differences compared to the results in 1996 and 2000 (NAEP, 2005). Within the 37 states and jurisdictions that participated in both the 1996 and 2005 assessments, nine increased their average scores and five decreased in 8th grade science scores (NAEP, 2005). Overall, science scores for 8th graders have remained unchanged at 149 out of a 300 score scale (NAEP, 2005). Achievement-level results are similar to the score results in that there have been no significant changes in the percentages of students performing at or above the proficient level and at or above the basic level compared with either previous assessment year (NAEP, 2005).

This lack of science achievement can also be seen on the international level in assessments such as the Trends in International Mathematics and Science Study (TIMSS) and the Program for International Student Assessment (PISA). Both of these assessments compare student achievement in various areas including science. Data from the 2007 TIMSS report shows that 8th grade American students scored higher (520) than the study's average (500), however, lagged behind many other industrialized nations such as Japan, England, Korea and Hungary.

Based on these assessments, both national and international, it would be hard to argue that reform focused mainly on research into what should be taught would be sufficient to make the achievement improvements called for in "A Nation at Risk". Research has shown that factors such as teacher behavior and strategies can have an effect on student motivation (Skinner, 1993) and that motivation can lead to improvement in math and science achievement (Singh, 2002). It seems that teacher behavior and instructional strategies would also be of value to research and help further understand how student achievement can be improved.

While there has been research into the relationship between student achievement and teachers' strategies, much of the available research has been directed at the effect different strategies have solely on student achievement. Since achievement is dependent upon so many variables, including motivation, it is important to understand which of these strategies is shown to have a positive effect on achievement, and which ones serve to motivate students to be successful.

Problem Statement

This study focuses on understanding the effect of instructional strategies in Life Science from the student perspective. Realizing the classroom is a dynamic setting, many factors can effect student achievement and motivation. However, much of the research has focused solely on what content should be taught and which instructional strategies have the most significant effect on student achievement. One area that has received little research attention is how students perceive these instructional strategies as effecting their motivation to achieve. Thus, student preference of these instructional strategies can have an effect on achievement. This study seeks to determine which instructional strategies are most preferred by 7th grade Life Science students.

This study will survey 7th grade Life Science students in a Midwest urban middle school. The participants of this survey will be asked to identify which of the five instructional strategies they feel has had the most significant and positive impact on their motivation to learn the content. The five instructional strategies include: *Enhanced Context Strategies, Collaborative Learning Strategies, Questioning Strategies, Inquiry Strategies and Manipulation Strategies*; which have all been shown to increase student achievement in science (Schroeder, 2007). The results of this survey will be quantitatively analyzed to determine which instructional strategies the participants feel have the most significant effect on their motivation to achieve in a Life Science class.

Significance of the Study

This study aims to inform 7th grade science instructors about which instructional strategies their students find most effective at motivating them to learn the content. Through this understanding, teachers will be able to take into consideration student motivation when planning lessons. In addition, administrators will be able to create professional learning opportunities that help teachers develop lessons and strategies that take into account students' perceptions of the way they learn the material.

Research Design

This study used a descriptive analysis design to determine student perceptions on preferred learning strategies. This design is most appropriate because it describes the given state of affairs as fully and carefully as possible (Fraenkel & Wallen, 2008). The independent variables include the education level, Life Science class, gender, age, and strategies. The dependent variable is the strategies the students choose that motivate themselves.

Research Question

The research question this study looks to address is:

1. Which research based instructional strategies do 7th grade Life Science students feel is most effective at increasing their motivation to achieve?

Research Setting and Participants

This study included information gathered from students in a Midwestern junior high school located in an urban area. There were 1,088 students enrolled in this school. There are 324 seventh graders enrolled in Life Science class though 109 were surveyed for this study. The student body's socioeconomic status ranges from high to low with the large majority of students being from middle class backgrounds. The study population consisted of 69.1 % Caucasian students, 13.4 % African-American, 14.1% Hispanic, and 4.6% students categorized as "other" ethnicity.

Instrumentation

Participants were selected for this study using a convenience sampling technique. These participants were easily assessable because they were a part of the researcher's community. Initial recruitment commenced with the Informed Consent which was sent home with the 7th grade Life Science students for parents to sign, giving permission for their child to participate in the survey. The second phase of recruitment included an informed assent which was presented to the students giving them the option to participate or not to participate in the study. Finally, the survey was administered after obtaining the informed consents. The Informed Assent and survey were given to the 7th grade students during their class time. Only those surveys including both an Informed Consent and an Informed Assent were used in this study; all other surveys were immediately shredded. However, the documents containing non-participation information were kept on file in a secure location through the end of the study.

The data for this study was collected using a Life Science survey developed by the researchers. A Likert scale of a four-point scale ranging from strongly agree, agree, disagree, strongly disagree was used. This model was based off a sample given in *The Survey Handbook* by Arlene Fink. This survey includes thirteen questions: five of the questions are addressed the five most effective learning strategies, five more questions used specific examples from the Life Science class that relate to the five learning strategies, two of the questions are false negatives to ensure the students are completing the survey truthfully, and then one question is gender related.

The false negative questions that were used in the survey were based on the learning- strategies questions. They were written in a negative style to ensure that the student taking the survey reliably answered each question to his or her preference in the Life Science course.

All students in the 7th grade Life Science course had the option to complete the survey during class time. The researcher, who also teaches 7th grade Life Science, administered the survey. The results from the surveys were computed and inputted into the Excel program.

Data Analysis

Descriptive statistics such as the mean and standard deviation, and a paired Samples *t*-test were calculated. The research question determines what strategies 7th grade Life Science students prefer that would help motivate them to achieve. The study investigated which strategies are most preferred and least preferred by the 7th grade students. All data was entered into and analyzed using SPSS.

Literature Review

Although people essentially learn the same way by processing information from our five senses (Reid, 2008), the combination of reasons as to why we learn, the methods in which we learn, and perceptions of learning are unique to each individual. In terms of research, these factors translate into motivation and engagement (reasons), strategies (methods), and self-reported reflection (perceptions).

Motivation and Engagement

Learning seems to be dependent upon the engagement of students; however, engagement is often considered synonymous with motivation. Motivation and engagement are not synonyms. Motivation involves inducing, provoking, or stimulating whereas engagement refers to participating and involving; a distinctly cause-and-effect relationship rather than synonymous.

In education, motivation is further divided into two categories: intrinsic, or internally driven, and extrinsic, or externally driven. Intrinsic motivation stems from a personal desire or stimulation and satisfaction, while extrinsic relies heavily on rewards (inducement) such as recognition or good grades. Engagement refers to an action such as participation in an activity, engrossment in a topic, or involvement in learning. While these components may be collaborators for student knowledge acquisition, they are not synonymous as motivation refers to the student vector or the energy and direction driving the student; and engagement is the kinetic energy of the student or the connection between energy (effort) and a given activity. However, this is problematic as present day adolescent students are generally described as bored, disengaged, or unmotivated (Ainley, 2004).

Extrinsic Motivation

Extrinsic, as the name suggests, is associated with an external source. These sources come in many forms such as reward and punishment, or praise and recognition. Motivation is often influenced in the early years by extrinsic rewards, often for the sole purpose of dictating appropriate classroom behavior and motivation. A reward-system is commonly established that rewards good behavior (sitting quietly in class or staying on-task) and punishes bad behavior (acting out in class or getting off-task in activities); most likely to establish expectations and desired behaviors (Moberly, Waddle, & Duff, 2005). As the students progress through their educational careers, extrinsic motivation in the form of punishment and rewards, such as those found in elementary classrooms, usually begin to taper off in the middle level grades. However, in some cases, the lines between intrinsic and extrinsic rewards are blurred. For example, praise is considered to be an intrinsic reward despite the external nature of the praise (Haywood, Kuespert, Madecky, & Nor, 2008).

Extrinsic motivation can also be counterproductive in the classroom or extend beyond the elementary level classrooms. Students can easily fall prey to the need for praise and when exposed to different teachers where praise is not as forthcoming, the student is less motivated (Moberly et al., 2005). Beyond the elementary classrooms, extrinsic motivation is still heavily relied upon in special needs classes continuing to address behavioral issues rather than educational (Witzel & Mercer, 2003). Extrinsic motivation can be a valuable asset in a teacher's arsenal, however, if over-used it can become a crutch or barricade for students. Witzel proposes a motivational model to gauge and self-moderate the use of extrinsic rewards as shown below in Figure 1. An introduced activity must be aligned with the students' abilities and in an appropriate context for the student to put forth effort. Then, if the balance is present, intrinsic motivation is stimulated as efficacy is perceived. Yet when these relationships are out of kilter, the teacher's response to student effort or submissions can be assimilated as intrinsic or extrinsic; thus, possibly creating a circular relationship which may bolster the students feeling of competency and confidence or in the worst case scenario, disengage the student.

Figure 9: Proposed motivational model to address the overuse or inappropriate use of extrinsic motivation

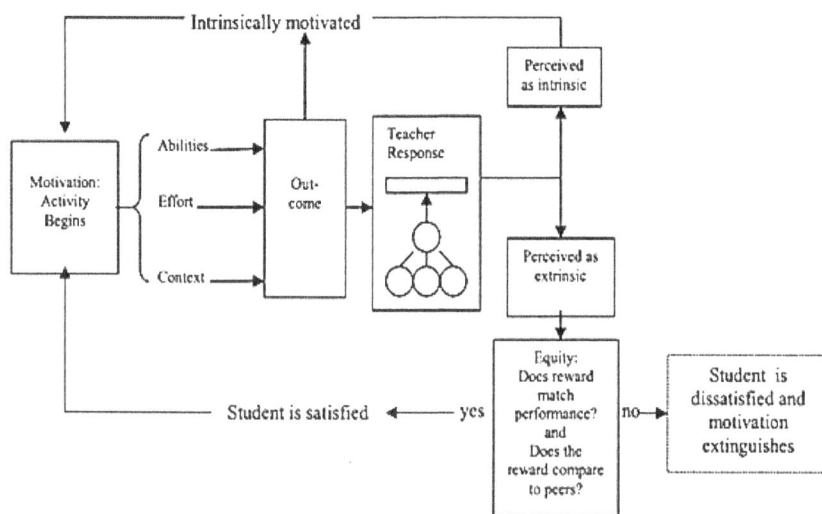

Extrinsic motivation is a learned response whereas intrinsic motivation is inherent. The innate desire to know and learn is evidenced by the first exploratory learning of the crawling child.

Intrinsic Motivation

Intrinsic motivation can be related to natural curiosity or desire to learn, simply for the sake of learning without a specific end goal such as a grade; however, the cultivation of these natural student resources have been hampered by classroom rigidity and expectations often set through extrinsic motivational factors such as rewards and punishments (Niemiec, 2009). Self Determination Theory (SDT) was the theoretical framework for this research focusing on student autonomy and resulting efficacy stemming from classroom environments in which the students were more or less autonomous. In classrooms where the students were autonomous and allowed to explore their curiosity and desire for learning guided by a teacher, the student-perceived efficacy increased; conversely, students in classrooms where the learning was teacher dictated and uniform for all students, efficacy decreased (Niemiec, 2009). Although there has been disparity with the use of SDT as applied solely to the classroom (Winn, Harley, Wilcox, &

Pemberton, 2007), the overall results of this study cannot be ignored; which states that students feel more confident in their abilities and learning when they have some measure of autonomy in learning.

Engagement

Engagement, like motivation, has multiple dimensions from battling disengagement to intellectual participation in a deeper level of knowledge acquisition (Schussler, 2009). The base level of engagement simply refers to participation or the act of being involved in an activity or task such as homework, studying, or on-task behavior in the classroom. On the other hand, intellectual engagement involves student-generated connections between the material and personal interest beyond the test (Schussler, 2009). The study by Schussler involved a Middle College, which is a public high school which collaborates with a local college(s). More specifically it acts like an alternative school (excluding the behaviorally challenged) but meant for students capable, yet disengaged from learning, and at risk of choosing to discontinue their education prior to graduation. Although this particular environment does not mimic the traditional high school, three elements were deemed necessary for students to be engaged:

- There are opportunities for students to succeed.
- Flexible avenues exist through which learning can occur.
- Students are respected as learners because teachers convey the belief that the students are capable of achieving academic success.

These three criteria would appear to be fundamental in any classroom but according to Schussler (2009), disengaged students perceive these criteria lacking in schools. In Middle Colleges, these three elements are encompassed throughout the curriculum utilizing academic challenges and subsequent support, instructional techniques that convey excitement for the content, and relevance of the learning. Instructional techniques with excitement for the content are often the portal to student(s) engagement; conversely, unimaginative instruction or lack of enthusiasm for the content contributes to disengagement, where even the most impressive extrinsic rewards may not be sufficient to overcome the students' academic lethargy in the classroom.

Unimaginative Instruction

Unimaginative instruction such as teaching directly from textbooks or failure to maximize the use of available technology could be considered weak teaching strategies and can contribute to the lack of student engagement (Baines & Stanley, 2003). Various research studies have explored methods of improving instruction through curriculum design and implementation, (Cheung, 2009; Reid, 2008; Reynolds, 2006; Sanacore, 2008; Schussler, 2009) but as studies have shown much of the research does not cross the curricular divide into the classroom (Scott, Asoko, & Leach, 2007).

Teacher Perspective

A study performed by Baines and Stanley included interactions with teachers inquiring how they knew they had a positive effect on students' learning and engagement (Baines & Stanley, 2003). The responses generally focused around improving test scores and discussions regarding the need to teach to the test to assure student success on standardized tests. In addition, the teachers voiced complaints about problem students whom disrupt classes and infringe upon time spent learning for all students. One teacher in particular was asked about incorporating alternative methods in classroom learning; she indicated she would very much like to try but fears for her job if she varies from the assigned curriculum and instructional designs; if it is not on the standardized test, the material is not to be covered. When the test scores decline, teachers fear losing their positions but schools tend to cut elective courses to focus more on the content. Students struggle with core-content classes according to the scores; taking away the classes that might actually be of interest to students further disengages students (Baines & Stanley, 2003). For example, the student might be interested in art and must maintain his or her grades to participate in the art show. This event may strongly motivate the student to do reasonably well in the core-content classes to enable participation in a desired activity. Based on the responses from this study, teachers expend minimal energy on creating lessons that interest and engage the students, and rather exert their focus on covering the required content in a measure of self-preservation.

Though teachers perceive students' engagement in vastly different ways, typically their views fall into six primary categories: behaving, enjoying, being motivated, thinking, serving a purpose, and owning (Harris, 2008). For some teachers, as long as the students are following the classroom rules and not being disruptive, they are engaged according to the behavioral category. For others, engagement is student participation and for the minority, engagement is embracing the learning through interest and ownership.

These graduations almost seem to mimic Maslow's Hierarchy and ascend from the basic behaviors in a classroom to ownership of knowledge as shown in Figure 2. It is also stated as always student-generated engagement responses, and rarely mentioned as teacher influenced engagement, which might imply that teachers perceive that they have little influence on student engagement beyond enjoying the classroom experience or activity (Harris, 2008).

Figure 10: Hierarchical Ascension of Teacher Perceived Student Engagement

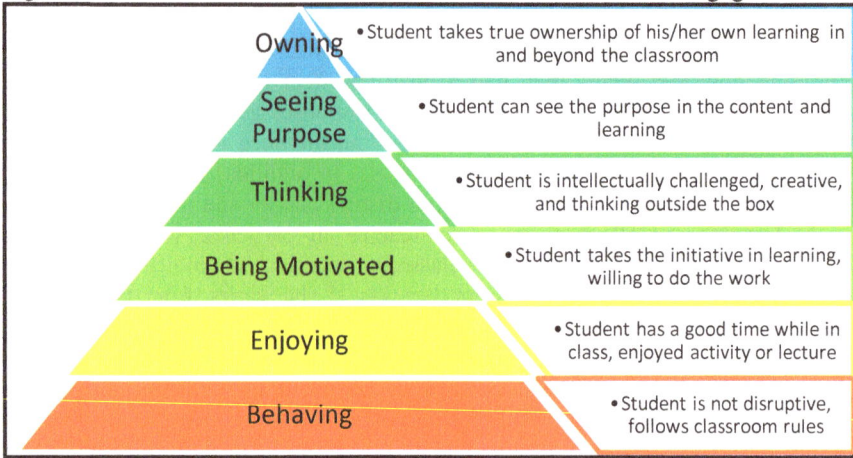

Owning	• Student takes true ownership of his/her own learning in and beyond the classroom
Seeing Purpose	• Student can see the purpose in the content and learning
Thinking	• Student is intellectually challenged, creative, and thinking outside the box
Being Motivated	• Student takes the initiative in learning, willing to do the work
Enjoying	• Student has a good time while in class, enjoyed activity or lecture
Behaving	• Student is not disruptive, follows classroom rules

Both of these studies were limited in participant numbers so the claims cannot be deemed universal or generalized; however, if there is commonality beyond this study, it does not bode well for creating lifelong learners.

Student Perspective

The previously mentioned study by Baines and Stanley also surveyed the school experience from the students' perspective revealing the majority of students were dissatisfied with the school experience for a number of reasons such as textbook reliance (Baines & Stanley, 2003). This study included 52 students who were asked to journal for five or more days and write about their day-to-day experiences such as their perceptions of the curriculum, how their teachers taught, what they learned, and their feelings, or intake, on what they learned. The overwhelming majority felt that school was irrelevant, boring or worthless; this was the common sentiment regardless of whether or not the student achieved high marks or was considered at-risk.

Fifty of the students in the study reported that their teachers rely too much on the textbook with activities such as fill-in-the-blank worksheets; while the other two students did not share this perception and reported that their teacher(s) rarely used the textbook if ever. Their reflections mentioned the teacher bringing in supplemental readings or videos pertaining to the learning, and then conducting whole-class discussions. Students frequently queried why they were not taught anything that was of interest for what they had to learn; this extended to vocational programs because the tradition curriculum was perceived as irrelevant to their interests. The strongest levels of dissatisfaction were at the far ends of the spectrum with the gifted students and those academically at risk. Dissatisfaction is a precursor to disengagement and lack of motivation in any of the categories previously mentioned.

Motivation and engagement are distinctly different; however, they are needed in conjunction with each other for a successful academic experience and are ultimately a cause- and-effect relationship regardless of where the student falls on the academic spectrum. Furthermore, the classroom environment has a profound effect on student engagement or lack thereof. Although the distinctions between engagement and motivation are acknowledged, for the purposes of this study the cause-and-effect relationship between motivation and engagement will be collectively referred to as motivation; getting the students interested and subsequently involved in their own learning. While it is evident that motivation and engagement are vital components in a student's achievement, because the classroom is such a dynamic setting there are other factors that can affect a student's achievement. Different instructional strategies can have different levels of effectiveness in helping students learn the material (Schroeder, 2007). Because of the effect instructional strategies can have on student achievement (positive, negative, or apathetic), this study determined what strategies have been shown to have a positive effect on student achievement. In addition, the five strategies chosen were selected according to which had the largest effect size on achievement.

Effective Instructional Strategies

A number of previous studies have investigated the effect of different instructional strategies on student achievement. Since there are so many studies on effective teaching strategies, a variety of meta-analysis studies have been conducted to analyze and draw conclusions on which methods have the largest effect overall. One such study by Wise and Okey (1983) examined multiple studies which analyzed the influence of experimental teaching methods and techniques in elementary through secondary grade levels. It took a closer look at collaborative and inquiry learning styles on student achievement in science, as compared to traditional strategies such as lecturing. The experimental teaching methods and techniques were categorized into 12 groups. The results of this study showed a mean effect size of 0.34. These results indicated that overall, these experimental methods and techniques showed improvement in student achievement.

A more current meta-analytic study by Schroeder (2007) consisted of sixty-one "U.S. research studies published from 1980 to 2004." The effect sizes of the grouped science instructional techniques were as follows: Questioning Strategies (0.74); Manipulation Strategies (0.57); Enhanced Material Strategies (0.29); Assessment Strategies (0.51); Inquiry Strategies (0.65); Enhanced Context Strategies (1.48); Instructional Technology Strategies (0.48) and Collaborative Learning Strategies (0.95). Detailed descriptions of the top five instructional strategies are provided below.

Enhanced Context Strategies

Enhanced Context strategies are defined as teaching by relating learning to students' previous experiences, knowledge or engaging students' interest through relating learning to the students'/school environment or setting. Examples of this strategy would include using problem-based learning, taking field trips, utilizing the schoolyard for lessons, or encouraging reflection (Schroeder, 2007). This instructional strategy requires the teacher creating lessons in which the students' prior knowledge of the content is built upon, thus activating the schema of the child, so they can relate to the teaching of new or unfamiliar material.

One specific study which analyzed the effectiveness of this strategy on improving upon student achievement, examined the correlation between design-based science and student learning (Fortus, 2004). In this study students were taught three different lessons using a design-based approach in which the artifact created by the students represented the development of their scientific knowledge. For each of these lessons students were asked to apply their learned scientific knowledge to construct models or posters. The results (Effect Size =2.2) of this study indicate that Enhanced Context strategies have a significant impact on science achievement.

Collaborative Learning Strategies

Collaborative Learning strategies are defined as arranging students in flexible groups to work on various tasks. Examples of this strategy would include conducting lab exercises and discussions (Schroeder, 2007). This instructional strategy involves the teacher having students work in small groups to accomplish a goal and learn or practice the content.

A specific study which investigated the effectiveness of this instructional approach examined how levels of cooperation within science lab groups affected science achievement (Chang, 1994). The control groups of this study were taught the content using traditional (non-cooperative) methods while the experimental groups worked collaboratively with each individual assigned a role in the group. Grades from lab reports and quizzes were used in determining the effectiveness of the approach. The results of this study indicated that there was a significant correlation between collaborative work and student achievement ($r=0.46$, $p <$ .05).

Questioning Strategies

Questioning strategies are defined as varying the pacing, cognitive levels of questions, or delivery position. Examples of this instructional approach would be increasing wait time, including higher cognitive-level questions, and posing comprehension questions to students at the start of a lesson or assignment (Schroeder, 2007). This instructional strategy entails the teacher using questions as formative assessments at the beginning of a lesson to determine students' prior knowledge and to activate existing knowledge of the content. Formative assessments build up to the culmination of the material where there is normally a summative type of assessment, such as a chapter or unit test. So this type of questioning could also be formative if it is included at the end of a day's lesson to determine if the topic(s) at hand need to be revisited the next day, or if the material has been learned adequately.

One particular study of this instructional approach looked at the effect of advanced questioning and prior knowledge on science learning (Osman, 2001). In this study, science students were assigned to one of three groups. The control group was taught a basic lesson with introduction (B). There were two experimental groups. The first group was taught the basic lesson plus three orienting questions (B+Q). The second group was taught the basic lesson with three orienting questions and a rationale for the value of the questions (B+Q+R).

Students in the B+Q group answered 56% of post-test questions correct, while students in the B+Q+R group answered 61% of post-test questions correct. Comparing these values to the B group which only answered 46% of post-test questions correct would indicate that the use of Questioning strategies is an effective method to increase science achievement.

Inquiry Strategies

Inquiry strategies can be defined as the use of student-centered instruction that requires less teacher directed step-by-step instruction than the traditional instruction. Examples of this strategy in a science class would be using guided or facilitated inquiry activities or laboratories (Schroeder, 2007). The implementation of this instructional strategy would include the teacher having students design, carry out, and analyze a scientific experiment where students draw their own conclusions. This differs from the conventional method where students are known to follow a set procedure in which the steps and outcomes of the lab are predetermined by the teacher.

A previous study which examined the effectiveness of inquiry strategies in science classrooms analyzed the effect of inquiry-based science in middle grades as a method of reform urban education (Marx, 2004). In this analysis, the authors analyzed student achievement of over 8,000 Detroit-area science students enrolled in Inquiry-based and Technology-infused instruction. Based on pre- and post-test scores, students in these classes showed gains in achievement each year in content knowledge. The average effect size of this instructional strategy for science content over the three year period was 1.1, indicating a significant improvement in science content knowledge.

Manipulation Strategies

Manipulation strategies can be defined as providing students with opportunities to work or practice with physical objects. Examples of this instructional strategy consist of developing skills, using manipulatives or drawing or constructing something (Schroeder, 2007). This strategy would be used in the classroom by a teacher allowing his/her students to practice a concept taught using physical representations of the material; for example, reviewing the components of a cell by building a scale-model of the cell.

One study which investigated the effectiveness of manipulatives in science instruction analyzed the cognitive gains made by students using concrete versus traditional instructional strategies (Saunders, 1987). The students taught using concrete instruction learned the content primarily through "hands-on" lessons which involved gaining knowledge through sensory experiences. In contrast, the traditional group learned primarily through reading, writing, and lecture formats. Results of this study showed that learners from the concrete instructional group performed significantly better on post-tests than learners from the traditional group; with mean achievement scores of 490 and 434, respectively.

Motivation, as previously described, is strongly influenced by students; they are in control of their motivations and make decisions on the level of motivation and effort they are willing to expend. When the students indicate a preference for a specific type(s) of teaching strategy, they are more likely to be motivated. According to research from teachers' perspectives, these teaching strategies are the most effective for motivating students but not necessarily from the students' perspective

Summary

Motivation and engagement are different when it comes to teaching students. Teachers need to know how to motivate and then keep them in engaged. Students can also be motivated intrinsically or extrinsically. Teachers have to ask themselves: Is the individual student motivated through rewards or do they have a natural drive to learn? It is known that teacher and student perspectives differ. Teachers are expected to teach towards standardized tests, thus feeling they lack the sufficient time to implement inventive lessons that students prefer. Students believe their teachers follow the textbook too much and need to incorporate different strategies into their teaching. Based on prior research, the top five strategies that are the most effective in teaching are: Enhanced Context strategies, Collaborative Learning strategies, Questioning strategies, Inquiry strategies and Manipulation strategies. In this research study, the students will have an opportunity to choose the strategies they feel best motivate them to learn in 7th grade Life Science class.

Results

The survey used to gather data consisted of thirteen questions that contained ten instructional strategy statements. Five of them were based on detailed classroom examples of the instructional strategies, and the other five were the definitions of the instructional strategies. Two false negative statements were inserted into the survey to rule out a student(s) that could potentially just be marking down random answers. Then one gender related question was incorporated as well, asking them to circle "1" for female, and "2" for male. Students' responses from the Likert scale were collected with a "1" being Strongly Disagree, "2" Disagree, "3" Agree, and "4" Strongly Agree. After all the data was collected and coded into SPSS it produced information results as to which instructional strategies the students prefer that most effectively increase their motivation to achieve in a Life Science class. The information was further translated to conclude if one gender over another prefer specific instructional strategies.

Analysis of the survey results indicated that students prefer Manipulative Instructional Strategies the most and Questioning Strategies the least. Collaborative Learning Strategies was also a popular strategy with the students. Even though the Questioning Strategies were the least favored by the students, they still encompassed over half mean score.

The analysis showed that the means for student response were 3.62 (s.d. = 0.650); 3.21 (s.d. = 0.914); 3.06 (s.d. = 0.773); 2.88 (s.d. = 0.802); 2.85 (s.d. = 0.951); 2.81 (s.d.=1.032); 2.76 (s.d.=.849); 2.60 (s.d.=.914); 2.52 (s.d.=.929) and 2.50 (s.d.=.899) for Manipulative, Enhanced Context, Collaborative Learning, Questioning and Inquiry Strategies, respectively.

Table 1: Average Mean and Standard Deviation of Instructional Strategies

Instructional Strategies	Mean	SD
I'm excited to understand the material when completing hands-on activities in class, like labs.	3.62	.650
I'm excited to understand the material when I get to work in small groups to complete an assignment	3.	.914
I'm excited to understand the material when my teacher uses examples that relate to my own life or something I already know a lot about.	3.06	.773
I was enthused about learning when we observed the process of diffusion by watching iodine move through a membrane to change the color of starch.	2.88	.802
I'm excited to understand the material when participating in activities to generate my own questions and investigations.	2.85	.951
It helps me learn when teachers ask me different types of questions during class to check for my understanding.	2.81	1.032
I was enthused to learn when we were comparing the cell to a factory to learn about the different cell parts and how they work together.	2.76	.849
I was excited to learn when we worked together to complete a PowerPoint presentation on the stages of cell division.	2.60	.914
I was enthused to learn about the different types of cells, observing pictures of them, and trying to identify their characteristics.	2.52	.929
It helps me understand the Life Science material if teachers ask me questions at the end of class about what I just learned, like an exit pass.	2.50	.899
I'm not excited to learn when we are asked to work in groups.	1.52	.867
I am not excited to learn when we are asked to complete hands on activities.	1.45	.739

Our research question examined which instructional strategies do Life Science students feel is most effective at increasing their motivation to achieve. We used a descriptive statistics analysis of the students' survey responses to determine the mean value for their opinion of each instructional strategy. Table 1 shows the mean values of the students' responses. The results showed that students, overall, feel instructional strategies using manipulatives motivates them the most to achieve (Mean=3.62). However, students felt Questioning Strategies motivated them the least to achieve (Mean=2.50). The mean values for the Enhanced Content Strategies are 3.06 and 2.76, Inquiry Strategies are 2.85 and 2.52, and Collaborative Learning Strategies are 3.21 and 2.60. The reasoning behind the two different mean scores is due to the fact that on the survey the students had to respond to a statement that was the definition for the strategy and another question that was a specific example of the strategy that they would experience within the classroom.

Among the students that were surveyed, there was not a significant difference in average mean between males and females. A Paired Samples T-Test was conducted to compare means for each of the instructional strategies based on gender. The results of this test are presented in Table 2. There was not a significant difference between males and females for any of the instructional strategies ($p < 0.05$).

Table 2: Paired Samples t Test for Instructional Strategies by Gender

Instructional Strategies	t	df	sig. (2-tailed)
Enhanced Content Definition	-19.95	108	.000
Enhanced Content Example	-13.78	108	.000
Collaborative Content Definition	-10.81	108	.000
Collaborative Content Example	-16.84	108	.000
Questioning Content Definition	-11.80	108	.000
Questioning Content Example	-11.19	108	.000
False Negative	-.297	108	.767
Manipulation Content Definition	-30.27	108	.000
Manipulation Content Example	-17.03	108	.000
False Negative (2)	.506	108	.614
Inquiry Content Definition	-10.49	108	.000
Inquiry Content Example	-13.73	108	.000

Discussion

Previous research states that a critical problem we encounter in the education field is that adolescent students of today are generally described as bored, disengaged, or unmotivated (Ainley, 2004). There is ample research that claims to have the most effective teaching strategies narrowed to Enhanced Context, Collaborative Learning, Questioning, Inquiry, and Manipulation (Schroeder, 2007). The student participants of this study, from a Midwestern urban middle school named Kingsley Junior High, strongly agreed that manipulatives motivate them to learn and keep them engaged in the curriculum. The statement is based from our data findings which revealed the majority of the students surveyed believed this was true for them. Similar findings in a previous study by Saunders (1987) explained that students learning given the "hands-on" approach made gains in their scores when compared to students who were taught with the traditional instructional style.

Students in this research study survey were given one particular example of a hands-on lab conducted thus far in the school year, and were also asked to mark whether they agreed or disagreed that the Manipulation strategy definition motivated them as well. The results, Manipulation Strategy being the top motivational strategy chosen by males and females, remains consistent with what the teacher/researcher observes in the classroom. The students are very excitable during lab days when they enter the room and notice supplies set up and procedures listed on the board and sheet on their lab table. Most of the time, they are ready to dive straight into the exploration of the lab and are anxious when given scaffolded instructions.

As mentioned in the Literature Review, prior research claims that the five motivational strategies we used in our study were considered the most influential motivation strategies based from the perspectives of teachers. They confirmed that each of these strategies were equally as important. In correlation with our own research, even though the Questioning strategies were the students' least favorite, it still encompassed over half our mean score; summarizing that there was not a critically impactful difference in the mean of the Manipulation and Questioning strategy.

Nevertheless, the findings suggested that the students were least motivated by the Questioning strategy. This technique involves teachers varying timing, positioning, or cognitive level questions as formative assessments along the way (Schroeder, 2007). The teacher/researcher notes that even the students identified as "gifted" struggle with higher-level-thinking and reasoning; this would then almost be apparent that the lower kids definitely struggle with this type of teaching method. When students dislike or are uninterested, whether it be because they are confused or struggling, they will surely not be motivated to learn the content (Stanley, 2003).

Conclusion & Implications

The science classroom is a dynamic setting in which many factors can effect student achievement. By examining which of five instructional strategies students feel has the greatest impact on their achievement; this study hopes to reveal the role instructional strategies play in student motivation and achievement in science class.

After conducting our research we found that students feel instructional strategies which use manipulatives motivate them the most to achieve in science class. Student responses also indicate that questioning strategies motivate the students to achieve the least. The students' responses seemed to vary with the remaining instructional strategies: Enhanced Context, Inquiry, and Collaborative Learning. These results indicate that students felt they are most motivated to achieve in a science class where learning is taking place using hands-on activities and manipulatives.

The results of this study could have been affected by a number of limitations. First, while student achievement is effected by their motivation, a number of factors undoubtedly play a role in their achievement. Specifically, parental involvement, socioeconomic status, attendance, peer-social aspect, and amount of time spent participating in extracurricular activities as well as many other factors certainly effect student achievement. Although this study demonstrates that students feel certain instructional strategies motivate them differently to achieve; because other factors play a role in student achievement, it is not possible to conclude how much of an effect instructional strategy choice has solely on student achievement.

Another limitation of this study was the sample size. There are 324 seventh grade students at Kingsley Junior High School that are enrolled in Life Science Classes. This study surveyed 109 of these students, roughly one-third of the population. This relatively small sample size limits the generalizations that can be drawn from the results.

A final limitation of this study in relation to the sampling was an error in the survey presented to the students. The survey ran over onto a second sheet of paper and it was given using both sides of the paper, front and back. The Likert scale descriptions {Strongly Disagree, Disagree, Agree, Strongly Agree} were not at the top of the second sheet of the survey. As a result, some students had to keep flipping back to page one to see the Likert scale or some students tried to memorize the scale to answer the second page of the survey. Since the layout of the survey was flawed, it is possible that some of the students memorizing the order of the Likert scale may have remembered a (1) being "Strongly Agree" instead of "Strongly Disagree". To summarize, the data collected for the second page of questions may have been skewed if the students did not refer back to the Likert scale on page one of the survey.

The results of this study indicate that students feel instructional strategies motivate them differently to achieve in science class. This is significant to science teachers who may take this information into consideration when designing and planning science lessons. Inclusion of the more effective strategies in their instruction may help teachers keep their students motivated and increase achievement. Administrators can also provide professional development opportunities to their teachers which teach them about these strategies and how to use them effectively.

Based on the limitations of this study individuals interested in researching this topic should focus their research on how much of an effect student motivation has on their achievement. Comparing the effect of motivation to other factors such as parental involvement and attendance could, in turn, guide additional research. Future research could also differentiate between motivation and engagement. This study treated the terms synonymously; however as previous studies have indicated, there is a difference between the two. Thus, additional research could also be conducted to determine if these instructional strategies have the same effect on engagement as this study found them to have on motivation.

References

Ainley, M. (2004). What do we know about student motivation and engagement? Australian Association for Research in Education, Melbourne.

American Association for the Advancement of Science. (1993). Benchmarks for science literacy. New York: Oxford University Press

Baines, L. A., & Stanley, G. K. (2003). Disengagement and Loathing in High School. Educational Horizons. 81(4), 165-68.

Chang. (1994). The effects of levels of cooperation within physical science laboratory groups on physical science achievement. Journal of Research in Science Teaching, 31(2), 167.

Cheung, D. (2009). The Adverse Effects of Le Chatelier's Principle on Teacher Understanding of Chemical Equilibrium. Journal of Chemical Education, 86(4), 514-518.

Ediger, M. (2001). Assessment and High Stakes Testing. Access ERIC: FullText (ED4492340)

Fink, Arlene. (2003). The Survey Handbook 2nd edition. California: Sage Publications, Inc.

Fortus. (2004). Design-based science and student learning. Journal of Research in Science Teaching, 41(10), 1081.

Fraenkel, Jack & Wallen, Norman. (2008). How to Design and Evaluate Research in Education 7th edition. New York: McGraw Hill.

Harris, L. R. (2008). A Phenomenographic Investigation of Teacher Conceptions of Student Engagement in Learning. Australian Educational Researcher. 35(1), 57-79.

Haywood, J., Kuespert, S., Madecky, D., & Nor, A. (2008). Increasing elementary and high school student motivation through the use of extrinsic and intrinsic rewards access ERIC: FullText.

Marx. (2004). Inquiry-based science in the middle grades: Assessment of learning in urban systemic reform. Journal of Research in Science Teaching, 41(10), 1063.

Moberly, D. A., Waddle, J. L., & Duff, R. E. (2005). The use of rewards and punishment in early childhood classrooms. Journal of Early Childhood Teacher Education, 25(4), 359.

National Center for Education Statistics. (2004). Comparing NAEP, TIMSS, and PISA in mathematics and science. Retrieved October 11, 2009, from http://nces.ed.gov/timss/pdf/naep_timss_pisa_comp.pdf

National Center for Education Statistics. (2005). Science: The nation's report card. Retrieved October 11, 2009, from http://nces.ed.gov/nationsreportcard/science/

National Commission on Excellence in Education. (1983). A nation at risk. Retrieved October 11, 2009, from http://www.ed.gov/pubs/NatAtRisk/recomm.html

National Research Council. (1996). National science education standards. Washington, DC: National Academy Press

Niemiec, C. (2009). Autonomy, competence, and relatedness in the classroom: Applying self-determination theory to educational practice. Theory and Research in Education, 7(2), 133.

Osborne. (2003). What "ideas-about-science" should be taught in school science? A delphi study of the expert community. Journal of Research in Science Teaching, 40(7), 692.

Osman. (1994). Effects of advance questioning and prior knowledge on science learning. The Journal of Educational Research, 88(1), 5.

Reid, N. (2008). A scientific approach to the teaching of chemistry. Chemistry Education Research and Practice, 9, 51. doi:10.1039/b801297k

Reid, N. (2008). A scientific approach to the teaching of chemistry. Chemistry Education Research and Practice, 9, 51.

Reynolds, J. (2006). Learning-Centered Learning: A Mindset Shift for Educators. Inquiry. 11(1), 55-64. Sanacore, J. (2008). Turning Reluctant Learners into Inspired Learners. Clearing House, 82(1), 40-44.

Saunders. (1987). A comparison of concrete and formal science instruction upon science achievement and reasoning ability of sixth grade students. Journal of Research in Science Teaching, 24(1), 39.

Schroeder. (2007). A meta-analysis of national research: Effects of teaching strategies on student achievement in science in the united states. Journal of Research in Science Teaching, 44(10), 1436.

Schussler, D. L. (2009). Beyond content: How teachers manage classrooms to facilitate intellectual engagement for disengaged students. Theory into Practice, 48(2), 114.

Scott, P., Asoko, H., & Leach, J. (2007). Student conceptions and conceptual learning in science. In S. K. Abell, & N. G. Lederman (Eds.), Handbook of Research on Science Education (pp. 31). Mahwah, New Jersey: Lawrence Erlbaum Associates, Inc. Publishers.

Singh. (2002). Mathematics and science achievement: Effects of motivation, interest, and academic engagement. The Journal of Educational Research, 95(6), 323.

Skinner. (1993). Motivation in the classroom: Reciprocal effects of teacher behavior and student

Winn, S., Harley, D., Wilcox, P., & Pemberton, S. (2007). Reconceptualizing student motivation: Accounting for the social context beyond the classroom

Wise, K.C., & Okey J.R. (1983). A meta-analysis of the effects of various science teaching strategies on achievement. Journal of Research in Science Teaching, 20, 419.

Witzel, B. S., & Mercer, C. D. (2003). Using rewards to teach students with disabilities. Remedial & Special Education, 24(2), 88.

Chapter 9: Instructional Practices for Teaching Writing

Betsy Cease, Jean Glick, Kristy Karmenzind & Cara Norris

The Problem and Its Background

Over the years teachers have seen the frowns and heard the groans of their students when they announce it is time for writing. For some students, writing is a time of frustration as they stare at their papers and have no idea where to begin. Others know how to start their writing, but not how to organize it. In addition, students often balk when it comes to editing what they have written. Many students come into the classroom lacking life experiences and print-rich environments in their homes which makes the writing process even more difficult. Students who struggle with writing may also be poor readers, their confidence may be low, and their vocabulary might be lacking with vivid words.

Teachers understand the importance of having their students practice writing every single day. However, many of them often struggle to teach writing in a way so that students don't get burnt out or bored. With state and federal mandates from No Child Left Behind on mathematics and literacy, many teachers have chosen to focus on the reading aspect of literacy and the teaching of writing has been pushed aside. However, many teachers are rediscovering the importance of including writing in fostering a literate classroom environment. There are many different instructional practices when it comes to teaching writing. The researchers have decided to focus on two specific writing practices that may impact student motivation.

In this study, two classrooms that have students participating in the Six Trait writing program will be compared with two classrooms participating in the Lucy Calkins writer's workshop program. Information regarding the students' motivation towards writing will be gathered in each classroom. This study is important because it will give insight as to whether or not the type of writing program used in the classroom affects students' motivation toward writing. If teachers are able to find a writing program that will increase student motivation towards writing, it is likely that students will want to write more often. Just like the well-known phrase, "Practice makes perfect," students will become better writers the more they write.

Rationale for the Study

Despite the existence of many writing programs, few studies have been conducted to compare the Six Trait writing approach and the Lucy Calkins Writer's Workshop model in increasing student motivation. Observations have shown that student motivation directly impacts the classroom. Students who are not motivated tend to be off task and often are the cause of behavioral distractions for others. If these distractions are taking place, the amount of time students are independently writing and practicing writing skills is severely decreased.

Literature Review

Exploring Teacher Instruction

"The art of teaching is the art of continuing to learn. Teachers are the most important learners in the classroom" (Write Traits 6-Trait Instruction and Assessment Professional Development Research Base, 2009). This quote suggests that teachers must continually learn even while they are in charge of instructing students. But what happens when teachers notice a lack of motivation and achievement in their students, specifically in the area of writing? Does their instruction influence student achievement and motivation? Instruction is one of the most important factors influencing students. Often teachers feel frustrated with the quality of student writing they collect and wonder why their students aren't better writers. Sometimes they attribute this to the lack of student motivation and other times they do much self-reflection and realize the type of instruction they offer their students may also influence both the motivation and quality of writing students produce.

One thing that cannot be argued is the importance of writing ability in regards to students' academic success. This is why it is so important for teachers to figure out what exactly motivates students to perform in writing (Lam & Law, 2007). Often, motivating students to write begins with the instructional practices that a teacher uses. However, there are many times when teachers do not feel prepared to teach writing and do not know what best teaching practices to use.

Six instructional components that have been linked to increasing student motivation in writing are "challenge, real-life significance, curiosity, autonomy, recognition, and evaluation" (Lam & Law, 2007 p. 146). The Teachers College Reading and Writing Project (TCRWP) uses *Units of Study for Teaching Writing, Grades 3-5* by Lucy Calkins as a sample writing curriculum for educators in order to teach them how to incorporate these components into their classroom. These units of study teach students to write using several traits that are found in good writing. They are centered around a combination of direct instruction, guided practice, and independent practice (Teachers College Reading and Writing Project at Columbia University Research Base, 2009). Students will not put a lot of effort into a task when they know they will not have a very high chance of being successful. In the same way, students will not put much effort into something that is too easy because these tasks have little value and no sense of pride comes from such work (Lam & Law, 2007). TCRWP is teaching educators how to support students through direct instruction, guided practice, and independent practice so that students' writing is challenging and engaging, but not overwhelming (Teachers College Reading and Writing Project at Columbia University Research Base, 2009).

The scaffolding that is offered also brings students to gain a sense of autonomy. Teachers first teach students a certain strategy through a mini lesson. Then students are given an opportunity to practice the strategy in front of the teacher or with a writing partner. Eventually, the students get to a point where they take ownership of the strategy and use it often during independent practice. The teacher teaches the students to be their own captains of their writing and make their own decisions about what to do next. (Teachers College Reading and Writing Project at Columbia University Research Base, 2009). Such an experience also increases students' self-efficacy because the teacher is providing scaffolding so that students can move from easy to increasingly harder tasks. Students who have higher self-efficacy will not give up as easily during writing tasks. Intrinsic motivation is also increased when students have the opportunity to make choices and control their own results (Lam & Law 2007).

Throughout the *Units of Study* developed by TCRWP, students are taught how to generate ideas and then choose some of those ideas to develop even further into published pieces. This program is very motivating because students are given opportunities to come up with their topics and write about things that matter to them. Teachers using this program are taught how to use this real-life significance component in writing instruction (Teachers College Reading and Writing Project at Columbia University Research Base, 2009). This lets students see the meaning in what they are doing instead of leaving them wondering why they have to write about a certain topic (Lam & Law, 2007). The examples of mini lessons that teachers are given, also show how to teach in a way that sparks students' curiosity. Students become eager to know how to make their writing better (Teachers College Reading and Writing Project at Columbia University Research Base, 2009).

Finally, the *Units of Study* show teachers how to use the recognition and evaluation component as well. Students who are praised for effort and who realize that their success was due to this effort, are more motivated to engage in more grueling tasks in the future (Lam & Lam, 2007). The *Units of Study* show teachers how to celebrate the students' work at the end of a unit. Also, teachers are taught how to conference with students and give them feedback about their work. Teachers are shown how to compliment students and then give them tips about how to improve their writing. Students can also discuss their writing with their writing partners and get feedback. Peer modeling and feedback given by peers can help students develop their "self-perceptions of competence" (Pajares, 2003, p.140). Students feel like they can accomplish good writing after hearing valuable feedback from others. When evaluation is given without feedback, as is sometimes done in traditional programs, students tend to focus on just getting a good grade rather than how to improve (Lam & Law, 2007). Teachers are taught how to give specific feedback in the *Units of Study*. They specifically tell the students what they want him or her to do during a writing conference. In this way, students improve their writing without having to guess why they got points deducted or what the teacher wants them to do (Teachers College Reading and Writing Project at Columbia University Research Base, 2009).

The TCRWP program is one way that prepares teachers to use instruction that helps motivate students to write. Teachers learn to teach writing in a way that produces confident writers. When students are confident in their writing abilities, their motivation to write increases as well (Pajares, 2003).

Student Motivation

Student motivation is effected by many different factors. It can be driven by students or by the instructor. If the instructor has control over the class of students, he or she has an important job to do by setting a positive environment for learning to take place. One result of a positive classroom environment is motivation. The teacher can set the stage for student motivation by allowing the students to take ownership in the classroom and with their own learning.

There are different types of motivation. Extrinsic motivation is when students are working toward a goal not associated with the task. Two examples of extrinsic motivation are a student receiving a piece of candy for turning in their homework or giving a student verbal praise. Another type of motivation is intrinsic motivation. Intrinsic motivation is when a student works toward a goal because it interests them or they find meaning in doing the activity. Students become intrinsically motivated when they see how the outcome of the assignment or activity is going to benefit them or others around them.

There are countless ways that students can be intrinsically motivated. One way is giving students choices in the classroom. Students who were given the choice of setting their own groups for collaborative assignment showed greater intrinsic motivation. These students also felt a greater sense of classroom community (Ciani, Summers, Easter, & Sheldon 2008). When students feel a sense of community or belonging in the classroom they are more willing to let other people know about them. This is very important when students are sharing their writing with peers. Students also feel motivated when they have the ability to choose their own writing prompts (Johnson, 2004). Students want to have the ability to write about what they know about. When students have background knowledge on the topic they are writing about, it gives them a little bit of confidence they may not have otherwise had.

It is important for a teacher to have a balanced approach to motivating students (Sanacore, 2008). Even though we want our students to be intrinsically motivated we still need to give them some praise. Students who are doing the work because they want to learn still enjoy and thrive on that recognition. Some of our students do not come to us intrinsically motivated to learn. As educators we have to do some work to see what it will take to motivate that student. Some students will not be motivated by the material being taught; the educator may have to start with extrinsic motivators and as the students are becoming successful start to reduce them.

When teachers are working to intrinsically motivate students, it is important to give them genuine experiences. If students have a real reason to write, they will then see the importance of producing quality work. Giving students this opportunity is crucial to a worthwhile writing program (Wilson, 2008). Students know when they are being asked to do busy work and they do not enjoy doing it. If they see a real reason to write or see what is in it for them they are more apt to engage in the activity. Students want more than a grade from what they are doing, they want to be able to see an end product that they can be proud of.

Students' motivation is crucial to a meaningful educational experience. If they are not motivated to learn the learning will be superficial and short term. Students who are intrinsically motivated will take their learning to heart and will continue to use their knowledge. These behaviors contribute to the students keeping the information long term.

Six Trait Writing

In the early 1980's, some educators in the northwestern United States felt they needed to have a common set of guidelines for use in the teaching of writing. Student writing was compared across several states and the samples collected showed that there were certain characteristics lacking. By studying successful student writing samples, there were qualities found that helped develop the Six Trait Writing model. This model teaches writing as a process and allows students to focus on one element of writing at a time. This method breaks the task of learning to write effectively into small manageable chunks. Elements such as Ideas and Content, Word Choice, Fluency, Voice, Organization and Conventions are taught each week for six weeks and

> help students take charge of their own writing process: understand the difference between strong and weak writing-and use that knowledge to write stronger drafts; and revise and edit their own writing because they can 'read' it and know what to do to make it better. (Write Traits 6-Trait Instruction and Assessment Professional Development Research Base, 2009, p.2)

Using this kind of common language benefits both teachers and students as they work on improving writing. Students who can take charge of their own writing process and feel confident as they write are more motivated to work on their writing.

Writing Workshop Model

The Writing Workshop model also offers an interactive approach to teaching writing in which students can learn and practice the importance of rehearsal, drafting/re- vising, and editing their own work (Jasmine & Weiner, 2007). Through the context of their own writing, children are able to select topics of their own interest, write for authentic audiences, and still learn the conventions and mechanics of writing. In order to maximize student motivation, there are three conditions that follow in a workshop:

- A predictable structure: a whole-group discussion or demonstration at the start of each workshop, followed by quiet time for independent writing and conferring with the teacher and peers
- A regular schedule for writing
- Student discretion about topic, process, pace, approach, and audience

The last condition is the prime motivator for students in the writer's workshop (Atwell, 2003).

In the past, writing was not taught as much as it was assigned for students to do. The final product was emphasized, not the process. Many times this approach stifled the creativity of children and many lost motivation to write. The writing process approach, first developed by Graves in 1983, focused on instruction, which allowed teachers to help students brainstorm ideas, solicit feedback, revise their work , then edit and proofread the final product before publishing. (Jasmine & Weiner, 2007). The Writing Workshop Classroom is also built on the foundations of using quality children's literature to help provide students with the ability to make connections to their own lives and to imitate a favorite author's style into their own writing. Lucy Calkins, an instructor of the Teacher's College Reading and Writing Project in New York, extended the concept of this kind of writing to include a more student centered approach that included extensive modeling by the teacher in whole group mini lessons, peer conferencing, time for students to work on their own writings, and sharing and celebrating throughout the publishing process (Jasmine & Weiner, 2007). By involving students throughout the whole writing process, they are given much time to consider, revise, and reread what they had written.

Writers thrive when they're motivated to work hard, have regular opportunities to practice and reflect, and benefit from the knowledge and experience of a teacher who writes and knows about writing. The Writing Workshop model suggests using mini lessons that are tailored to teacher observations of student needs. These short, focused lessons help students who are ready to process the information and apply it to their own writing. A good mini lesson is inspiring, practical, relevant, and conversational. Effective Writer's Workshop mini lessons can fit into four categories: lessons about gathering and developing topics, lessons about drafting and revising principles, lessons about different genres, and lessons about conventions (Atwell, 2003).

As students are engaged in various steps of writing, the teacher observes and confers with students on an individual basis. The responder's role is to listen, tell back, and ask questions to help the writers discover meaning and build on what they know and have written. Students must also be encouraged to take an active role during conferencing because writers know more than what appears on the page they draft. After a question is asked, the force of listening helps draw words out of the writer and they will find themselves saying things they did not know they knew (Jasmine & Weiner, 2007). As Atwell describes it, "conferences are occasions for the writing teacher to uncover kids' intentions, problems, and plans, and to demonstrate hands-on approaches and solutions." (2003) Using common language that all students know, understand, and can apply is necessary to expedite conferences between students and teachers and make them more effective.

It is interesting to note that the Six Trait Writing process is used during the conferencing section of the Writer's Workshop model. This mentions that using the common language of ideas, voice, word choice, etc. is necessary to expedite conferences between students and teachers and make them more effective. Using these traits with a rubric helps make expectations clear and allows the students specific goals to master. By combining these two models during the Writer's

Workshop, it suggests that student motivation and improvement in writing may be achieved by both of these models and that they are not a separate entity.

Although a few studies have examined factors that influence student motivation and achievement in writing, an individual's personal judgment of his or her ability to reach a set goal, also plays a large part in the attainment of self-regulation (Helsel & Greenberg, 2007). Self-regulation refers to self-generated thoughts, feelings, and actions that individuals use to help themselves attain personal goals (Helsel & Greenberg, 2007). Students who are able to self-regulate are usually more motivated to set goals, and manage time effectively. "This self-regulation supports one of the aspects of writer's workshop that I personally believe helps fuel students' love of writing most is the flexibility that the schedule allows" (Helsel & Greenberg, 2007, p. 758)

Summary

There are several studies that have examined various aspects of instruction for writing, and many materials on student motivation. However the question remains for educators; how can teachers encourage their students to become a community of writers who are motivated to write and share their writing? The research suggests that as students become more familiar and comfortable with their writing, they begin to take ownership in the whole writing process and feel good about their writing. To achieve the ultimate goal of intrinsic motivation, students must first take ownership of their writing.. The focus of this research is to discover what method of instruction best encourages student motivation. This study gives serious consideration to two main methods of teaching writing and the effects they have on student motivation.

Methodology

Research questions

Is there a difference between teaching writing using the writing workshop method and teaching students how to write using the Six Trait Writing Model? Does one of these models lend itself to motivating students to write? These central questions were the focus of the study. The researchers were looking for ways to improve writing instruction by continuing to help motivate students. Current trend data indicates that there will be a difference between how motivated students are, based on the model of writing they were taught.

Participants

This study will be conducted in midsize school district in Illinois. The population of this city is 33,857. The participants were selected from an intermediate school which includes 657 fourth, fifth, and sixth grade students.

According to the school report card for 2008-2009 our school population was 657. The racial/ethnic background includes 94% White, 0.6% African American, 0.6% Hispanic, 1.2% Asian/Pacific Islander, 1.1% Native American and 2.1% Multi-racial. The low-income rate of the student body is 51%. There is a limited

English proficiency rate of 0.5%. The mobility rate is at 11.5% and the attendance rate is 94.7%.

The participants in this study include 44 students from two fourth grade classrooms and 47 students from two fifth grade classrooms. These 91 students are enrolled in the researchers' classrooms. All four classrooms are self-contained and have a wide range of abilities. Academic abilities range from low first grade to high sixth grade. One student in the group is visually impaired, while 14 students have an Individualized Education Plan (IEP). There are 42 girls involved in this study and 39 boys. From the sample, 53% of the students receive free or reduced lunches. Ninety-six percent of the sample is white/non-Hispanic, leaving the other 4% consisting of Hispanic, multi-racial, and American Indian/Alaskan.

The students used in this study were chosen from the researchers' classrooms. All students had the option to have their data used in this study by signing an assent form. All students received the same classroom instruction.

The teaching experience of the researchers ranges from teaching 20 years to five years, with an average of 9 years of experience.

Instrumentation

In this study, an enthusiasm chart which is similar to a scatter plot was created as a simple, quick, yet effective method of measuring students' thoughts and feelings about their writing instruction. The chart was given monthly with a baseline chart started in September. Data was collected at the same time each month and the results were compiled on one enthusiasm chart. The enthusiasm chart was designed as a tool that students could use to share their thoughts and feelings about writing. Scatter plots are used to provide a visual understanding of how two variables are related (Lane, 2007). This tool was chosen to see the correlation between students' motivation to write compared to the writing instruction. The data from the two writing programs was then compared to determine whether students were more motivated by one type of writing instruction over the other.

The enthusiasm chart was set up similar to a scatter plot. The classes that received Writer's Workshop instruction were given an enthusiasm chart with writing [in general] on the y axis and Writer's Workshop on the x axis. The y axis was labeled "I don't like to write," "Writing is OK," and "I love to write." The x axis was labeled "Writer's Workshop is awful," "Writer's workshop is the same [as what I've done before]" and "Writer's workshop is awesome." The classrooms that received the Six Trait writing were given an enthusiasm chart that was exactly the same except the Writer's Workshop label was changed to Six Trait Writing. Students marked their papers using both the *x* and *y* axis according to how they felt about writing in general and that model specifically. The data for each writing program was compiled. The researchers totaled the number of students that marked each category on the enthusiasm charts, and then divided that number by the total number of students involved in the program. This number was then multiplied by 100 to get the percent of students who marked each category on the chart.

The reliability of the instrument remained the same each month and it was given by the same classroom teacher. Students were not influenced in any way, but just instructed to mark their charts and turn them in. Teachers were careful to not give any bias toward either model but instead administered this chart in the same manner each month. The only materials used were the enthusiasm chart and pencils to mark their papers.

Chart one: Enthusiasm Chart for Six Trait Writing

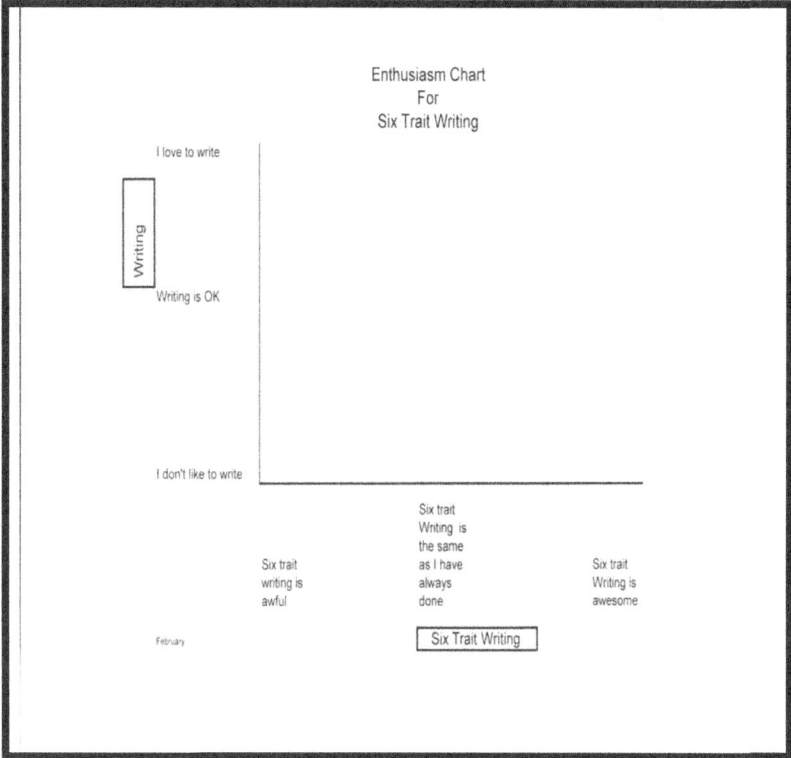

Enthusiasm Chart
For
Six Trait Writing

I love to write

Writing

Writing is OK

I don't like to write

Six trait
Writing is
the same
as I have
always
done

Six trait
writing is
awful

Six trait
Writing is
awesome

February

Six Trait Writing

Chart two: Enthusiasm Chart for Writer's Workshop

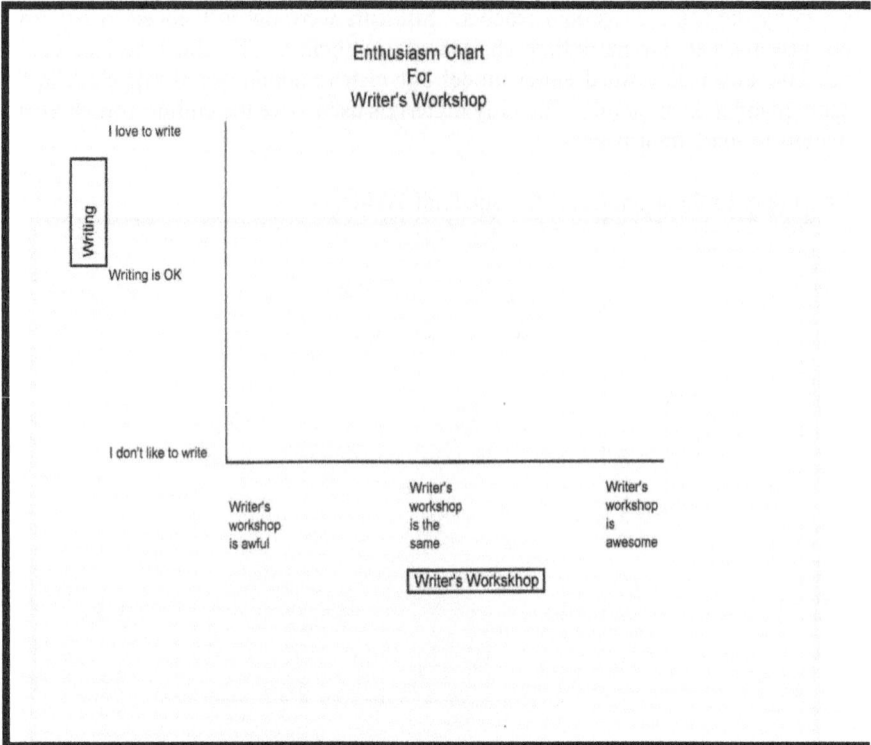

Enthusiasm Chart
For
Writer's Workshop

Results

Each month the researchers collected data using the enthusiasm chart. The student data from the fourth and fifth grade classrooms using the writer's workshop program was combined as was the data from the fourth and fifth grade classrooms using the Six Trait writing program. The researchers counted the number of students that responded in a particular category and divided that by the number of students who completed the enthusiasm chart. This gave a percentage to represent each variable. The variables are students' feelings about themselves as writers, students' feelings towards writer's workshop, and students' feeling towards Six Trait writing. Once the results were attained, the researchers were able to look at the percentages and compare the variables to see what correlations surfaced.

After obtaining percentages from the enthusiasm chart, the researchers input the data into an Excel worksheet to compile the averages for each variable. The table created was then turned into a bar graph to visually compare categories for correlation and trends. By looking at the bar graph and then concentrating on the averages for each category, several discoveries were made. When looking at the categories in Writer's Workshop, the percentage of students who thought it was awesome was the highest at 58%. Even though 13% of students in the Writer's Workshop setting did not like to write, only about 7% thought the program was awful. The percentages were similar between students who thought writing was OK (35%) and students who thought Writer's Workshop was the same as what they've had in the past (36%) (Figure 1).

Figure 1: The percentages of comparing students' motivation using Writer's workshop and 6 Traits writing program

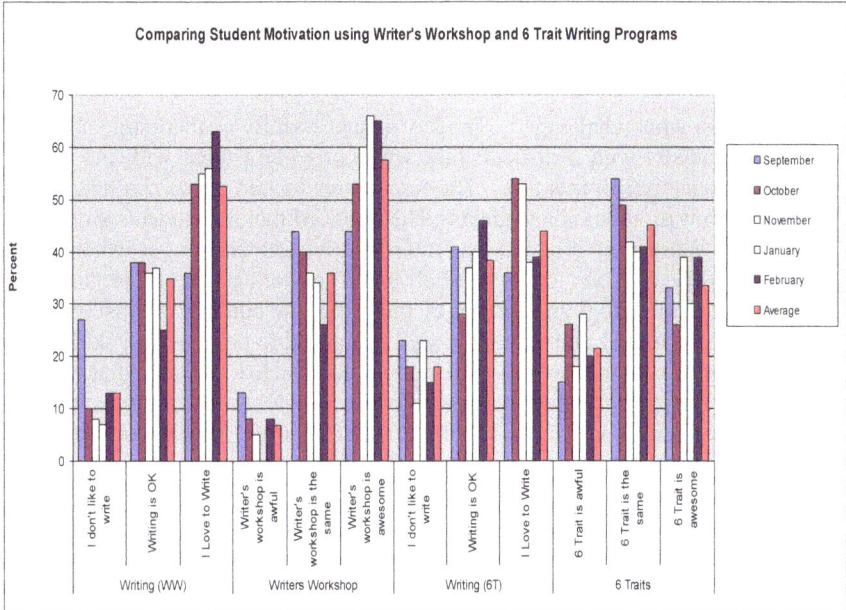

These numbers are a statistical representation that correlates with what the researchers saw in the behavior of the students in the Writer's Workshop program. Due to certain aspects of the program researchers found that these numbers also reflect the research that was done on this program.

When looking at the categories associated with the Six-Trait Writing program, the percentage of students who thought it was awesome was 33% which was lower than the 44% of students who loved to write. Eighteen percent of the students involved in this program did not like to write and 21% of students thought the program was awful. Overall, the largest percent of students (45%) fell into the category of thinking the Six-Trait writing program was just OK.

There were a higher percentage of students who loved to write in the Writer's Workshop setting compared to the students in a Six-Trait Writing setting. Similarly, there were a higher percentage of students who thought Writer's Workshop was awesome compared to the number of students who thought Six-Trait Writing was awesome. The difference between these two groups was about 24%. The percent of students that thought Six-Trait Writing was awesome was not the highest. Instead more students thought it was ok rather than awesome. On average, 15% more students thought the Six-Trait writing was awful compared to the students in Writer's Workshop.

Discussion

Six instructional components have been linked to increasing student motivation in writing: "challenge, real-life significance, curiosity, autonomy, recognition, and evaluation" (Lam & Law, 2007 p. 146). By using these six components, we can begin to discuss the reasons why the data showed us that Writer's Workshop is more motivating.

Challenge

Students thrive when challenged. The key to successfully challenging students is to provide students with a difficult task while providing them with the support they need to accomplish this task. The researchers looked at the challenges each writing program provided the students. They noticed that the students working in the Writer's Workshop program had more individual challenges whereas the students working with Six Traits were all asked to work on the same task. The Writer's Workshop program challenges the writer to outgrow themselves as a writer. The class would all be taught a skill and asked to practice that skill. When the teacher had a conference with each student, the teacher decided what teaching point would benefit that student most. While every student in the class was working within the same genre of writing, the skills each student practiced were differentiated according to need. They challenged students who had met the whole class objective to extend their writing in new ways. Students who were struggling to meet the whole class objective had the larger objective broken down into more manageable pieces during their conferences to help them be successful. The teachers helped support the students with this by giving the students their own "tool boxes". This was just a list of ways the writer could take their writing beyond where it was.

The students participating in the Six Trait writing program were all asked to focus on the same task. One concept was focused on for a period of time and if the student had mastered that concept they were not pushed beyond that point. Since the researchers found that providing challenging writing experiences was a motivator, the fact that fewer students were excited about the Six Traits program suggests that the lack of individualization in this program leads to less motivation.

Real - Life Significance

Throughout the Writer's Workshop program, students are asked to look at the world from a new perspective and find topics in their own life experiences to write about. Considering students were writing about their personal experiences, they were able to stay focused on writing for an extended period and took ownership of their writing pieces. Students also studied mentor texts which provided them with real life models to influence their craft. Students seemed more motivated to create something that another author was successful at publishing. Also in this program, students are taught to realize that not everything they write is publishable, but they can always go back and look at previous writing to change it or make it better at a later time. Just like real authors, students come to realize that writing takes time.

In the Six Trait writing program, students were usually given prompts to start off their writing. As they developed their piece, they brought in their own experiences to personalize their writing. Mentor texts were also used to model writing traits for the students. However, the link between the process that real life authors go through to write and the writing that the students did in class was not conveyed to the writers in this program.

Both programs encouraged students to write for authentic audiences. The fact that students knew someone would eventually be reading their writing kept them motivated and focused to improve their writing. In the Writers Workshop program, students shared their writing through the celebration process. Writers in the Six Trait program wrote to pen pals and sent letters to their favorite restaurants. Overall, both programs had the real-life significance component which is why both programs showed over 30 percent of the student involved thought the programs were awesome.

Curiosity

According to Lam & Law (2007), curiosity is another important component when it comes to choosing instructional tasks that motivate students. Tapping into students' curiosity "usually involves novelty, surprise, and uncertainty" (Lam & Law, 2007, p. 147). The results of this study show that more students thought the Writer's Workshop setting was awesome than did students in the Six-Trait setting. It seems that the curiosity component of the tasks in each of these programs might have contributed to these results.

In the Writer's Workshop program, students were specifically asked to revise their writing and to try writing various sections in several different ways. For example, students wrote three leads to their stories, one focusing on setting, one focusing on a small action, and one focusing on mood. Often students were not used to doing this. Prior to this program, they would write something and make very few changes---maybe change a word here, add a period there. The Writer's Workshop setting required them to look at their writing with a new lens and make major changes in order for them to outgrow themselves as writers. This task was both new and uncertain for many of the students, thus sparking their curiosity.

While the 6-Trait writing program did not discourage revising, the challenge of revision was not as explicit in this program as it was in Writer's Workshop. Students may have been encouraged to reread their work and edit it, but were not specifically told to try different parts of the writing in several different ways. The novelty and surprise of this was lacking which may have decreased the students' curiosity in the writing tasks altogether.

Students involved in the Writer's workshop program were also provided with many mentor texts and were told to write just like the authors of these books. The teachers taught the students that good writers look at the work of other authors to see if the authors used any strategies that they could apply to their own work. This idea of writing just like the authors of their favorite books also sparked the curiosity of the students. They were eager to search through picture books and other compositions to see what they could apply to their own writing.

Mentor texts were also used in the Six-Trait writing program. The teachers read books to students to show them good examples of word choice, organization, voice, etc. However, the students were not specifically taught to look at the works of other authors to gather strategies for their writing. Students did not spend as much time immersing themselves in the works of other authors, looking for strategies that those authors used. The way in which the mentor texts were used in the Writer's Workshop program may have increased the students' curiosity more than the way in which they were used in the Six-Trait program.

Autonomy

Another instructional component that has been linked to increasing student motivation is autonomy. One meaning of autonomy is self-government, but it can also mean independence or one's ability to "call the shots". This relates well to writing. In the area of Writer's workshop, the students and teachers had created anchor charts that were hung on the wall upon completion. These anchor charts included instructional strategies to keep students writing even if they got stuck. These step-by-step directions let students feel in control of their pace and allowed them to continue their writing while waiting for teacher feedback. In essence, the students became their own teacher and were able to make individual decisions based on their own perception of their writing. This individualization of the writing process helped students remain motivated as they completed their writing tasks.

However, Six Trait Writing did not allow the students the same kind of autonomy. Since all students were working on the same trait at any given time, there was little, if any, incentive for them to move on. If students became stuck while writing using the Six Trait approach, they usually needed teacher guidance before they could proceed to the next step in the writing process. Although students were allowed the freedom to write at their own pace and choose what they wrote about, they did not have enough self-efficacy to move much beyond where the rest of the class was.

The lack of autonomy in this program could play a role in the fact that not as many students in the study rated it as "awesome." Instead more students thought Six Trait Writing was just "OK."

Recognition

Recognition is also an aspect of writing that can influence the motivation of the writer, as written by Lam and Law (2007). The authors believe that students who are recognized for effort and growth are more motivated to engage in other, more difficult tasks. If recognition is meaningful to the student and authentic, the student will see the benefit to their hard work and be more likely to be intrinsically motivated, rather than extrinsically motivated. Looking at the data, we have seen that, overall, writer's workshop tends to be a more motivational program. By comparing the recognition component of each program, we can consider this aspect as a possible reason for the difference.

In the writer's workshop program, recognition is an integral piece. At the end of each unit, students participate in a celebration in order to recognize, not only their work, but the work of their classmates. The celebration can change; however, there are specific pieces that are essential. Students have the opportunity to share in the writing of their classmates. This can be done by having small groups of students take turns reading their pieces to each other or by having students quietly rotate to the work of their classmates. In either situation, the person listening or reading their classmates' work has an opportunity to write comments about the pieces. Each writer then has an opportunity to get feedback from an authentic audience. This proves to be a positive experience for the writer because they get to see that their classmates recognize all of the hard work that they have put into this piece, which helps to motivate them to work even harder on their next piece as they anticipate the upcoming celebration.

Another way that students can recognize each other is through writer's gifts. Each student makes a small memento or gift as a thank you to their writing partner. Throughout the writing process their partner has worked close by them to help them make their piece the best it can be. To honor that, students may create a bookmark or write a note to that person to show their appreciation. As the celebration comes to a close, each student is awarded a certificate to signify the completion of a project and their work is posted somewhere to make it accessible to others in the school.

The Six Trait program also has ways of recognizing student work. At the end of their skill focus, student work is posted for others to enjoy. These students also spend time sharing their work with either the whole class, small group, or a writing partner. While they get to experience the work of other students, these writers do not have the chance to compliment and encourage each other in a meaningful way. Because of this major difference, the researchers believe that the decrease in students finding Six Trait writing awesome compared to that of Writer's Workshop is associated with the recognition students receive.

Evaluation

One component comes from the amount and kind of meaningful evaluation students received during the writing process. In the Writer's Workshop, students were consistently receiving relevant feedback based on their performance. It was an on-going process in which students were encouraged and taught how to make their writing better. Since students understood the correlation between the feedback and their writing, they had a clear picture how to keep improving their writing (Teacher's College Reading and Writing Project, 2009). The feedback changed with every conference based on the improvements students made. On the other hand, the feedback given during the Six Trait was usually based on the one particular skill that had been taught for that piece of writing. Therefore that one area was the focus of the evaluation that week. The feedback was also given towards the end of the writing process instead of being on-going which made the information less meaningful at times. This seems to be yet another reason the number of students who thought 6 Trait writing was awesome came out lower than Writer's Workshop.

When analyzing the data, the researchers discovered several areas of concern such as the following:

- Sometimes students placed their dot in the middle of two categories, making it difficult at times to discern where the student really meant to place it.

- Some students also misinterpreted what writing actually meant. They were more concerned how writing hurt their hand than the type and process of writing.
- The genre of writing being taught influenced the students' opinion of how they felt that month. For example, students seemed more interested to write fiction than expository essays.
- Some students didn't take the chart seriously and immediately just placed their dot without thinking.
- The enthusiasm chart was not given at the same time each month in each classroom.

Interpretation and Practice Decisions

After reviewing the results of this study, it seems more likely that teachers would choose to use the Writer's Workshop program instead of the Six Trait program. When looking at the two writing programs, students seem to feel more motivated by Writer's Workshop. As teachers, we want to empower our children and give them the opportunity to use their voices. Writing Workshop is a great way to make sure students are getting that opportunity.

The Units of Study by Lucy Caulkins that are used in Writer's Workshop are repeated throughout grades 3-5. It would be interesting to see if the repetition of the same units effects student motivation throughout the course of the three years. Future studies could be focused on investigating long term changes in attitudes for students in a Writer's Workshop program. Another research question would be whether or not a student' motivation changes if they were to change from a Writer's Workshop program to a Six Trait program. Similarly, further research could be done to see if the writers in the Six Trait program experienced an increase in motivation if they were placed in the Writers Workshop setting in the future. These types of studies might be useful in reinforcing the idea that the type of program used really does influence students' attitudes toward writing and their motivation.

References

Atwell, Nancie (2003). Hard Trying and These Recipes. *Voices from the Middle.* 11(2) 16-19.

Ciani, Keith D, Summers, Jessica J, Easter, & Sheldon. (October 2008). Collaborative learning and positive experiences: does letting students choose their own groups matter? *Educational Psychology*, 28*(6)*, 627-641

Glenn, Wendy J. (2007). Real writers as aware readers: Writing creatively as a means to develop reading skills. *Journal of Adolescent & Adult Literacy.* 51(1), 10-20.

Heskett, T. (2002). *Using the Six Trait Writing Model.* (Rev. ed).Westminster, CA. Teacher Created Materials, Inc.

Helsel, L., Greenberg, D. (2007). Helping struggling writers succeed: A self-regulated strategy instruction program. *The Reading Teacher.* 60 (8), 752-760.

Jasmine, J.; Weinder, W. *The Effects of Writing Workshop on Abilities of First Grade Students to Become Confident and Independent Writers.* Early Childhood Education Journal, 35(2), 131-139.

Johnson, Martin. (2004). "This one is more me!" What children think about writing test stimuli involving choice. *Literacy,* 90-96

Lam, S.-F., & Law, Y.-K. (2007). The roles of instructional practices and motivation in
writing performance. *The Journal of Experimental Education, 75*(2), 145-164.

Pajares, F. (2003). Self-efficacy beliefs, motivation, and achievement in writing: a review
of the literature. *Reading & Writing Quarterly, 19*(2), 139-158.

Sanacore, Joseph. (2008). A turning reluctant into inspired learners. *The Clearing House*, 82(1), 40-44.

Teachers College Reading and Writing Project at Columbia University Research Base. (n.d) Retrieved November 4, 2009
http://rwproject.tc.columbia.edu/assets/base/rw/rwcontent/ResearchBase oftheTCRWPWritingCurriculumVersion7.pdf

Wilson, Amy A. (2008). Motivating young writers through write-talks: real writers, real audiences, real purposes. *The Reading Teacher*, 61(6). 485-487.

Write Traits 6_trait Instruction and Assessment.(n.d)Professional Development ResearchBase. Retrieved November 4, 2009 from http://www.greatsource.com.

Chapter 10: Caught in the Middle: Teachers' Perceptions of Differentiated Instruction in Middle School

Julie Nourie, Joy E. Clauson & Suzy F. Dees

Background

Classrooms today are more diverse than ever. Inclusion of special education students in general education classes, lack of funding for gifted education, increasing numbers of students whose first language is not English, new legislation, and a host of other factors seem to make differentiated instruction not only a common term used in educational companies, but also an increasing necessity in all classroom across the United States. The United States National Center for Educational Statistics (2003) reports that approximately 6 million students in the United States received special education services in 2001-2002 school year. Nearly four million are acquiring English as a second language. In addition to ELL learners, student diversity also can be seen in economic factors as well. Approximately 36% of students in the United States qualify for free or reduced lunch services. This information demonstrates the wide array of needs that students bring with them into classrooms across our nation.

Differentiated instruction in its most simplistic state provides students with options for receiving information, comprehending the information, and demonstrating their learning (Tomlinson, 2001). In the 1970's, individualized instruction was a desired practice and thought to be an effective approach to teaching. However, there are differences between today's differentiation and yesterday's individualized instruction. Differentiation does not require a separate plan or lesson for each child within the classroom, which makes it much more manageable, and therefore more effective than individualized instruction (Tomlinson, 2001). Differentiated instruction provides numerous approaches and opportunities for students to encounter content, process material, and various ways to assess the content learned (Tomlinson, 2001). Differentiation also allows teachers to differentiate according to student differences such as readiness, interest, and rates of learning (Good, 2006). As one can imagine, differentiation requires a teacher to know his or her students and be in tune with their changing academic needs, as well as social and emotional needs. This process is just that - a process that is ever changing and differs for each student and each subject area. Many schools or districts may group students according to learning abilities through tracking, however at the classroom level the teacher is able to assess and meet students' needs accordingly by knowing the students' specific needs, interests, and rates of learning.

Study participants at this school have long been committed to providing quality instruction for their students. In 2003, teachers were asked to implement a different method of differentiated instruction in their classroom each month, a request that was documented by the principal in the School Improvement Plan (SIP) and followed by individual teams of teachers. Trying out the various strategies showed teachers that differentiation did not require them to work harder to create effective lessons but rather saving valuable instructional time by allowing students to meet goals and state standards more quickly. Teacher buy-in was high, and there was a general consensus that this school was doing its part to reach all levels of learners.

As years passed, however, enthusiasm for differentiated instruction waned. With the introduction of No Child Left Behind and its high-stakes tests that require schools to show Adequate Yearly Progress (AYP) as well as state-mandated Response to Intervention (RtI), this study teacher participants have retained their favorite DI lessons. These teacher participants also scrapped the rest in favor of one-size-fits-all lesson planning meant to address the standards quickly so that the school can move on to the next benchmark represented on the state tests. Like other teachers, teacher participants in the study see true differentiation as labor-intensive from lesson creation to implementation (VanTassel-Baska & Stambaugh, 2005). Pre-assessment and compacting, two forms of differentiation, require extra planning and are "really [teachers'] work…and don't become students' work until they represent true learning for them" (Winebrenner, 2001). While the teacher participants in this study value student learning, the thought of extensive planning for a small part of the curriculum is not appealing. Today, professional development opportunities for teacher participants in this study which include workshops, peer mentoring, and district mandated collaboration time are all designed to help them meet the needs of the varied learners in their classrooms. Still, differentiation is an instructional method that has largely been left behind.

According to O'Meara (2010), teachers are able to discuss, on many levels, the "what" of differentiation, but not able to apply it. She goes on to explain that differentiation is a process, though not linear, that is responsive to students' needs and within the context of their learning and is, at the core, based on assessment. Most teachers agree that differentiation is a good idea and that they should be doing more of it. Over the past few years, the researchers have observed a waning of differentiated practices in their various educational settings. With the advent of federally mandated programs like Response to Intervention (RtI) and schools not making Annual Yearly Progress (AYP), teachers are feeling beat up by the system. The increased demands on teachers can lead to a perception of Differentiated Instruction (DI) as an additional burden rather than a means to accomplishing all of the aforementioned programs and of best teaching practices. This study focused on examining teacher's perceptions of the effectiveness of

Differentiated Instruction in their junior high school as well as within their own classroom.

Teachers and special education providers will benefit from this study as it will provide them with feedback regarding other professionals' perceptions and implementations of Differentiated Instruction (DI). It will also provide teachers with a reflective opportunity to analyze their own DI practices and beliefs, as well as add to their knowledge of Differentiated Instruction. Administrators will also benefit from this study because it will provide them with teacher responses that will allow them to make changes and provide the necessary support to achieve a more responsive approach to differentiated instruction.

Review of the Literature

Differentiated Instruction: A Definition

Of all the current trends in education, differentiating instruction is one teaching method that all teachers claim to know how to do and swear they are currently implementing in their classrooms. Press them to define Differentiated Instruction (DI), and those questioning would receive a myriad of answers. Some would say that DI is a way to make curriculum more interesting and relevant to students so as to help them succeed academically, while others will claim DI is using assessment to drive their instruction to ensure that each student is getting exactly what he or she needs in order to achieve in school. While both definitions are correct, they paint only part of the picture that is DI. Most teachers can probably identify DI, but the issue of defining it is more complicated because it encompasses so many different theories and practices. O'Meara (2010) claims that because DI is so steeped in theory, it "leaves many teachers able to talk about differentiated instruction yet still wondering how to do it" (p. 2).

While this is true, many experts have attempted to break down the definition of DI to make it more palatable for teachers. Tomlinson (2001), for example, states, "At its most basic level, differentiating instruction means 'shaking up' what goes on in the classroom so that students have multiple options for taking in information, making sense of ideas, and expressing what they learn" (p. 1). Most teachers would agree that, generally, this is how they view DI as well, though they crave the "practice" to this theory. In one of her many texts, Tomlinson (2001) goes on to simplify DI, dividing it into two categories: what it is (qualitative, driven by assessment, and student-centered), and what it is not (individualized instruction, chaotic, and one-size-fits all), and in doing so, gives general practice to previous theories (pp. 2-5). O'Meara (2010) shares many of Tomlinson's theories on DI, including the belief that it is responsive to students' needs, inextricably tied to assessment, and should focus on learning as a whole rather than a set of fragmented skills that can be broken off and taught in isolation (p. 3). VanTassel-Baska and Stambaugh (2005), too, offer further the explanation of DI, noting that it requires teachers to shift their pedagogical theories to "the belief that students learn at different rates, possess different abilities and interest, and acquire knowledge through different avenues" (p. 213). This change in teaching philosophy, then, readies teachers for differentiation and all it has to offer students and teachers in the 21st century classroom.

History/Purpose of DI

The idea of differentiating instruction for each student based on his or her needs is not novel to this generation of teachers. According to O'Meara (2010), the term Differentiated Instruction was coined in the 1950s. Back then, teachers commonly, though mistakenly, thought that Differentiated Instruction was synonymous with individualized instruction (O'Meara, 2010). That idea continued into the 1970s and perpetuated the thought that teachers needed to create different lesson plans for each of their students (Tomlinson, 2001). This approach to DI also encouraged teachers to fragment their curriculum so that it catered to the precise needs of each student at a certain point in their education. Doing so negated the idea that DI for each student should be thought of in terms of the whole; O'Meara (2010), like Tomlinson, advocates that, "differentiation requires a focus on the big picture as opposed to isolated skills" (p. 3).

With several advocates like Tomlinson, O'Meara, and others in the field, teachers today are more educated in regards to differentiated instruction. Still, the strong opinions formed when teachers were faced with the insurmountable task of planning 25 different lesson plans for 25 different students linger. Nowadays, the stakes for student success are at an all-time high, with threats of high-stakes testing and teacher retention being tied together. In his article, George (2005) states that, "In the face of these challenges, educators committed to public education must find ways of providing excellence and challenges to all students" (p. 185). Differentiated Instruction is the vehicle that can make this achievement possible.

Response to Intervention, or RtI, has become the key to solidifying DI as a part of the nation's collective pedagogy. Walker-Dalhouse, Risko, Esworthy, Grasley, Kisler, McIlvain, & Stephan (2009) cite RtI as "a method for identifying students who will profit from differentiated and appropriate instruction in the classroom" (p. 84). Teachers surely understand the enormity of educating each student to succeed, though the method of instruction that will consistently garner high levels of success is more difficult to figure out. O'Meara (2010), too, sees Differentiated Instruction and RtI as two halves to a whole instruction:

> They are two parts of a circle, creating one whole process of curriculum and instruction. The student response to instruction or intervention is studied and measured. Based on those results, the instruction is differentiated. The student response is again studied and assessed and instruction is adapted to best meet the needs of the student. The process is cyclical. (p. 122)

From this perspective, the tie between DI and RtI is undeniable.

Types of Differentiated Instruction

In education today, there are nearly as many different ways to differentiate in the classroom as there are teachers teaching. Once teachers have the knowledge and tools to implement DI, the only limit to instructional planning is each teacher's creativity. Tomlinson (2001) gives shape to this instructional planning, dividing differentiated instruction into three categories: content, process, and products.

Content, to any teacher, is what is taught. For many teachers, the idea of modifying a district-mandated curriculum is taboo, even if that content does not fit student need. Differentiating content does not have to mean the abandonment of that which textbook adoption committees deem sacred, but teachers must be experts in their content area in order to differentiate their curriculum. O'Meara (2010) states that, "a stumbling block with differentiated instruction can occur when the teacher does not have the level of mastery of the content required to differentiate" (p. 38). In knowing all aspects of their content, teachers can "adapt *what* [they] teach . . . or modify *how* [they] give students access" to content (Tomlinson, 2001, p. 72). Specific adaptations to content might include content acceleration, compacting, or learning contracts.

Differentiating process is, in many ways, less daunting to teachers than modifying curriculum. The process for learning presented by the teacher is frequently said teacher's choice; there is often no mandate as to how acquisition of knowledge or skill happens, just that it does. Teaching students in the heterogeneous environment that DI promotes differentiates process of learning because, according to George (2005), "heterogeneous classrooms help ensure that all students are exposed to a complex, enriched curriculum, and to spirited instruction" (p. 188). Tomlinson (2001), too, promotes this kind of instruction, defining process of learning as "sense-making" (p. 79). When students collaborate with other students, they are trying to merge new information into their existing schema, thus "making sense" out of new information and assimilating it. Interacting with students that have different abilities, especially where students are collaborating, allows for differentiation of process. This kind of flexible grouping, along with choice activities, reading and writing workshops are all specific avenues for differentiating process.

While formative assessment, defined by O'Meara (2010) as "ongoing assessment for the purpose of instructional decision making" (p. 89) should be continual and could occur within any of Tomlinson's (2001) three categories of DI, it is usually associated with the process of learning. According to O'Meara, "indicators of progress during the learning are essential to maintain differentiated instruction" (p. 89). At base level, formative assessment lets the teacher know, at any given moment, how well students understand what is being taught. So powerful is formative assessment that Marzano (2003) claims "appropriate and systematic use of formative assessment could drastically improve the achievement of U.S. students" (p. 37). Using formative assessments to drive instructional decisions often happens during the process of learning because it steers differentiation in the right direction and, thus, caters to the needs of each student.

To some teachers, differentiating product is the most adaptable form of differentiation; most teachers have creative ideas as to how students can present what has been learned. Tomlinson (2001) states that "product assignments should help students—individually or in groups—rethink, use, and extend what they have learned" (p. 85). Summative assessments are included with products and may be differentiated to show deeper understanding of a common concept. For example, O'Meara (2010) describes a summative assessment where on-level learners are given one question and gifted students are given a different one that requires they show a deeper understanding of a concept. O'Meara (2010) goes on to explain that "In both cases, there are higher-level questions. In each pair of questions, the question does not require more work to answer, but it does require deeper thinking" (p. 108). Differentiation of product can ensure that each student is able to demonstrate learning at a level that is appropriate for his or her ability.

Obstacles, hurdles, and challenges to the implementation of DI

There are countless books, articles, and published resources on how to differentiate instruction. Availability of differentiated instruction resources is at an all-time high and includes things such as frameworks of DI, templates for unit and lesson plans, sample assessments, how-to guides, learner inventories, etc. Why, then, would teachers elect to not differentiate?

In their article on the REACH framework for DI, Rock, Gregg, Ellis, and Gable (2008), cite "excessive workload responsibilities, demands for substantial content coverage, and negative classroom behavior" as stumbling blocks to teachers attempting to differentiate in their classrooms.

Shumm & Avalos (2009) echo the idea that demands for extensive content coverage is an obstacle to differentiation, but also indicate grading policies, lack of funding, and resistance to change as additional reasons for teachers' lack of differentiation implementation.

Tomlinson (2005) states that teachers have not experienced Differentiated Instruction in their roles as learners nor have they seen examples of what differentiation actually looks like in the classroom, and are therefore unable to draw on effective models in their implementation of DI. "Teachers need to see living examples of implementation, done by teachers who inspire them and to whom they can go for support as well" (Blaz, 2008, p. 143). Without these effective models, DI remains in the realm of theory and stays somewhat inaccessible to teachers. Tomlinson (2005) identifies four barriers to successful implementation of DI:

> lack of reflection on students as individuals, a lack of clarity about what students should know, understand, and be able to do as the result of a segment of learning; inadequate repertoires of instructional approaches that invite student-centeredness and flexibility; and lack of skills to manage and facilitate flexible instruction. (p.11)

One way to overcome these barriers, according to Tomlinson (2005), is to create staff development which is reflective and models the core components of DI in order to bring about substantive change in standard teaching practices.

Hertberg-Davis and Brighton (2006) indicate that differentiation is not a quick fix and that a significant amount of time is needed for "realization, implementation, and actualization" (p. 91). Not all educators are patient with the process and give up before the benefits can be fully realized. Internal factors to the teacher "such as conflicting beliefs about the meaning of differentiation and the nature of schooling, insufficient depth of content knowledge, and shallow pedagogical understandings" (Hertberg-Davis & Brighton, 2006, p. 91) can all inhibit the willingness to engage in differentiation of curriculum, instruction, and assessment.

Misconceptions regarding differentiation challenge the ability of teachers and administrators to advocate the use of differentiation in the classroom. King-Sears (2008) debunks two common reasons teachers give for not differentiating for students with disabilities. The first fallacy is that students with disabilities are not able to comprehend the general education curriculum and the second is that "teachers are required to cover the curriculum, regardless of student learning" (King-Sears, 2008, p. 56). To assume that students with special needs are not able to comprehend the general education curriculum is to make a very dangerous assumption. It is the role of the educator to help students find their voice, even when, at first glance, it appears the student is not capable of comprehending. Forging ahead with the curriculum, regardless of student learning ultimately leaves everyone behind as students do not then have the scaffolding on which to build the next concept.

Teachers' views on differentiation tend to reflect the views of the administration. In their study on middle school principals' influence on differentiated instruction, Hertberg-Davis and Brighton (2006) determined that the principals who supported teachers in their effort to differentiate were more likely to have staff consistently differentiating in their instruction. Support, according to Hertberg-Davis and Brighton (2006), included discussing differentiation with teachers in multiple settings, providing release-time for collaboration and planning, a common language surrounding DI, and feedback on DI following observations of differentiated lessons. Conversely, Hertberg-Davis and Brighton (2006) determined that a lack of administrator interest in and support for DI was generally followed by the teachers with the same view of DI as time consuming and not worthy of focus in the classroom.

A common theme in the literature surrounding barriers to implementation of differentiation seems to include misconceptions surrounding DI, a feeling of needing to cover vast amounts of curriculum, and a lack of on-going support for DI.

Finding a Balance: Initiating, Supporting and Developing DI

There are several key components found in recent literature that reportedly determine the successfulness of differentiated instruction and the quality of differentiation within classrooms. Teachers must make a support plan for themselves, support one another, and be given support from others in order for DI to reach an effective level.

There are multiple components to successful implementation of differentiation. Differentiation calls for modifying the use of curriculum, content, materials, and or the delivery methods (Tomlinson, 2001). Whether a teacher is changing all or some of these components, the primary duty of differentiation often seems to reside on teachers' shoulders. Therefore, teachers need an immense amount of support, on different levels, to achieve this continual cycle of differentiation, as differentiation takes time and much effort (Yatvin, 2004). According to Wormelli (2007), one way in which teachers can provide a continual support for themselves is by equipping themselves with an understanding of how the human mind learns. Wormelli (2007) explains that teachers are educated on this; however they often forget to apply what they have learned to their daily practices in their classrooms, or the teachers do not stay current with new information regarding cognitive sciences. The growing information and research surrounding cognitive sciences allows a teacher to better understand how to reach all students because he/she understands how the human mind learns. For example, students who have connections and well established background to the content being encountered are able to learn more effectively. A teacher's ability to "prime the brain" and structure lessons can significantly help students in their learning process as well. Another key component to reaching all learners is by thoroughly understanding and applying what is known regarding emotional connections. Teachers who build a safe community and are aware of their students' emotional development can build a classroom of learners that are more willing to take risks and ultimately learn better (Wormelli, 2007). The research of cognitive science also explains and explores the primacy and recency effect, effectiveness of hydration while learning, and novelty of instructional design (Wormelli, 2007).

Another way in which teachers can provide support for themselves is by calling on colleagues. Tomlinson (1999) explains that teachers who call on colleagues to expand ideas, critique lessons, plan lessons, and troubleshoot are more effective in differentiating in their own classrooms. Building a colleague support system also reduces isolation and discouragement as teachers attempt to maintain steam through the differentiation process. Tomlinson (1999) also indicates that making a partnership with the building principal can be a critical component for a teacher's successful implementation and growth of DI as well as a catalyst for administrator interest (Tomlinson, 1999). Yatvin (2004) supports the idea that one of the best resources an educator has when practicing differentiating is the support of his or her colleagues. Working with like-minded colleagues allows a concept like DI to grow and improve over time. When observed by a peer, the peer can see the lesson from a different perspective and offer constructive feedback to improve instruction.

Yet another component for successful differentiation with the classroom is to gain the support of parents of their students, which begins with their education of the differentiation process (Tomlinson, 1999). Most parents of school aged children today did not experience differentiation in their classrooms as students. They might remember being singled out or placed in color coded groups and associate those experiences with DI, which is not the goal or intent of DI (Tomlinson, 2005). By including parents in the process and showing parents how the child's needs are being met, the teacher will gain the parents' support, which will only increase the child's learning experience (Tomlinson, 1999). Parents and community members need to learn the benefits and necessities in today's world to embrace the practices of differentiation. By embracing differentiation and changing the traditional teaching structure and practices, teachers can better prepare students for life in a democracy where they will interact frequently with those of all ethnicities, cognitive abilities, and religions (George, 2005).

It is easy to find ways in which teachers must better themselves or provide a support system for themselves, however education is not merely the responsibility of one person, therefore, it is critical that teachers be provided a strong support system from their administration as well. In Hertberg-Davis and Brighton's (2006) study, several key components were found. Principals that supported differentiation verbally and through actions had a significantly higher influence on teachers' attitudes and implementation of differentiation. Attending workshops with teachers, being an active participant and observer in the differentiated classrooms, and attending team meetings, are all key actions that made an effective school wide program and acceptance of DI. Just as Wormelli (2007) shares the need to create a safe environment in order for learning to occur, principals must do the same. Principals must protect their teachers as they become better teachers and implementers of DI. Teachers must know and believe that they will have the support of their principal no matter the troubles or obstacles they encounter along their learning path. Encouragement, enthusiasm, and a hands-on approach are necessary to support teachers (Hertberg-Davis & Brighton, 2006) on their differentiation journey.

Effective leaders understand the difficult nature of change and balance change with support. A strong sense of community is essential to employ the changes that allow differentiation to become a common and continual practice. The greatest necessity for teachers to be effective in classroom change, like DI, is administrative support (Tomlinson & Allan, 2000). When administration is involved in the differentiation process they understand the demands and process of change. By being involved, they understand their responsibility to provide a structure that allows for the successful implementation of DI. Class schedules and school day routines must allow for regularly scheduled time for teachers to collaborate, problem-solve, and carry out the plans for differentiation (Nordlund, 2003). Yatvin (2004) states that teachers who do not share plan time together find few opportunities to discuss their practices, ideas, or struggles and often must seek collegiality at other times. More often than not, this results in teachers not collaborating at all. While regularly-shared planning is essential for the continuation of day-to-day planning and implementation of DI, long-term planning days scheduled throughout the year are also critical to allow teachers to participate in planning sessions and seek the support of district specialists (Tomlinson & Allan, 2000).

Nordlund (2003) suggests that collaborative teams be formed and take time to get to know one another and gain the respect of one another through a variety of structured surveys and team building exercises. Team attitudes are critical to a school's progressive moment towards differentiation. Not only does working as a team provide opportunities to plan lessons and problem-solve together, but it also creates a synergy that spreads, causing a ripple effect and continual forward motion (Nordlund, 2003). It is essential that all teachers and staff are working towards a common goal and remain committed to the individual needs of each student (Nordlund, 2003).

Gaining support from wider collegiality is yet another resource for teachers when attempting to provide a support structure for themselves as well as for administrators providing support for their staff (Yatvin, 2004). National organizations as well as educational cooperative and state programs offer training and in-services regarding specific elements and implementation of DI. With today's technology, there are also numerous contacts and support outlets through online services, websites, and the increased ability to connect with well-known authors and experts in the area of DI (Yatvin, 2004).

Summary of the Literature

By defining differentiated instruction and exploring its history and purpose, teachers are better able to understand the rationale behind its validity in the classroom. True, there are obstacles to the implementation of DI of which teachers and administration must be aware in order to be successful in their endeavor to help students experience legitimate academic success in their classes. In order to be successful in the implementation of DI, teachers need support in the way of staff development, time to collaborate with peers, and support from the administration. Teachers cannot pretend that DI will go away with each progressive political party and as something that is optional; DI is simply considered to be what good teachers do on a regular basis. DI is a forward movement in education that requires teachers to view it as a necessity in order to bring as many students to the educational table as possible.

Methodology

This research study was conducted through an anonymous online survey utilizing Survey Monkey. It attempted to investigate teacher perceptions of Differentiated Instruction within their school as well as their classrooms. The researchers attempted to quantitatively measure teachers' perceptions by assigning a numeric value to each survey question response. The SPSS data analysis program was used to organize and calculate this information. Results and conclusions are depicted through charts and graphs.

The population for this research includes 74 certified junior high teachers in a Midwestern school in central Illinois. The teachers who were invited to participate in this study range in age from twenty two years of age to sixty five and consist of both male and female participants. The instrument that was used for this quantitative study is a survey consisting of twenty eight questions that aim to gather teacher perception of differentiated instruction.

Research Questions

1. What are teacher's perceptions regarding differentiation within their own classrooms?
2. What are teachers' perceptions of support for differentiated instruction?
3. What, if anything, hinders a teacher's implementation of Differentiated Instruction?

Operational Definitions

Differentiation - a proactive approach in which a teacher "plans and carries out varied approaches to content, process, and product in anticipation of and response to student differences in readiness, interest, and learning needs" (Tomlinson, 2001).

Perception - used in this study as teachers' beliefs, feelings, and associations connected with differentiation.

Response to Intervention (RtI) - "a general education initiative which requires collaborative efforts from all district staff, general educators, special educators and bilingual/ELL staff where student academic and behavioral needs must be identified and monitored continuously with documented student performance data used to make instructional decisions"
(ISBE, 2008 http://www.isbe.net/pdf/rti_state_plan.pdf)

Support – anything that is going to help teachers in continuous implementation of differentiated instruction including professional development, peer collaboration and mentoring, materials, school culture, etc.

Results

Seventy-four teachers were invited, via e-mail, to participate in a survey that measured perceptions of differentiated instruction in their classrooms and the school as a whole. Thirty-eight teachers started the survey. Of those thirty eight, nine teachers did not complete more than the first section of the survey, resulting in a total of twenty nine participants. Education level and experience were the only demographics identified for the purposes of this research. Table 1 indicates that the majority of the participants (86.2%) in this study have been teaching more than 10 years, resulting in only 13.8% having taught 10 years or less. The majority of participants (89.7%) also possess a Master's Degree, leaving the remaining 10.3% possessing a Bachelor's Degree.

Table 1: Participants teaching experience and education

Category	Percent
Years of Experience	
0-4 years	6.9
5-10 years	6.9
11-16 years	37.9
17+ years	48.3
Level of Education	
Bachelor's	10.3
Master's Degree	89.7
Doctorate Degree	0.00

Research Question #1: What are teacher's perceptions regarding Differentiation within their own classrooms?

When surveyed, 27 participants responded to all questions, 29 participants responded to one or more question (Table 2). Most participants feel differentiation is achieved through content modification or adaption and/or differentiation of assessment. Differentiation of content and assessment were thought to be as equally effectively implemented within individual classrooms.

Whereas a slightly smaller population of participants believe that differentiation is achieved mostly through their instructional approaches.

Table 2: Perceived Effectiveness of DI in the Classroom

Types of DI	Strongly Agree		Agree		Disagree		Strongly Disagree		Avg.
	%	# of Part.	%	# of Part.	%	# of Part	%	# of Par.	
DI of Content	25.9	7	63.0	17	7.4	2	3.7	1	1.89
DI of Instructional Approaches	53.6	15	35.7	10	7.1	2	3.6	1	1.61
DI of Assessment	25.9	7	59.3	16	14.8	4	0.0	0	1.89

Chart A shows that participants felt that differentiation within their classrooms was mostly achieved through content and assessment, averaging 1.89. Likewise, Table 2 shows the percentages and number of participants who agree differentiation is achieved through content and/or assessment. Table 2 also shows the population of participants who "Disagree" or "Strongly Disagree" that differentiation is mostly achieved in their classrooms through these methods. Specifically, only 3 participants reported that they "Disagree or Strongly Disagree" that they effectively differentiate through the content, whereas the majority of participants (88.9%) "Agree" in their feeling that differentiation is effectively carried out within their own classrooms through the content, or curriculum. Strikingly similar results were gathered in regards to differentiation being effectively implemented through means of assessment. However, more participants reported feeling that their implementation of differentiation though their instruction (delivery of skills, information, and processes) was most effective. The average score of effectiveness of Differentiation based on instructional approaches was 1.61 (Chart A), however, 53.6% of participants reported "Strongly Agree" (Table 2).

When surveyed, participants were asked several questions pertaining to their differentiation of content, instruction, and assessment and their perceptions of their effectiveness. Analyzed responses from participants showed an overall perceived effectiveness of Differentiation of Content being an average of 1.783 and a standard deviation of .681608 (Table **3**). These results show that most of the participants fall between the "agree" and "strongly agree" variables, with only .68 variance to each side of the mean.

Chart A: In My Classroom, I feel Differentiated is Mostly Achieved Through

In my CLASSROOM, I feel differentiation is mostly achieved through:

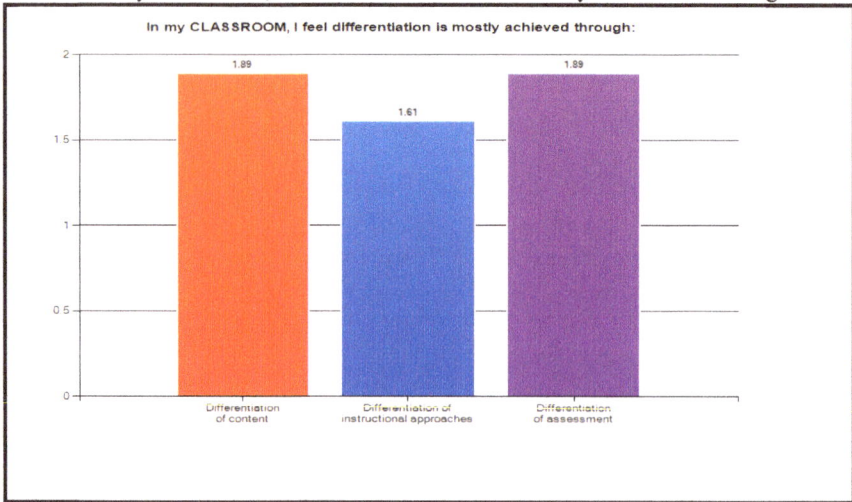

Table 3: Differentiated Instruction Regarding Content

Questions	Mean	SD
I bring in differentiated content material.	1.58	0.82
How effective do you feel in your implementation of DI of Content (standards-based core curriculum)?	1.82	0.54
Within my classroom, I feel differentiation is mostly achieved through the differentiation of content.	1.88	0.69
Teachers' overall perceived effectiveness of Differentiation of Content.	1.78	0.68

Analyzed responses from participants showed an overall perceived effectiveness of Differentiation of Instruction being an average of 1.61 and a standard deviation of .72 (Table 4). These results show that most of the participants fall between the "agree" and "strongly agree" variables, with .72 variance to each side of the mean, slightly higher than perceived effectiveness of Differentiation of Content.

Table 4: Differentiated Instruction Regarding Instruction

Questions	Mean	SD
I plan my lessons/units using a DI model.	1.79	0.77
How effective do you feel your implementation of differentiated INSTRUCTION is? (delivery of skills, information, and processes)	1.39	0.62
Within my classroom, I feel differentiation is mostly achieved through Differentiation of instructional approaches	1.60	0.78
Teachers' overall perceived effectiveness of Differentiation of Instruction	1.61	0.72

Analyzed responses from participants showed an overall perceived effectiveness of Differentiation of Assessment being an average of 1.70 and a standard deviation of .65 (Table 5). These results show that most of the participants fall between the "agree" and "strongly agree" variables, with only .65 spread to each side of the mean.

Table 5: Differentiated Instruction Regarding Assessment

Questions	Mean	SD
I assess my students using various methods.	1.48	0.57
I use formative assessments to determine the direction of my teaching.	1.72	0.75
How effective do you feel your implementation of differentiated ASSESSMENT (formative and/or summative measurement of what students know or are able to do) is?	1.67	0.66
In my classroom, I feel differentiation is mostly achieved through differentiation of assessment	1.75	0.78
Teachers' overall perceived effectiveness of Differentiation of Assessment	1.70	0.65

Research Question #2- What are teachers' perceptions of support for Differentiated Instruction?

Overall, teacher participants report a feeling of support for differentiated instruction in their school. Chart B and Table 6 indicate that the majority of teachers responding to the survey agree, to some degree, that they are supported in their DI efforts (75.4%) while fewer (24.7%) disagree that support is present.

In regards to the different kinds of support for DI that teachers receive, the participants responded that there is much support from colleagues for implementing DI in the classroom, with 89.7% agreeing with this thread of the question (Table 6). Similarly, most survey participants (89.6%) agreed that administration is knowledgeable about DI (Table 6). In addition, 65.5% of respondents believe that quality materials and/or resources are available to help differentiate instruction in the classroom (Table 6), but perceived support in the form of training for DI in the classroom is not as strong. Table 6 shows that 62% of participants perceive support in this area. Table 7 shows that the perceived support for differentiation is reported to have a mean of 2.158. Most participants responded that they "Agree" that they are supported in the various areas. The perceived support for DI did show a standard deviation of .85 indicating a range of responses.

Chart B: Support for Differentiated Instruction in My School

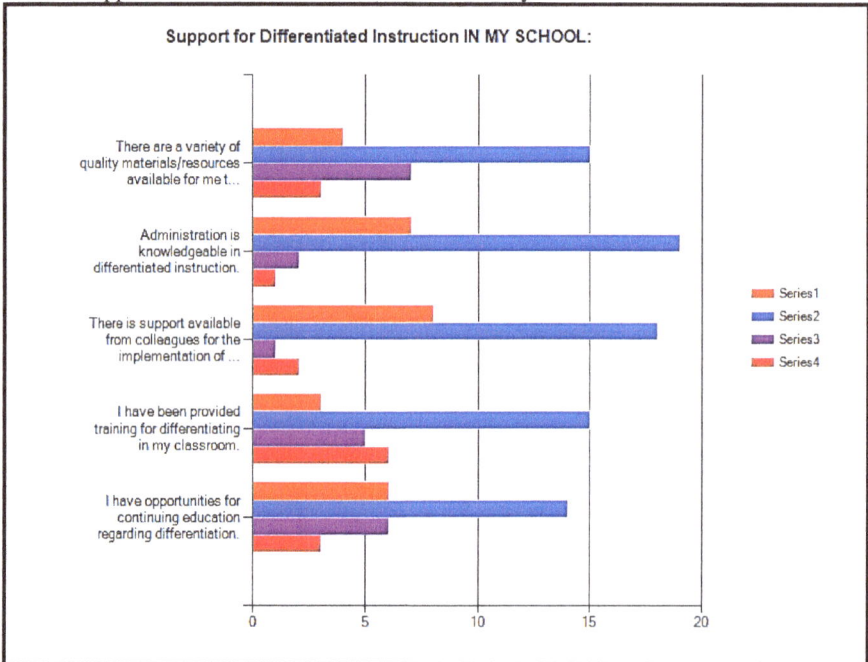

Table 6: Teacher Perception of Support for Differentiated Instruction in their School

Question or Category	Strongly Agree	Agree	Disagree	Strongly Disagree
There are a variety of quality materials/resources available for me to use for me to differentiate in my classroom	13.8	51.7	24.1	10.3
Administration is knowledgeable in differentiated instruction	24.1	65.5	6.9	3.4
There is support available for colleagues for the implementation of differentiated instruction.	27.6	62.1	3.4	6.9
I have been provided training for Differentiating in my classroom	10.3	51.7	17.2	20.7
I have opportunities for continuing Education regarding differentiation	20.7	48.3	20.7	10.3
Overall Support for Differentiated Instruction IN MY School	19.2	56.2	14.4	10.3

Table 7: Overall Perceived Support for Differentiated Instruction

	Mean	Mode	Standard Deviation
Perceived Support for DI	2.158	2	0.85

Research Question #3 – What if any, correlation is there between teachers' perception of DI implementation and the level of perceived support?

Table 8 shows that over 95% of the teachers in the survey agreed or strongly agreed that they feel effective in their implementation. Less than 5% of teachers disagreed that they feel they are effective in their implementation of Differentiated Instruction. One respondent skipped this section of the survey and one respondent skipped one question in this section of the survey. Table 8 indicates that 75.3% of participants feel supported in their efforts to Differentiate Instruction in their school and 24.7% of participants do not feel supported in their efforts to Differentiate Instruction.

Table 8: Overall Perceived Effectiveness in DI Implementation & Support for DI in Participants' School

Question or Category	Strongly Agree	Agree	Disagree	Strongly Disagree
Overall Perceived Effectiveness in DI Implementation	35.8	59.3	4.9	00.0
Overall Perceived Support for DI in Participants' School	19.2	56.2	14.4	10.3

According to the data in Table 9, the teachers' perceived overall effectiveness in implementing Differentiated Instruction and the perceived level of support for Differentiated Instruction is not statistically significant at the .05 level.

Table 9: Correlation between Perceived Support and Perceived Effectiveness of DI

Pair 1	Paired Differences			95% Confidence Interval of the Difference				Sig. (2-tailed)
	Mean	Std. Deviation	Std. Error Mean	Lower	Upper	t	df	
Support - Effectiveness	.48148	1.00139	.11127	.26006	.70291	4.327	80	.000

Discussion

This study addressed teachers' perceived effectiveness in Differentiated Instruction at a Junior High School in central Illinois. Within the study components that were identified and investigated were DI of *content, instruction,* and *assessment,* as well as the perceived level of support regarding DI.

Research question #1 addressed teachers' perceptions regarding Differentiation within their own classroom. The results depicted in Chart A show that most participants reported that they would agree that they are effective in their implementation of DI though *content, instruction,* and *assessment within their own classroom.* This portion of the study stemmed from Tomlinson's (2001) division and categorization of differentiation into three categories: content, process, and products. Tomlinson (2001) states that differentiated instruction provides numerous approaches and opportunities for students to encounter content, process material, and various ways to assess the content learned.

Table 2 shows that the majority (53.6%) of participants felt strongly regarding their effectiveness of Differentiation when pertaining to the instructional approaches they practiced within their classrooms. The category of Differentiation of Instruction held the more "Strongly Agree" responses than the categories of "Differentiation of Content" or "Differentiation of Assessment." This indicates that, although all three categories demonstrated a similar combined score for "Agree" and "Strongly Agree," the category of Differentiation of Instructional Approaches show 53.6 % "Strongly Agree" and Differentiation of Content and Assessment both indicate 25.9% "Strongly Agree." Teachers' overall perceived effectiveness of DI regarding instruction was found to have a total mean of 1.61, with a standard deviation of 0.72 (Table 4).

When broken down further, this study also investigated teachers' perceived effectiveness regarding each sub category: instruction, content, and assessment. This was done by analyzing individual responses to particular questions that pertained to each of the three components of differentiation (instruction, content, and assessment).

As demonstrated in Table 3, when concentrating on "Differentiated Instruction Regarding Content," a mean of 1.58 was calculated regarding teachers bringing in differentiated content materials, this meaning that most teachers either "Agree" or "Strongly Agree" with the statement that they bring in differentiated content material.

The area that showed the most disagreement among participants was the area of Differentiation of Assessment. 14.8% of participants responded that they "Disagree" that Differentiation is mostly achieved through differentiation of Assessment within their classroom (Table 2). This is double the "Disagree" response of DI regarding instruction and DI regarding Content. According to O'Meara (2010) ongoing assessment is essential for the purpose of making educated decisions concerning instruction.

When looking into perceptions regarding differentiated instruction in the specific area of assessment, this study revealed that most participants use a variety of assessment methods, but fewer participants are using the assessments to determine the direction of their teaching (Table 5). Although achieving differentiation of instruction through means of assessment did not reveal as high of scores of perceptions as other areas, the mean score of teachers' overall perceived effectiveness in this area was still 1.705, with a standard deviation from the mean of 0.65 (Table 5).

The disagreement shown among participants within the area of "Differentiation of Assessment" depicted 14.8% of participants responded that they "Disagree" differentiation is mostly achieved through differentiation of assessment within their classroom (Table 2). This is double the "Disagree" responses of instruction and content.

According to O'Meara (2010), ongoing assessment is essential for the purpose of making educated decisions concerns instruction. O'Meara (2010) states the importance of assessment in the achievement of effective Differentiation within classrooms. She argues that formative assessment is essential as it provides necessary indicators of progress that teachers need in order to maintain effective implementation of differentiation. Furthermore, Marzano (2003) stresses that by properly using formative assessments to drive instructional practices, student achievement would drastically improve in the United States. Despite what the current research shows regarding the connections between differentiation and assessment, the responses gathered demonstrate that this area is the weakest among participants, which identifies a weak component in these participants' implementation and mastery of differentiation.

In regards to question two, which gauges teachers' perceptions of support for differentiated instruction both generally and specifically, results show that the teachers overwhelmingly feel supported in their DI efforts, with over seventy-five percent either "Agreeing" or "Strongly Agreeing" with this part of the survey (Table 6).

Examining the breakdown of this data by the specific kinds of support surveyed, the area teachers feel the most confidence is in the administration's knowledge of DI, with nearly ninety percent of participants "Agreeing" or "Strongly Agreeing" that the administration knows much in regards to DI (Table 6). As noted in the literature study, Hertberg-Davis and Brighton (2006) claim that principals who support teachers in their efforts to differentiate instruction generally have more staff members implementing DI in their classrooms. Tomlinson (1999), too, indicates that having a building principal who is on board with and understands the importance of DI is critical in teachers' success in implementing this kind of instruction; a principal's educational philosophies permeate all corners of any school's pedagogical climate.

Further, support from administration is especially important when implementing training for DI; having access to this kind of professional development simply would not be possible without the support of administration. The majority of survey participants (62%) felt that training for DI had been provided (Table 6). Tomlinson & Allan (2000) advocate long-term planning days during the school year as one of the most effective ways to train teachers, and implementation of such training must be the job of the building principal. Hertberg-Davis and Brighton (2006) emphasize the importance of administrators attending DI workshops alongside teachers to show acceptance of and commitment to DI, which then helps promote a school-wide acceptance of DI. While the majority of the teachers surveyed felt training for DI was available, it is also important to note that training as a support for DI implementation in the classroom is also the thread of the question that had the largest number of teachers "Disagreeing" that this support was available, with over twenty percent "Strongly Disagreeing" with that statement (Table 6).

Perceived support from their colleagues was another area in which staff indicated a high degree of confidence, with almost ninety percent of respondents "Agreeing" or "Strongly Agreeing" here (Table 6). According to Tomlinson (1999), the opportunity to brainstorm and collaborate with colleagues already using DI in the classroom regarding lesson planning and troubleshooting allows teachers to expand their thinking and, thus, be more effective at differentiating their lessons. Yatvin (2004) also cites collegial support as vital for development of DI; being able to share and critique colleagues' ideas allows teachers' ideas regarding DI to evolve and grow.

Nearly seventy percent of survey respondents "Agreed" or "Strongly Agreed" that opportunities to continue their education to add to their knowledge of DI exist (Table 6). Wormeli (2007) emphasizes the importance of staying current with new research in the cognitive sciences, information that is often left out of local professional development methods-type classes. Wormeli (2007) goes on to explain that teachers often forget ideas gleaned from any kind of professional development activities if they do not immediately use them in the classroom.

Research question #3 asks "What, if any, correlation is there between teachers' perceptions of Differentiated Instruction implementation and the level of perceived support? The survey results, as shown in Table 8, indicate that, overall, the teachers who participated in the survey felt they are effective in implementing DI. 19.9% of respondents "Strongly Agree" and 32.9% "Agree" to the overall effectiveness in DI implementation. Table 1 displays that an overwhelming majority of participants have over eleven years of teaching experience (almost half of the participants have over seventeen years' experience) coupled with a Master's degree. The level of teaching experience in the pool of participants supports O'Meara's (2010) contention that in order to effectively differentiate, teachers need to first have mastered their content area. The longer they have been teaching, the more comfortable the teachers are implementing strategies like differentiation. The teachers participating in the survey fit that stereotype. It is interesting to note that one participant skipped the entire section on implementation, yet continued on with the rest of the survey.

The research of Hertberg-Davis and Brighton (2006) indicates that support (from colleagues and administration) is vital to the success of DI implementation. This support can come in a variety of forms such as professional development, common planning time, common language surrounding differentiation, and feedback from colleagues and administration following observations of differentiated lessons, activities, or assessments. Table 8 indicates that over three-fourths of participants feel supported in their efforts to Differentiate Instruction in their school, one of the contributing factors to teachers not feeling comfortable with differentiated instruction. The calculated point of significance of .00 (in Table 9) is less than the acceptable point of significance .001, therefore proving the null hypothesis. Table 9 illustrates, through the two-tailed test, that there is no correlation between teachers' perceived overall effectiveness in implementing Differentiated Instruction and the perceived level of support for Differentiated Instruction.

Conclusions and Implications

Of the ninety-five certified teacher participants who were invited to participate in this research study on differentiated instruction, thirty-eight began the survey process. However, only twenty nine participants completed the survey. Out of these twenty-nine participants, 37.9 % possessed eleven to sixteen years' experience while 48.3% held seventeen or more years of experience. In addition to years' experience, 89.7% of participants held a Master's degree. The years of experience and level of education support the researchers' understanding that teachers who are experts in their content are better equipped to be effective in their implementation of differentiation. Furthermore, there is a general perception that teachers who have sought out post-graduate education are more willing to try newer methods, such as DI, in the classroom.

The majority of participants felt the most perceived effectiveness of DI was their differentiation of instructional approaches. This aligns with the fact that teacher participants have had the most training in this area of instructional approaches, therefore, researchers conclude that the more training and support teachers receive the more empowered teachers feel to implement DI in their classroom. The uncertainty regarding differentiation in assessments reflected in the survey responses may be reflective of the fluctuating nature of assessment practices in education today. There seems to be a push for using formative assessments to guide instruction, but not an abundance of professional development on how to implement that shift in thinking.

This study's researchers conclude that teachers' participants feel supported from their colleagues in their efforts to differentiate. This perceived support can be credited to the long history of supportive administrators who value differentiated instruction along with the fact that the school operates in teams and has an atmosphere of sharing. Not only does the Junior High School were this study participants teach have a history of supportive administration, they still report feeling strongly sustained in their efforts to differentiate. Although the researchers paired *t* test did not reveal a significant correlation between perceived effectiveness of DI and perceived support for DI, there is a high level of perceived support and perceived effectiveness at the Junior High School. Despite these results, this study researches still believe that the more supported teachers feel, the more effective teachers will be in their implementation of DI, which is also in agreement with the literature.

References

Blaz, D. (2008). Differentiated assessment for middle and high school classrooms. Larchmont, NY: Eye on Education.

George, P. (2005). A rationale for differentiating instruction in the regular classroom. *Theory into Practice, 44*(3), 185-193.

Hertberg-Davis, H.L. & Brighton, C.M. (2006). Support and sabotage: Principals' influence on middle school teachers' responses to differentiation. *The Journal of Secondary Gifted Education, 17(*2), 90-102.

King-Sears, Margaret E. (2008). Facts and fallacies: Differentiation and the general education curriculum for students with special educational needs. *Support for Learning, 23*(2), 55-62.

Marzano, R.J. (2003). *What works in schools: Translating research into action.* Alexandria, VA: Association for Supervision and Curriculum Development.

Nordlund, M. (2003). *Differentiated Instruction: Meeting the educational needs of all students in your classroom.* Lanham, MD: The Scarecrow Press.

O'Meara, J. (2010). *Beyond differentiated instruction.* Thousand Oaks, CA: Corwin Publishing.

Rock, M.L., Gregg, M. Ellis, E. & Gable, R.A. (2008). REACH: A framework for differentiating classroom instruction. *Preventing School Failure, 52*(2), 31-47.

Tomlinson, C.A. (2001). *How to differentiate instruction in mixed-ability classrooms.* Alexandria, VA: Association for Supervision and Curriculum Development.

Tomlinson, C.A. (1999). The differentiated classroom: Responding to the needs of all learners. Alexandria, VA: Association for Supervision and Curriculum Development.

Tomlinson, C.A. (2005). Traveling the road to differentiation in staff development: Teacher leaders can help educators hurdle four key barriers to implementation. *The Journal of National Staff Development Council, 26*(4), 8-13.

Tomlinson, C. A. & Allan, S. (2000). *Leadership for differentiating schools and classrooms*. Alexandria, VA: Association for Supervision and Curriculum Development.

The United States National Center for Educational Statistics (2003). Retrieved from http://nces.ed.gov/pubs2003/overview03/tables/table_10.asp

VanTassel-Baska, J., & Stambaugh, T. (2005). Challenges and possibilities for serving gifted learners in the regular classroom. *Theory into Practice, 44*(3), 211-217.

Walker-Dalhouse, D., Risko, V., Esworthy, E., Grasley, E., Kaisler, G., McIlvain, & Stephen, M. (2009). Crossing boundaries and initiating conversations about RtI: Understanding and applying differentiated classroom instruction. *The Reading Teacher, 1*(63), 84-87.

Winebrenner, S. (2001). *Teaching gifted kids in the regular classroom: Strategies and techniques every teacher can use to meet the academic needs of the gifted and talented.* Minneapolis, MN: Free Spirit Publishing, Inc.

Wormeli, R. (2007). *Differentiation: From planning to practice grades 6-12.* Portland, ME: Stenhouse Publishers.

Yatvin, J. (2004). *A room with a differentiated view: How to serve all children as individual learners.* Portsmouth, NH: Heinemann.

Chapter 11: Job Related Factors that Impact Teacher Attrition

Colleen Rowsey & Pam Wilson

Introduction

The teaching profession can yield many rewarding moments. Helping children become successful can be a very gratifying experience. However, teachers can also undergo extreme amounts of stress as they deal with behavior problems, non-academic issues, and parent problems. It is not very often that a teacher's day ends when the last bell rings. Many teachers get overwhelmed by the amount of work both physical and emotional that is brought home each day. Teachers often have little plan time to feel sufficiently prepared, and feel unsupported by their superiors. As a result, many teachers leave the profession. Teacher attrition appears to be at an all-time high. In June 2007, the National Commission on Teaching and America's Future indicated that nearly one-third of new teachers leave after one year, and 50% of teachers will leave within the first five years. According to Dr. Sharif Shakrani (2008), the Co-director of the Education Policy Center at MSU, "Nearly 1,000 teachers leave the field of teaching every school day. (p. 1)" The high levels of teacher attrition can lead to multiple problems for students, schools, and school districts. Students do not have the advantage of being taught by experienced teachers. In return, if students do not feel connected to their teachers, or are not taught by a qualified teacher, they may be at risk for failure or drop-out. Schools have to scramble to make new hires each year. School districts spend money trying to hire and train new teachers; "teacher turnover and attrition cost the nation's school districts about $7 billion annually for recruiting, hiring and training new teachers"(p. 2).

There have been numerous attempts to create programs and policies to help beginning teachers. Induction programs are popular within many school districts. Having a more superior teacher work with a beginning teacher can yield many rewarding benefits. According to a study by Cherubini (2007) induction programs help first year teachers to remain motivated and to feel a better sense of belonging with other colleagues. When paired with a strong mentor, induction programs can also build the confidence of a first year teacher so that he or she can exercise leadership abilities as well.

Another attempt to help beginning teachers is the creation of materials suited for the needs of new teachers. Out of a study done by Vanderpyl (2007) came the formation of a website geared to help new teachers. The site offers behavior management tips, motivational topics, as well as information on how to deal with stress.

Even with the previous attempts aimed to help new teachers, the question remains; why is teacher attrition so high? This research project was designed to determine what issues give teachers the most stress during their academic year. It was also designed to see how motivation, job-satisfaction, and work-load are related to factors such as age and years of teaching experience. By discovering how these factors are connected, some light can be shed on the most stressful issues teachers face, and what assistance needs to be provided so that teachers can overcome these problems. Keeping experienced, quality teachers should be a goal of all educational districts as it directly benefits the youth of our society.

Methodology

Participants

The sample study used in this study was 25 elementary certified teachers. The subjects taught vary among the participants. The experience of teaching experience ranged from first year to 30+ years. There were 15-25 females, and 1 male participating. Their ages range from 23-60. Ninety two percent of the participants were Caucasian, 4% African-American, and 4% Asian/Pacific Islander. The participants teach at a school that had an enrollment of 422 students for the 2009-2010 school year. The participants came from a district that had student enrollment of about 5522 for the 2009-2010 school year. There were 360 certified teachers in the district. Seventy-nine percent of those teachers are female, and 21% are male. The average number of teaching experience years for the district is 15.2. Forty eight percent of teachers in the district have a Master's degree or above.

Instrumentation and Data Collection

The instrument used to collect data was a Likert-scale survey developed by the researchers. The first section on the survey consisted of demographic section that asked the participants to fill out general information such as age, numbers of years of experience, gender, and marital status. The rest of the survey was divided into three parts with 21 questions total. The first part contained eight questions about job satisfaction, the second part contained questions about motivation, and the third part contained eight questions about work-life. Each question required participants to rate their answers on a scale of 1-5. The scale had the following values: 1=strongly disagree; 2=disagree; 3=somewhat agree; 4=agree, and 5=strongly disagree.

The data was analyzed using the statistical program SPSS. Inferential statistics such as the *t*-test and an ANOVA test were used to determine if the data was significant. The tables and graphs were used to interpret the relationship between the three variables and teacher attrition.

Quantitative research is effective because it "employs methods that attempt to categorize and assign numbers to an experience or event" (Parsons & Brown 2002, p. 50). The quantitative method was chosen for this research in order to categorize the data collected, and find relationships among the variables that may lead to teacher attrition. By using statistics, the variables of job satisfaction, motivation, and work-load can be connected to age, years of experience, and number of years teaching. These descriptive statistics can "provide the action researcher with an economical tool for organizing and describing data" (p. 51).

Research Questions

This study aimed at answering the following questions:

1. Does job satisfaction play a role in teacher attrition?
2. Can job motivation be a factor in the duration of teaching careers?
3. Does work-load contribute to teachers leaving the profession early?
4. Does the number of years teaching have an impact on the satisfaction or motivation of teachers?

Definition of Terms

The terms satisfaction, motivation, work, and attrition are key to this study. Webster's Dictionary defines the terms satisfaction, motivation, work, and attrition as follows:

> Satisfaction: contentment, gratification.
>
> Motivation: to be provided with a motive.
>
> Work: task, job.
>
> Attrition: a reduction in numbers as a result of resignation.

Literature Review

Job Satisfaction

Teacher attrition continues to be a problem in our education system today. As more teachers near retirement, it is important to discover the reasons why teachers are leaving the profession and ways to prevent it. In our study we plan on looking at job satisfaction, motivation, and work-load to see if these three things are factors in teacher attrition. We believe all three will show a positive relationship with teacher attrition. Previous studies show teachers need to feel satisfied at their job and receive support from administration and parents. Praise was also found to be a good motivator among educators. Lighter work-loads or more plan-time may also entice teachers to stay in the profession. All of the studies agree on one thing, teacher attrition is a problem that needs to be addressed in order for our educational system to be successful in the future.

Baker and Perie (1997) argue that, "Daily interaction between teachers and students is at the center of the educational process; attracting and retaining high quality teachers is, thus, a primary necessity for education in the United States" (p.1). Job satisfaction is defined as an affective reaction to an individual's work situation. If teachers are not happy, then they will not stay in the profession thus lowering the quality of our educational system in the United States. Perie and Baker state that satisfaction with teaching as a career is important because it directly effects student achievement. Teachers that do not feel supported in their work may be less motivated to do their job to the best of their ability.

In a study conducted to analyze the relationship among teacher work orientation, organizational commitment, and job satisfaction of public-school teachers, the results showed work orientation was directly related to job satisfaction (Reyes, 1990). A positive relationship between tenure and job satisfaction was found, which is to be expected as the more years spent at a school the more likely the teacher will have a sense of commitment towards the organization. The data also showed the fewer the total years of teaching experience the teachers have, the more committed they are. This study confirmed that teachers having a utilitarian (i.e. merit pay and career ladder programs) work ethic were less satisfied and committed to their schools. In conclusion, to have an increase in job satisfaction; teachers need administrative support and intrinsic motivation.

Butt, et. al (2005) state that, "The factors that contribute to, or detract from, the desirability of pursuing a career in teaching are numerous" (p. 456). It is because of this very reason the Transforming the School Workforce (TSW) Pathfinder Project was created. The TSW Pathfinder Project was designed to secure significant reductions in the weekly hours worked by teachers and increase the proportion of a teacher's work week spent either teaching or tasks directly related to teaching. Questionnaires, interviews, focus groups, observations, and analysis of reports were completed by teachers at eight of the schools performing in the project. The purpose of the study was to explore the differences in teachers' job satisfaction and work-load in primary, secondary and special schools after implanting the TSW Pathfinder Project. The data proved there was greater job satisfaction among primary and special school teachers after implementing the project. Among secondary teachers there was a relationship between a fall in hours and an improvement in their job satisfaction. The study concluded job satisfaction is closely linked to good leadership, strong support, and enhanced teacher autonomy and while number of hours worked may impact satisfaction it is not a major contributing factor.

In another study, Baker and Perie (1997) explained that, "Teacher satisfaction has been linked to teacher attrition, as have some factors associated with satisfaction (e.g., teacher control, student behavior)" (p. 3). They used Item Response Theory to question elementary and secondary teachers on their levels of job satisfaction. Responses were categorized into one of three categories of satisfaction; high, moderate, or low. Private schools had a higher concentration of teachers with high levels of satisfaction, while public school teachers were fairly evenly distributed across the three levels. Approximately, 34 percent of teachers that gave responses indicated they would not choose the teaching profession again. In addition, this same group felt it was a waste of their time to be an educator. It was found that teachers with three years of experience or less tend to have higher levels of satisfaction than those with 4-9 years of experience. Compensation levels were not found to be a contributing factor in job satisfaction among teachers regardless of type of school. It was found that, "Several factors stood out as being more strongly associated with teacher satisfaction including parental support, student behavior, principal interaction, staff recognition, teacher participation in decision-making, and control of classroom" (p.4). Interestingly, elementary school teachers that agreed with the statement "Parents support teachers' work" were highly satisfied with their jobs. Those that disagreed had low satisfaction levels with their jobs reinforcing that parent support is an important factor in keeping teachers in the profession. As you can see from Perie and Baker's research, workplace conditions are strongly associated with teacher job satisfaction and more needs to be done to support teachers in their efforts.

Motivation

Motivation is the activation of goal-oriented behavior and may be internal or external. Improving teacher motivation can have a positive impact on student achievement. Bishay found it to be true that, "Students seem to recognize the effectiveness of teachers who are satisfied with their teaching performance" (p.150). This can lead to higher self-esteem in students and more nurturing teachers. Unmotivated teachers tend to do the bare minimum in terms of job requirements and do not make the extra effort to form strong relationships with their students.

There are several factors that contribute to a teacher's motivation. The freedom to try new ideas, public perception of school, and intrinsic work elements are motivators among educators (Bishay, 1996). Teachers need to have administrative support, parent/community support and constructive feedback. Often times teacher's lack the praise they feel they need and deserve. This can become disheartening and the effort put into teaching does not seem to be worth the sacrifice. Bishay's study found that, "Teachers who held an in-school job other than teaching, or who were advisors to a team or club, consistently reported higher levels of job satisfaction" (p. 149). Increased responsibility can lead to satisfaction because of the greater involvement, challenge, or control. The more valuable a person feels to his/her school, the more motivation they will possess to make it a better place.

In addition to positive reinforcement, there are other things that can increase motivation. Smaller classes are a benefit to teachers as they allow for more discussions and participation from students, which many teachers enjoy (Bishay, 1996). Not to mention less children in a classroom means less behavior problems, planning, and parent interaction, all things that can be a struggle for beginning teachers. The grading and paperwork can also take its toll on motivation. In Bishay's study many women felt the burden of paper work added to their stress levels on the job. Those that have other family obligations outside of the classroom particularly struggled with motivation and job satisfaction. When there is dual pressure of family and work, the latter is what tends to suffer. Experienced and beginning teachers both struggle with getting things done for their classroom and at the same time maintaining a life outside of school.

Work-Load

For many educators it is common knowledge that a teacher's day does not end when the last bell rings. In order to fully be prepared, many teachers need to spend extra time outside of the school day on their profession. In a study done by Drago, the relationships between the measures of working time was explored, it was discovered that while the average teacher was contractually required to work 6.5 hours a day, the amount of time teachers were spending on school-related work was averaging close to 8.25 hours a day (1999). It is not only time in the classroom that occupies a teacher's time, but also countless other hours doing school-work outside the contractual day. "Classroom contact time is only one of a number of activities that occupy teachers in their daily work. Others include homeroom, guidance, hall, lunchroom and playground monitoring, extra-curriculars, meetings, preparation, marking, and much more all falling outside formal teaching in the classroom" (Harvey & Michelson 2000, p.3). The devotion of time to a teacher's work is extensive. In Harvey & Michelson's study teachers, administrators, and managers were asked questions such as "How often do you feel rushed?" "Do you feel that you are constantly under stress?" "Do you worry that you don't spend enough time with family and friends?"(p.5) According to the data collected, 60.6% of teachers feel rushed every day. Nearly 40% feel they are always under stress. 34.4% feel they don't have time for fun outside of their profession. Furthermore, it was discovered that teachers spend a mean time of 58 minutes a day on work-related activities at home.

With all the extra time being put into their profession, it is no wonder teachers often feel great amounts of stress. Many teachers have families and other obligation at home. The extra work brought home leaves little time for these other responsibilities: Harvey and Michelson concluded, "They (teachers) have to work outside school hours and at home, but they are more likely to face time pressures then and there in the view of other commitments that they have in the limited time available" (p. 5). The stress teachers feel from extreme work-loads can lead to things such as poor performance, family and mental issues, and eventually even leaving the profession. Charlie Naylor speaks of these issues in his article and says "teacher workloads are excessive, and that the negative effects of stress are having considerable impact on teachers. The effects include declining job satisfaction, reduced ability to meet students' needs, significant incidences of psychological disorders leading to increased absence from work, and a high proportion of claims for disability caused by stress"(Naylor 2001, p.10).

Teacher Attrition within the First Five Years

Stress levels decrease as number of teaching years increase. As educators gain more experience, creating lessons, behavior management, and involvement with parents become easier. The challenge today is keeping new teachers in the profession long enough to experience the decrease in stress. Often times the first five years are so overwhelming, teachers feel they have no other option than to leave the profession in attempts to search for a career more suitable to their needs.

In addition to the lack of experience in the teaching field, new teachers are lacking the proper education to succeed. Teacher induction programs are not teaching the necessities needed to survive in managing a classroom. There is a lack of training in instructional materials, child learning theories, observation of other classes, and classroom practice prior to student teaching (Graziano, 2005). Every year 200,000 teachers are hired for the first day of school. By the end of the year, 22,000 teachers have quit the profession. Those that make it past the first year are not always in it for the "long haul". About 30 percent of new teachers leave the profession after three years and around 45 percent leave after five years. What is the main cause for these new teachers leaving? "Poor administrative support, lack of influence within the school system, classroom intrusion, and inadequate time" are a few of the main things mentioned in Graziano's article (p. 41). Teachers working in low-income schools are more likely to leave the profession as there is more stress and less support. Working in such conditions can be mentally draining and eventually takes a toll on the educator thus pushing him/her to pursue a different career.

Today, teachers face more challenges than ever before. Funding cuts have put a hold on some mentoring programs and class sizes are larger than ever. In addition to all of this, RTI (Response to Intervention) programs have become mandatory in schools as a part of the No Child Left Behind Act. This means educators have more on their plate than ever before and most often there is inadequate training for these new government sponsored programs. As a result, more and more teachers continue to leave the profession seeking something less stressful and not as time consuming. Through our research questions we hope to discover the relationship between job satisfaction, motivation, work-load, and number of years teaching to teacher attrition and hopefully discover ways that it can be prevented in the future.

Results

Results from the survey show that overall teachers are satisfied with their jobs and feel they have an impact on today's youth. Salary does not appear to play a role in job satisfaction regardless of experience as the responses show few teachers feel they need supplemental income outside of school (see Table 1).

Table 1: Job Satisfaction – Years Teaching

Satisfaction Questions (Means) Years	1-5	6-10	11-15	16-20	26-30	31-36	Total Mean
I am satisfied with my job.	4.50	4.00	4.00	4.20	4.33	3.60	4.11
I need to supplement my salary with supplemental jobs.	1.50	2.75	2.25	2.40	1.33	2.60	2.42
The style of supervision of my administrator is effective.	3.00	3.00	3.00	2.40	2.67	2.40	2.73
The flow of information Around my school is effective.	3.00	2.75	3.50	2.80	3.00	2.60	2.96
I have adequate time and support for professional growth.	3.00	3.25	2.75	3.80	3.00	3.00	3.12

The statement, "The style of supervision of my administrator is effective" showed a difference between new and experienced teachers. Teachers with 16 or more years of experience disagreed with this statement with means ranging from 2.40-2.60. The results for the flow of communication and adequate time for professional growth had mean averages of 2.96 and 3.12 between all levels of experience. Looking at job satisfaction in relation to number of years teaching shows the newer the teacher, the more satisfied he/she is likely to be in the field of teaching.

The overall motivation of participants in the survey proves to be high (see Table 2). The total mean average of 4.04 for the statement, "I feel I can impact the youth of today" confirms teachers strongly agree with this regardless of years of experience. On the topic of "On most days I'm motivated to go to work" the total mean was 4.12. The lowest mean for this statement was for teachers with one to five years of experience. Almost all of the participants disagreed with the statement, "I often feel defeated at the end of the day." Some of that could be contributed to the high total mean regarding the statements, "Educating the young is important to me" and "My job allows me to utilize my skills and talents." Educators that feel they have an impact on today's youth and are making an effort will more than likely be motivated to come to work.

Table 2: Motivation – Years Teaching

Motivation Questions (Means) Years	1-5	6-10	11-15	16-20	26-30	31-36	Total Mean
I feel I can impact the Youth in my community.	4.00	4.25	4.25	4.20	3.67	4.00	4.04
On most days I'm Motivated to go to work.	3.50	4.50	4.00	4.20	4.00	4.00	4.12
I often feel defeated at the end of the day.	2.50	2.25	3.00	2.20	1.67	2.40	2.42
Educating the young is important to me	4.50	5.00	5.00	4.60	4.67	4.60	4.73
My job allows me to utilize my skills and talents.	4.50	4.75	4.00	4.40	3.67	3.80	4.15

Participants were in agreement on several of the statements under the work-life section of the survey. The results showed the average amounts of time people surveyed spend on school work outside of the contractual day is around 10 hours per week (see Table 3).

Surprisingly, teachers with one to five years of experience also had a mean average of 10 hours per week. Teachers with 11-15 and 16-20 spend the most time on school work outside of the contractual way with means around 15 hours per week. The total mean for the statement, "I have difficulty leaving issues at work." was 3.46. Teachers with 6-10 years of experience had the lowest mean of 2.25 for the same statement. The total mean for, "I'm exhausted at the end of the day." is 3.31. Again, teachers with 11-15 years of experience had the most agreement with that statement with a mean of 4.25. The highest means for behavior problems in the classroom occurred in teachers with 11-15 and 31-36 years of experience. The total mean of 3.58 shows that teachers surveyed feel they are effective at handling behavior problems in their classrooms. Concerning, "I effectively communicate within the school day with parents." teachers had a total mean of 2.12, which shows their disagreement with this statement. The data collected suggests number or years teaching does impact feelings regarding work-life.

Table 3: Work-Life-Years Teaching

Work-Life Questions (Means) Years	1-5	6-10	11-15	16-20	26-30	31-36	Total Mean
Number of hours per week worked outside of contractual day.	2.00	1.50	2.75	3.00	2.33	1.80	2.35
I have difficulty leaving Issues at work.	4.00	2.25	4.00	3.00	3.33	4.00	3.46
I'm exhausted by the end Of the school day.	3.00	2.75	4.25	3.00	2.67	3.20	3.31
Behavior problems occur on a daily basis in my classroom.	1.50	2.00	3.25	2.80	2.67	3.20	2.85
I'm effective at handling behavior in my classroom.	4.00	4.00	3.00	4.00	4.00	3.40	3.58
I effectively communicate within the school day with parents.	3.00	2.25	1.75	2.20	3.33	1.20	2.12

There were differences between responses for the satisfaction questions in terms of age of teacher (see Table 4). Teachers between ages 61 and 70 had a mean of 3.00 for the statement, "I would be pleased if my child became a teacher." In contrast, teachers ages 20 to 30 had a mean of 4.50 for the same question. Teachers ages 20 to 30 and 41 to 50 disagreed the most with the statement, "The style of supervision of my administrator is effective." Younger teachers also felt strongly that the flow of information around their school is ineffective. Their mean for this statement was 2.25. Similarities were found between the statements on supplemental jobs and professional growth.

Table 4: Job Satisfaction - Age

Satisfaction Questions (Means) Age	20-30	31-40	41-50	51-60	61-70	Total Mean
I am satisfied with my job.	4.25	4.00	4.00	4.29	4.00	4.12
I need to supplement my Salary with supplemental jobs.	2.25	2.25	2.40	2.85	1.00	2.42
I would be pleased if my Child became a teacher.	4.50	3.75	3.85	3.86	3.00	3.88
The style of supervision of my administrator is effective.	2.50	3.25	2.50	2.86	3.00	2.73
The flow of information Around my school is effective.	2.25	3.50	2.80	3.29	3.00	2.96
I have adequate time and support for professional growth.	3.00	2.75	3.30	3.14	3.00	3.12

According to survey results, age does play a role in teacher motivation (Table 5). The teachers' ages 20 to 30 had a higher mean for the statement, "I feel I can impact the youth in my community." Means of 4.75 show this age group of teachers also felt strongly that educating the young is important and their skills and talents are utilized at their jobs. In contrast, teachers ages 61 to 70 did not feel as strongly towards the same statements having means of 4.00 for each. Educators ages 20 to 30 and 51 to 60 are most likely to feel defeated at the end of the school day with means 2.75 and 3.00. Across all age levels, motivation is high among the participants in the survey.

Table 5: Motivation - Age

| Motivation Questions (Means) | | | | | | Total |
Age	20-30	31-40	41-50	51-60	61-70	Mean
I feel I can impact the Youth in my community.	4.25	4.00	4.00	4.00	4.00	4.04
On most days I'm motivated to go to work.	4.00	4.25	4.00	4.29	4.00	4.12
I often feel defeated at the end of the day.	2.75	2.00	2.10	3.00	2.00	2.42
Educating the young is important to me.	4.75	4.75	4.80	4.71	4.00	4.73
My job allows me to utilize my skills and talents.	4.75	4.50	3.80	4.14	4.00	4.15

The survey shows age did impact responses towards work-life statements (see Table 6). Older teachers, ages 61 to 70 spend 11-15 hours per week on school work outside of the contractual day. Younger teachers ages 20 to 30 only spend 5 to 10 hours per week on school work. Teachers between the ages of 20 to 30 and 51 to 60 have the most difficulty leaving issues at work with means of 3.50 and 4.29. Older and younger teachers both agreed with the statement, "I'm exhausted by the end of the school day." The most disagreement with this statement if within teachers ages 31 to 50. The younger teachers felt they had control of their classroom and behavior problems were minimal. Older teachers seem to struggle more with behavior problems on a daily basis but also feel they have the skills to handle them effectively. In terms of the statement, "I effectively communicate within the school day with parents." teachers ages 61 to 70 agree with this statement. All other teachers disagree and feel there is not enough time in the day to keep up on communication with parents.

Table 6: Work-Life- Age

| Work-life Questions (Means) | | | | | | Total |
Age	20-30	31-40	41-50	51-60	61-70	Mean
Number of hours per week worked outside of contractual day.	1.75	2.25	2.50	2.57	3.00	2.34
I have difficulty leaving Issues at work.	3.50	3.00	3.10	4.29	3.00	3.46
I'm exhausted by the end of the school day.	3.25	2.75	2.90	4.14	4.00	3.30
Behavior problems occur on a daily basis in my classroom.	2.25	2.75	2.50	3.57	4.00	2.84
I'm effective at handling behavior in my classroom.	4.00	3.25	4.00	2.86	4.00	3.58
I effectively communicate within the school day with parents.	2.25	2.75	2.00	1.57	4.00	2.12

Marital status has an impact on job satisfaction (see Table 7). Single educators have a mean of 5.00 and are strongly satisfied with their job. A mean of 3.00 shows they are also more likely to have to supplement their salary with supplemental jobs than teachers who are married. In regards to administration style and communication within school, single teachers are more satisfied having means of 3.50 for each compared to 2.67 and 2.88 for married teachers. Single teachers also feel they have more time and support for professional growth. On the whole, single teachers are more satisfied with their jobs than married teachers.

Table 7: Job Satisfaction – Marital Status

Satisfaction Questions	Mean Married	Mean Single
I am satisfied with my job.	4.04	5.00
I need to supplement my salary with supplemental jobs.	2.37	3.00
The style of supervision of my administrator is effective.	2.67	3.50
The flow of information around my school is effective.	2.88	3.50
I have adequate time and support for professional growth.	3.08	3.50

Being single can also impact the amount of motivation a person has towards his/her teaching career (see Table 8). Single educators have a mean of 5.00 and are motivated to go to work. Married educators are also motivated to go to work however have a lower mean of 4.04.

The statements regarding impacting youth, the importance of educating the young and utilizing ones skills and talents all had means of 5.00 for single teachers. Unmarried educators are also less likely to feel defeated at the end of the day. Similar to job satisfaction results, single people have more motivation towards school than those that are married.

Table 8: Motivation – Marital Status

Motivation Questions	Mean Married	Mean Single
I feel I can impact the youth in my community.	3.96	5.00
On most days I'm motivated to go to work.	4.04	5.00
I often feel defeated at the end of the day.	2.46	2.00
Educating the young is important to me.	4.71	5.00
My job allows me to utilize my skills and talents.	4.08	5.00

While differences are apparent between work-load and marital status, there are also some similarities that were found (see Table 9). On the average, single teachers work 11 to 15 hours per week outside of the contractual day compared to 5 to 10 of married teachers. Both groups have the same amount of difficulty leaving work issues at work. A mean of 4.00 shows single teachers are more exhausted by the end of the day compared to a mean of 3.25 with married teachers. There was a positive relationship with the statement, "Behavior problems happen on a daily basis in my classroom." Both sets of teachers had similar means in response to this statement. The mean of 3.67 shows that married people feel they are more effective at handling behavior problems in their classrooms compared to 2.50 for single people. Unmarried teachers also feel it is more difficult for them to communicate with parents during the time allotted in the school day. Marital Status had an impact on the results for participant responses regarding work-life.

Table 9: Work-Life – Marital Status

Work-life Questions	Mean Married	Mean Single
Number of hours per week worked outside of contractual day.	2.29	3.00
I have difficulty leaving issues at work.	3.46	3.50
I'm exhausted by the end of the school day.	3.25	4.00
Behavior problems occur on a daily basis in my classroom.	2.83	3.00
I'm effective at handling behavior in my classroom.	3.67	2.50
I effectively communicate within the school day with parents.	2.20	1.00

Discussion

Job Satisfaction

Prior research has suggested that job satisfaction plays a large role in teacher attrition. If a teacher is not satisfied at his or her job, there is a greater chance that teacher will leave the profession. Overall, the population we surveyed seemed satisfied with their jobs. However, when broken down into different categories of satisfaction, there are both consistencies and inconsistencies with previous research. Our findings in regards to the number of years of experience a teacher has and job satisfaction seem to go against some of the research we found. In a study conducted by Reyes (1990), results indicated that the more years a teacher spends at a school, the more commitment he or she will feel, and in a sense be more satisfied. In our results the newer teachers seemed to be the more satisfied ones with the highest mean of 4.5 for the question "I am satisfied with my job". This does, however, coincide with the results found by Baker and Perie (1997) that indicated teachers with 3 years or less of teaching experience tend to feel more satisfied than teachers with 4-9 years of experience. This might reflect the optimism a new teacher feels when first beginning a teaching job. The trials and issues they face may not overshadow their love of the job, and thus lead to a higher sense of satisfaction. Perhaps it is this satisfaction that induction programs should emphasize in order to help deal with the hard times new teachers face.

When taking a look at the specific categories of job satisfaction, two areas that were lower for all ranges of experience were "the style of my administrator is effective," and "the flow of communication around my school is effective." These results are similar to the findings from the Butt et.al study (2005). Job satisfaction seems closely linked to good leadership, administrative support, and good communication. These factors are important in making sure teachers feel supported and satisfied with what they do.

While the teaching profession is not one known for its hefty salaries, according to our population salary does not seem to play a part in job satisfaction regardless of the number of years of experience, age, or marital status. This closely mirrors the results found in the Baker and Perie study. They state that "salary shows no strong association with teacher satisfaction at either the elementary or secondary level" (pg. 23). While these results may be surprising, it could indicate that many teachers are dedicated to their profession regardless of low salaries. It is the desire to help students learn that leads them to experience satisfaction in their jobs.

Motivation

According to previous research, motivation is another link to teacher attrition. The population that we sampled seemed overall very motivated. Most of the questions on the survey asked participants about intrinsic motivation. This shows that most teachers are motivated simply by teaching. The question "educating the young in important to me" scored very high with the lowest mean being 4.50. Bishay (1996) echoes this belief and says "true job satisfaction is derived from the gratification of higher-order needs, social relations, esteem, and actualization" (pg. 147).

However when looking at the categories of motivation, one question that scored lower for teachers with 1-5 years of experience was " on most days I am motivated to go to work." The mean score for their group was 3.50. The next lowest mean was 4.00. This may suggest that while newer teachers may be happy with what they do, the other stressful factors of being a new teacher can lead to decreased motivation. This is an area that new teacher induction programs and mentor programs should be aware of. Perhaps this is where research like the one done by Cherubini (2007) could be beneficial in this area. The research findings indicated that new teachers felt motivated when they had chances for personal growth and professional leadership opportunities. When new teachers feel valued for their input as educators, it may lead them to be even more motivated.

With regards to the statement "Educating the young is important to me", the age range of 61-70 had the lowest mean of 4.00. This may indicate that the longer a teacher is in the profession, motivation could lesson. Perhaps school districts should not only focus in on supporting the newer teachers, but they should also be sure their older, experienced teachers have the support they need and are being motivated. VanderPyl (2007) makes a good suggestion when she says "The success of the experienced teachers is not to be taken for granted. Previously an untapped resource, seasoned instructors can be the most helpful to new teachers (pg. 2)." A good way to motivate the experienced teachers might be to pair them as a mentor with a newer teacher. Perhaps they can provide each other with the motivation each one needs.

Work-Load

It was no surprise to see that our sampled population put in extra work hours outside the contractual day. While the work day technically runs from 8:15-3:30, our participants worked an average of ten extra hours during the week. This coincides with the study done by Drago (1999) where teachers were putting in two extra hours a day on school related work. While the group in our study with 1-5 years of teaching experience was putting in an average of ten extra hours per week, surprisingly, the groups with 11-15, and 16-20 years of teaching experience had the highest average mean for extra hours at around 15. This shows that all teachers, regardless of how much experience they have, feel there is not enough time in the school day to get everything done.

Teachers with 11-15 years of experience had the most agreement with the statement "I'm exhausted by the end of the day." It is common for teachers in this range to have families at this time, and perhaps that adds to the exhaustion felt on top of teaching. This is similar to the results that Bishay's study (1996) indicated. The dual pressure of family and work can be a struggle for teachers. This important issue is echoed in the research done by Drago (1999), "Problems of teacher retention could intensify if the long hours of teachers in this sample are typical for the profession (pg. 38)."

Conclusion

Teachers surveyed in this study were fairly motivated and satisfied. When looking at specific aspects of these two categories, and at the work-load questions, it is obvious that there are still improvements that can be made in order to reduce teacher attrition.

The findings of this study indicate that while teachers may feel satisfied and motivated overall, there are still areas in which they need more support. Work-loads appear to be excessive across all age groups, years of experience and marital statuses. This can directly affect satisfaction and motivation, and eventually lead to teacher attrition. The findings in this study suggest that administrators and school districts need to develop support strategies for teachers of all ages and with all years of experience. Both the new and the experienced teacher need to be encouraged and looked after. These findings can also imply that administrators need to be aware of the satisfaction and motivational levels of their faculty. In doing so, they may be able to provide the help necessary to keep teachers in the profession.

Further research should be done in the area of teacher attrition in order to supplement these findings. Results from this study showed that teachers work many extra hours outside the work day. Further research could explore ways that teachers could better utilize the time given during the day to complete tasks. Further research could also be done to explore how much plan time is really sufficient for a teacher. Other possible routes for further research could be to explore what motivates teachers, both new and experienced. And, how effective are mentoring programs for both new and experienced teachers?

These findings can be beneficial to those developing teacher induction programs, as well as those who are interested in the satisfaction levels of teachers. If, as much literature suggests, teacher attrition can be connected to motivation, job satisfaction, and work-load, focusing on strategies and policies that can address these issues could be beneficial to all involved in the system of education.

References

Baker, P. & Perie, M. (1997, August 25). Job satisfaction among America's teachers: Effects of workplace conditions, background characteristics, and teacher compensation. Retrieved September 14, 2009, from http://nces.ed.gov/Pubsearch/pubsinfo.asp?pubid=97471

Bishay, A. (1996, Fall). Teacher motivation and job satisfaction: A study employing the experience sampling method. *Journal of Undergraduate Sciences*, 3, 147-154. Retrieved September 16, 2009 from http://www.hcs.harvard.edu/~jus/0303/bishay.pdf

Brown, K.S., & Parsons, R. D. (2002) *Teacher as reflective practitioner and action researcher.* Wadsworth: Cengage Learning.

Butt, G., Lance, A., Fielding, A., Gunter, H., Ravner, S., Thomas, H. (2005, November). Teacher job satisfaction: Lessons from the TSW pathfinder project. *School Leadership and Management*, 25(5), 455-471. Retrieved September 16, 2009 from ERIC database (Education Resources Information Center) on the World Wide Web: http://www.eric.ed.gov/

Cherubini, L. (2007). Speaking up and speaking freely: Beginning teachers' critical perceptions of their professional induction. *The Professional Educator. Brock University.* 29 (1), 1-12. Retrieved October 28, 2009 from: http://theprofessionaleducator.org/articles/archives/fall2007.pdf

DeAngelis, K., Presley, J. (2007). Leaving schools or leaving the profession: setting Illinois' record straight on new teacher attrition. *Policy Research Report: IERC*, 1-48. Retrieved September 22, 2009 from ERIC database (Education Resources Information Center) on the World Wide Web: http://www.eric.ed.gov/

Drago, R., Captain R., Costanza, D., Brubaker, T., Cloud, D., Harris, N., Kashian, R., Riggs, T. L. (1999, April). New estimates of working time for elementary school teachers. *Monthly Labor Review.* 31-40. Retrieved October 15, 2009 from: http://www.bls.gov/opub/mlr/1999/04/art4full.pdf

Gonzalez, L.E., Brown, M., & Slate, J. (2008). Teachers who left the teaching profession: a qualitative understanding. *The Qualitative Report*, 13(1). 1-11. Retrieved September 15, 2009 from http://www.nova.edu/sss/QR/QR13-1/gonzalez.pdf

Harvey, A. S., Michelson, W. (2000). Is teachers' work never done? Time-use and subjective outcomes. *Radical Pedagogy.* 1-8. Retrieved November 3, 2009 from http://radicalpedagogy.icaap.org

Naylor, C. (2001). Teacher workload and stress: An international perspective on human costs and systematic failure. *BCTF Research Report,* Sect. 3, 1-14. Retrieved November 3, 1009 from http://epe.lacbac.gc.ca/100/200/300/bc_teachers_federation/teacher_wor kload/html/2001-wlc-01-report.html

Reyes, P. (1990, July/August). Individual work orientation and teacher outcomes. *Journal of Educational Research*, 83(6), 327-335. Retrieved September 14, 2009, from ERIC database (Education Resources Information Center) on the World Wide Web: http://www.eric.ed.gov/

Shakrani, S. (2008). Teacher turnover: Costly crisis, solvable problem. *Education Policy Center, Michigan State University*, 1-4. Retrieved September 14, 2009, from ERIC database (Education Resources Information Center) on the World Wide Web: http://www.eric.ed.gov/

VanderPyl, T. (2007, May). Growing pains: Giving new teachers the tools and tips they need to survive the early years and combat attrition. p. 1-18. Retrieved from ERIC database (Education Resources Information Center) on the World Wide Web: http://www.eric.ed.gov/

Chapter 12: Effects of Teacher Preparation and First Year Support for Teachers

Kristy Siebert & Rebecca Frangella

Introduction and Statement of the Problem

The transition from college to teaching is one that is often quite difficult for new teachers. During student teaching, students are typically supported by not only cooperating teachers, but also university supervisors who collaborate to ensure the success of these students. When these newly accredited teachers are hired for their first jobs, they may experience a "real" classroom for the very first time. Establishing a routine, setting and enforcing behavior guidelines, developing curriculum, meeting national, state, district, and parental expectations, and meeting the needs of a diverse student population are now solely the new teacher's responsibility.

Research shows that many of these new teachers are leaving the field. Using research data from the National Center for Education Statistics, Ingersoll and Smith (2003) have estimated that the attrition rate for new teachers is 40% to 50% after five years. This exodus of teachers from the profession has led a number of researchers to examine the question of how our school systems can better support beginning teachers as they transition from college into the professional world.

When examining the reasons that teachers give for staying in their positions, Certo and Fox (2002) found that one of the top motivators was collaborative relationships with colleagues. An important factor in these relationships was that adequate time was provided for the new teachers and staff to build these professional connections. Many mentoring programs strive to provide the opportunity and the motivation to establish these relationships and have proven to be effective in the effort to retain new teachers (Smith & Ingersoll, 2004).

Also, research has found that teacher training impacts teacher attrition. For example, new research on Professional Development Schools (PDS) found that it has a positive impact on new teacher retention. This alternative to traditional student teaching extends the experiences that students have in schools and attempts to immerse students in a more authentic teaching setting. A longitudinal study by Latham and Vogt (2007) compared students who participated in PDS with those who participated in traditional student teaching. This study of elementary education students found that PDS prepared teachers were more likely to enter the field upon graduation and stay in teaching longer than traditionally prepared students.

With consideration for these findings, this research will explore types of mentoring and induction programs that may yield the most positive results in the quest to retain new teachers in the teaching profession. Also, it will examine the effect that PDS programs have on teacher projections of continuing in the field of education. This research will be useful to teacher education programs, hiring practices of school districts, and the support systems that schools provide to new teachers.

Literature Review

Attrition

Why do so many bright, promising teachers leave the profession almost as quickly as they enter into it? In the state of Illinois alone, the ISBE's Educator Supply and Demand In Illinois: 2001 Annual Report affirmed that the attrition rate for new teachers is about 30% within the first three years, and it estimates that the percentages go up to between 32% and 40% over five years of teaching in Illinois Public Schools (IPS). This exiting of teachers from the profession, or *attrition*, has quickly become a cause for concern. According to Ingersoll and Smith (2003) the estimated attrition rate of new teachers, particularly those who received no form of induction support from their schools, is 40% to 50% after only five years of teaching. *Induction* is defined as the first three years of teaching (Feiman-Nemser, 2001). This can have a lasting effect on a teacher's career. Ingersoll and Smith found the following forms of induction support to be most common in public schools: mentoring, supportive communication from administration, common planning time with other grade level or content area teachers, or seminars for beginning teachers. However, the existence of an induction program is not the single factor that determines whether or not teachers remain in the profession. A multitude of studies have been conducted on factors that have led to teacher attrition, particularly for those exiting teaching within the first five years of entering into the profession. As indicated from nationally representative data collected by the National Center for Education Statistics, using the Schools and Staffing Survey (SASS) as well as the Teacher Follow-Up Survey (TFS) (Ingersoll, 1999, 2001, 2002; Smith and Ingersoll, 2003), beginning teachers who left the profession exited for the following reasons:

- *A school staffing action,* such as cutbacks, layoffs, or school closings (19%)
- *Family or personal reasons,* such as pregnancy, health, or family moves (42%)
- *To pursue a better job or career* (39%)
- *Job dissatisfaction,* including low salaries, student discipline, lack of administrative support, and unmotivated students (29%)

While the first two reasons listed for teacher attrition cannot be prevented, educational reformers and administrators can have an impact on the last two factors—pursuit of a better job and job dissatisfaction. The country's teacher shortage has attained national media attention, but the focus needs to be centered on what can be done to *retain* current and future teachers, not simply on what causes them to leave. For example, when looking at the issue of job dissatisfaction, several of the causes for the anguish felt by new teachers need to be addressed. The National Education Association (NEA) conveyed that while some teachers feel overwhelmed by the scope of their position, others feel that the expectations are unclear (NEA, 2003a). Also reported by the NEA was the sentiment that teachers are significantly underpaid when compared to other professions requiring the same amount of education and that teachers are not valued for their societal contributions (NEA, 2002).

In a report for the National Commission on Teaching and America's Future (NCTAF), Richard Ingersoll refers to teaching as a "revolving door profession" (Ingersoll as cited in NEA, 2003b), as the ratio of teachers entering and exiting the profession each year are roughly the same. A qualitative examination as to why beginning teachers left the profession so early was conducted in a study by Gonzalez, Brown, and Slate (2008). In this study, the researchers used semi-structured interviews with former teachers who had been located via snowball sampling and selected for the study based on criterion sampling. The sample included eight certified school teachers from Texas, six females and two males between the ages of 25 and 26, who were no longer teaching after one year in the profession. When asked why they left the profession so soon after entering, the factors they noted included student discipline, salary, and administration. Their responses were similar to what has been identified by Herbert and Ramsey (2004) as contributing factors to the high attrition rate: salaries and incentives, working condition, professional development, and assignments. The implications from this study, though limited in scope due to the small sample size and inclusion of teachers from only one state, can be used by school administrators to re-evaluate schools facing high attrition rates. These administrators, as well as any others involved in creating supportive, nurturing environments for teachers, need to ask themselves, "What can be done to maintain the greater majority of teachers on a yearly basis?"

With such high rates of attrition among beginning teachers, it is important to identify the factors, individually and in combination, that may be linked to the *retention* of current and future teachers in order to improve upon the current teacher shortage. Therefore, this study focuses on establishing beginning teachers' perceptions of the supports provided to them in their first year of teaching as well as their projections for a future in the teaching profession.

Teacher Preparation

A variety of experiences are implemented with pre-service teachers as they are prepared for graduation, certification, and jobs in the field of education. These various experiences may have an impact on how well prepared these new teachers are for their first jobs and how long they stay in the field of education. Two methods of preparation are examined in this research in attempt to determine if either method is superior in helping new teachers feel prepared for and supported in their new teaching positions. This research also seeks to determine if either method may correlate to lower projected attrition rates among these new teachers.

The two methods discussed here are Professional Development Schools (PDS) and traditional student teaching. PDS programs are defined by Ridley, Hurwitz, Hackett, and Miller (2005) as "a collaboration between schools, colleges, or departments of education; P-12 schools; school districts; and union/professional associations" (p. 46). These programs seek to better connect theory and practice through highly supported field experiences that are incorporated throughout teacher preparation programs (Ridley et al., 2005). The goal of PDS programs is to give pre-service teachers more experience in the "real work of teaching" (Latham & Vogt, 2007, p. 155). In comparison, traditional student teaching consists of more campus-based work culminating in one semester of experience in a classroom. Cooperating teachers in the classrooms and university supervisors collaborate and work together with the pre-service teachers to form a triad in both traditional student teaching and PDS programs.

Many factors influence the experiences of pre-service teachers in both programs. According to Valencia, Martin, Place and Grossman (2009), the goals of pre-service teachers, cooperating teachers, and university supervisors may be disconnected. Pre-service teachers come to the classrooms with concepts and strategies from their university work that they are eager to implement. Unfortunately, the goal of cooperating teachers is often to incorporate the pre-service teacher into the routines and practices that have already been established with little room left for exploration by the pre-service teacher. University supervisors may be left to negotiate these differing goals while still upholding the requirements set forth by the university involved. This can lead to many missed opportunities for learning on the part of the pre-service teachers (Valencia et al., 2009).

Pre-service teaching experiences that were of longer duration and that focused on building support for the university student were found by Tusin (1995) to better prepare new teachers for their first year of teaching. Of particular importance was collaboration between the pre-service teacher and an experienced teacher who assisted the pre-service teacher in blending theory and practice while connecting coursework to a real classroom setting. The teachers in this study valued the support provided, went beyond the minimum requirements, asked for suggestions, and sought help. All seven teachers in the study considered their pre-service experiences to be essential to the success they experienced during their first year of teaching. In addition, these supportive relationships were found by Dinsmore and Wenger (2006) to be of significant importance in extended pre-service experiences as well as during the first year of teaching.

Extended clinical experiences were also the focus of Latham and Vogt (2007) in their research on PDS programs. They found that teachers who participated in a PDS program were more likely to go on to teach and stay in the teaching profession longer than students who participated in a traditional student teaching experience. However, instead of targeting supportive relationships, they theorized that pre-service teachers who were willing to devote more time to clinical experiences in classrooms may inherently possess a deeper commitment to the field of education.

Regardless of the explanation, PDS prepared teachers were found by many researchers to experience greater success in the field of education when compared to teachers who had participated in a more traditional student teaching experience (Dinsmore & Wenger, 2006; Latham & Vogt, 2007; and Tusin, 1995). Both teacher preparation methods (PDS and traditional student teaching) are included in the current study and examined with mentoring experiences during the first year of teaching. This is done in an attempt to determine how teachers' perceptions of support during their first year of employment are affected by each factor.

Mentoring

Many new teachers receive support in the form of mentoring during their first year or two of teaching (Smith & Ingersoll, 2004). Various programs provided by school districts can be classified under the heading of "mentoring." For example, the informal pairing of new teachers with experienced teachers, new teacher meetings, full-time mentors assigned to groups of new teachers and the formal pairing of new teachers with experienced teachers in similar teaching positions all qualify as "mentoring."

With attrition rates estimated to be 40-50% after the first five years of teaching (Ingersoll & Smith, 2003), one of the main goals of mentoring programs is reducing teacher attrition. One program that is successful at reducing the rates of attrition in new teachers is the Partners in Education (PIE) Program. The components of this program include "(a) intensive mentoring, (b) cohort group networking, and (c) ongoing inquiry into practice" (Kelley, 2004, p. 442). The intensive mentoring was provided one half day each week by clinical professors, while the cohorts of new teachers attended seminars twice each month to discuss relevant issues for the new teachers. New teachers were also required to be in graduate school during this first year of teaching. Ninety-four percent of the participants in this program were still teaching after four years.

Other factors that have been found to reduce the turnover rate of new teachers are having a mentor in the same educational placement, maintaining a common time during the school day to plan on a regular basis, and retaining a network of teachers with whom to collaborate (Smith & Ingersoll, 2004). The combined implementation of these factors proved to be much more effective than individual components implemented separately (Smith and Ingersoll, 2004). Of these components, collaboration carries particular importance (Fresko & Alhija, 2009; Chubbuck, Clift, Allard, & Quinlan, 2001; Fry, 2007). Collaboration provides new teachers with a safe, effective environment in which to ask questions and receive constructive feedback from more experienced teachers (Fry, 2007; Weiss & Weiss, 1999; Fresko & Alhija, 2009). It also provides time for new teachers to discuss and reflect with peers (Chubbuck et al., 2001). These opportunities provide new teachers with the support of a "professional community where all teachers are learners" (Feiman-Nemser, 2003, p. 28).

Another important area of mentoring is that of receiving information that will promote the growth of new teachers (Chubbuck, et al., 2001). After conducting her follow-up study of first year teachers involved in a clinical experience program, Tusin (1995) concluded, "Mentor teachers who are included as valuable partners in education provide a wealth of experiences...they help blend theory and practice" (p. 8). New teachers can couple their student teaching with the educational theory they were taught from their university; however, research has consistently shown that these two experiences are simply not enough to provide a stable foundation for teachers upon initially entering the profession. In addition to needing the support and feedback of experienced teachers, first year teachers also need to become acclimated with their new surroundings within the school as well as with the policies and procedures they are expected to follow and enforce.

As mentoring programs such those described have become more of a commonplace, new teachers' perceptions of support have increased and rates of teacher turnover have been reduced (Smith & Ingersoll, 2004). Unfortunately, not every new teacher has the opportunity to participate in a mentoring program (Weiss & Weiss, 1999). This disparity in opportunity may continue to exist until the most effective mentoring programs are identified, mandated, and funded.

Methodology

The current study examined several factors that may have an impact on new teachers as they begin their careers in teaching. These factors include teacher preparation, full-time district mentor support, 1:1 mentor support, and less formal mentor support in the form of new teacher in-service meetings. Data was collected from new teachers during the spring semester of the 2009-2010 school year. The purpose was to determine the potential effect of these programs as they apply to new teachers with the goal of reducing teacher attrition.

Participants

This study includes male and female teachers who are in their first year of teaching in two public school districts in the Midwest region of the United States. Teachers selected to participate included those who were in their very first year of teaching as well as teachers with prior teaching experience who had relocated to a new district. Both school districts are located in the same community but function independently of each other. One district, District A, contains fifteen elementary schools, three junior highs, and two high schools. The other district, District B, has an early education center, six elementary schools, one junior high, one high school, and an area career center for high school students from throughout the area. Together, the student population of these districts totals 18,500, with the larger district, District A, serving approximately 13,000 students and District B serving approximately 5,500 students.

Of the nearly 13,000 students enrolled in District A, almost 24% are low income. The student population is comprised of approximately 71% white, 12% black, 5% Hispanic, and almost 6% Asian/Pacific Islander. The remaining 6% of students fall under the classification of Native American or Multi-Racial (Illinois School Report Card, 2009). District B is serving a population of almost 50% low income students. The racial make-up of these students includes 58% white, 23% black, 8% Hispanic, 4% Asian/Pacific Islander, and about 7% Multi-Racial (Illinois School Report Card, 2009).

Throughout the duration of this study, approximately 136 new teachers were employed by these districts (102 in District A and 32 in District B). These new teachers are employed throughout the K-12 system with representation from elementary, junior high, and high school. The teaching degrees of these new teachers were from several universities.

The majority of the new teachers in these districts had preservice teaching experiences in one of two categories: Professional Development Schools (PDS) programs or traditional student teaching. The PDS programs place pre-service teachers in schools for two semesters while they complete their on-campus requirements. The traditional student teaching experience consists of one semester in a participating school. Participants in PDS programs have been found to enter and remain in the profession at a higher rate than traditionally prepared teachers (Latham & Vogt, 2007).

New teachers in both districts participated in the mentoring program that was offered in their district. These mentoring programs differed greatly in the level of support that was offered to new teachers. One district was implementing the second year of a two-year grant that allowed four teachers in that district to be released from their teaching duties to become full-time mentors. These mentors visited new teachers in their classrooms weekly to give feedback and reflect on teaching practices. In addition, this district offered teachers in their first year of teaching as well as those new to the district 1:1 mentors who are peer educators (ideally teaching within the same school and subject/grade level). District mentors, 1:1 mentors, and the new teacher also met on a regular basis to discuss the new teacher's growth. This was coupled with new teacher seminars that discussed areas of growth that were relevant to the new teachers.

In the other district, there is not a formal new teacher mentoring program. A new teacher orientation day is held at the beginning of the school year for all teachers who are new to the district. This includes first year teachers as well as experienced teachers who are teaching in the district for the very first time. Thus, any teacher, no matter how much prior classroom experience he or she may have had, is labeled as a "new teacher" by this district. A *helping teacher* is assigned to each new teacher as a "resource" person. This peer mentor is available if the new teacher has questions or wants feedback or advice from a colleague. The Regional Office of Education (ROE) for this district also provides a series of workshops specifically designed for new teachers using an induction and mentoring grant.

Instrument/Procedures

A web-based survey was presented to the new teachers of both districts through an email invitation. The survey asked new teachers about their pre-service teaching preparation as well as their opinions/perceptions about the support provided by their mentoring programs and first-year teaching experiences. In addition, the participants were asked to rate how likely they were to be teaching in five years. This projection is especially relevant when considering the research of Ingersoll and Smith (2003) who estimated the attrition rate of new teachers to be 40% to 50% after just five years of teaching.

Pre-service teaching preparation was included in the survey based on the work of Latham and Vogt (2007). These researchers conducted a longitudinal study at the university, located in the community, shared by the two schools included in this study. This study found that "PDS-prepared teachers entered the teaching profession more often and stayed in it longer" (p. 163).

Support provided during the first year of teaching was found by Chubbuck, Clift, Allard, and Quinian (2001) to be an important factor for novice teachers. In this research, many new teachers considered opportunities for analysis and reflection of their teaching practices to be quite important, especially when this analysis and reflection was supported by relationships with peers from all experience levels.

This study was conducted within the school districts where the new teachers were employed. With the cooperation of the administration in each district, new teachers were identified and contacted through district email. Upon receiving the emailed letters and reading through the informed consent information, recipients interested in participating followed a link to a web-based survey. Included in the on-line survey were ten questions. Three of the questions were multiple choice with an open-ended "other" option. These questions were:

1. Please indicate the pre-service teaching experience in which you participated: PDS Program, Traditional Student Teaching, or Other, please specify.
2. Please indicate the mentoring program(s) in which you are participating: New Teacher In-Service Program, 1:1 Mentoring, District Mentoring Progarm, or Other, please specify.
3. What factor has been most beneficial to you during this first year of teaching? Mentoring Program, Administrative Support, Pre-Service Teaching Preparation, or Other, please specify.

Six questions contained a six-point Likert scale from which the participants could choose the best answer. These six questions asked participants to rate:

1. how well their pre-service teaching experiences prepared them for their present teaching positions
2. the level of support their mentoring programs were providing
3. the importance of meeting/reflecting with peers/colleagues
4. how likely they would be to recommend their mentoring program to a new teacher
5. how likely it was that they would still be teaching in five years
6. how their mentoring program positively affected whether they will continue in the teaching profession

The last question was an open-ended solicitation to "provide any additional information that may be helpful in supporting future new teachers."

This survey was offered to new teachers in both districts during the spring semester of their first year of teaching in that district. Participants were given one week in which to respond at which time the data was collected from the on-line survey site to be analyzed.

Research Questions

1. To what extent do (a) voluntary mentoring, (b) formal mentoring, & (c) 1:1 mentoring contribute to the perceptions of support for first year teachers in public schools?

2. Which pre-service teacher preparation program (a) PDS Program, (b) traditional student teaching, or (c) other experience will be perceived as providing the highest quality preparation for first year teachers in public schools?
3. Which factor (a) mentoring, (b) administrative support, (c) pre-service teacher preparation, or (d) other experience will most strongly affect new teacher's projections for their futures in the teaching professions?

Definition of Terms

Professional Development School (PDS) Programs – Programs that extend the experiences of preservice teachers in schools while immersing them in real teaching experiences (Latham & Vogt, 2007).

Attrition – Leaving the profession of teaching after being employed as a teacher.

Mentoring – Programs which provide varying levels and types of support to new teachers as they begin their careers in the profession of teaching.

District Mentors – Teachers within a district who are fully released from their day-to-day teaching responsibilities to support and guide new teachers on a full time basis.

1:1 Mentors – Teachers who continue to teach full time while they provide support and guidance to new teachers on a limited basis.

New Teacher In-Service Program – Mandatory program required for all teachers in their first year with the district that involves recurring meetings with other new teachers in the building as well as with the administration.

Limitations of the Study

The researchers have identified the following limitations impacting this study:

1. The participants in this study were from one geographic area of the United States. The results cannot be generalized to all areas of the United States.
2. The majority of the data from this study was qualitative in nature. The opinions cannot be generalized to all new teachers.
3. The researchers were from the districts in which they gathered data. This may have influenced participation and responses of participants.
4. Participants in the study were not randomly selected, a convenient sample was used.
5. This study is not longitudinal in nature; therefore there is no way to determine if the number of first year teachers who completed the survey will still be teaching in five years.
6. The sample size for this study was relatively small.

Replications of this study should be conducted using a larger, random sampling of first year teacher and should include a longitudinal component so that the findings of the study can be generalized.

Data Analysis

In order to analyze the data for both first year teachers' perceptions of supports provided to them as well as their projections for continued futures in the teaching profession, a paired sample t-test was run. Likewise, the paired-sample t-test was also used to identify which pre-service teacher preparation program yielded the highest correlation with perceptions of the quality of preparation.

Total responses on the web-based survey regarding teachers' perceptions of the supports provided to them in their first year of teaching in a public school and their perceptions of the quality of their teacher preparation program were computed and represented in a table. Written responses to the open ended questions included in the survey were also noted. These open-ended comments collected from all participants were compared; similar themes were grouped collectively and further analyzed by the researchers. Outlier responses on the survey were recorded and examined as well. The results from this survey determined the validity of these researchers' hypothesis that first year teachers in public schools will feel more supported when they are part of a district with a formal mentoring program and/or participated in a rigorous teacher preparation program.

Results

The informed consent and invitation to participate in the web-based survey were sent to all teachers in both school districts who were in their first year of teaching within each district. Unfortunately, major cuts had just been announced in both districts within the two weeks preceding this invitation. In the larger district, all the teachers in the study had received Reduction in Force notices indicating that they were released from this district the week before the survey opened. The number of email invitations sent to teachers in the larger district was 102. In the smaller district, an article published in the local newspaper as well as reports broadcasted on area news stations stated that the district would be eliminating up to 26 teaching positions in order to curb expenses in the budget. Thirty-four invitations for the survey were sent out in this district. Thirty-two teachers from both districts responded to the survey. Of the teachers responding, the majority had participated in a traditional student teaching experience (71.8%) while 18.8% had participated in a PDS program, and 9.4% indicated an experience other than traditional student teaching or PDS (Table 1). When asked to rate on a six-point Likert scale how well their pre-service teaching experience prepared them for their current teaching positions, most of the respondents responded with a four or a five (75%). This rating signifies that the majority of the new teachers felt very well or exceptionally well prepared for their current teaching position.

Table 1: Pre-Service Teaching Experience

Type of program	Percent	Frequency
PDS Program	18.8	6
Traditional Student Teaching	71.8	23
Other	9.4	3
Total	100.0	32

While in their first year of teaching within the two districts, most of the respondents were participating in some form of district mentoring program (61.3%). The teachers were able to select all programs in this section that were applicable.   Over half of the respondents indicated participation in a 1:1 mentoring program (51.6%), approximately one-third (32.3%) were participating in a new teacher in-service program, and 16.1% were participating in another program. These other programs included taking classes at the Regional Office of Education,   bi-weekly meetings with administrators and other new teachers, support provided when asked for, and occasional new teacher programs.

When asked to use a six-point Likert scale to indicate the level of support their mentoring program was providing during their first year in their current district, 25% of the respondents indicated they had received minimal or little support from their district. One-quarter of the participants responded that they were receiving an adequate or average level of support. Half of the respondents (50%) indicated they had received either an above average or a superior level of support (Table 2).   Nearly one-third of the respondents (31.3%) indicated that they would be very likely to recommend their mentoring program to another new teacher while 12.5% indicated that it was not likely at all that they would recommend the program.

Table 2: Level of Support Provided by Mentoring Program

Levels of mentoring support	Percent	Frequency
Minimal	12.5	4
Little	12.5	4
Adequate	9.4	3
Average	15.6	5
Above Average	28.1	9

When asked how likely it was that they would still be teaching in five years, the majority of teachers responded with likely to very likely (81.2%). None of the 32 respondents selected "not likely at all" or "not likely" as a response to this question, indicating that at this point in their careers, they all see the possibility of teaching in the future (Table 3).

Table 3: Likelihood of Teaching in Five Years

Likelihood of teaching in five years	Percent	Frequency
Not Likely at All	0.0	0
Not Likely	0.0	0
Uncertain	9.4	3
Somewhat Likely	9.4	3
Likely	9.4	3
Very Likely	71.8	23
Totals	100.0	32

When asked how their mentoring program has positively influenced whether they will continue in the teaching profession, the most common response (25%) was a 4, meaning the mentoring program had an "above average positive effect" on their decision to remain in the teaching field. Over one-third (37.5%) rated this question with a 5 or 6, meaning that their experience with the mentoring program in their district affected them "positively" or "very positively." Still, the same percentage of participants (37.5%) responded with a 1, 2, or 3, meaning that they felt the mentoring program had "no positive influence" to an "average positive influence" over their decision to remain in the teaching profession (Table 4). These high numbers may be attributed to the fact that the participants from the smaller district do not participate in a formal mentoring program.

Table 4: Positive Influence of Mentoring Program

Mentoring program influence	Percent	Frequency
No Positive Influence	9.4	3
Minimal Positive Influence	15.6	5
Average Positive Influence	12.5	4
Above Average Influence	25.0	8
Positive Influence	21.9	7
Very Positive Influence	15.6	5
Totals	100.0	32

To determine how schools can be most helpful to new teachers during their first year of teaching in a public school, respondents were asked to indicate which factor was most beneficial to them during their first year in their district (Table 5). About one-third (34.4%) indicated that their mentoring program had been most beneficial, while peer support and administrative support were each identified by 25% of the respondents as being most important. Peer support and reflecting with a peer was also indicated by 53.1% of the respondents as being extremely important when asked to rate this specific item. Only 15.6% of the respondents indicated that their pre-service teaching experience was the most beneficial factor during this year of teaching.

Table 5: Most Beneficial Support during This Year

Beneficial support this year	Percent	Frequency
Mentoring Program	34.4	11
Administrative Support	25.0	8
Pre-Service Teaching Preparation	15.6	5
Peer Support	25.0	8
Totals	100.0	32

Finally, respondents were asked to provide any additional information that might be helpful in supporting future new teachers. These are the comments that were provided:

- Mentoring programs are great!!! Wish we had one in my district.
- Being able to talk with experienced teachers in your department is the biggest key because they can provide insight into the specific lessons or subjects you will be covering. They can make suggestions that will work in your classroom and can help with evaluations and instruction.
- The position which I am currently teaching in is not one in which I did any specific student teaching. I have certifications in: Deaf & Hard of Hearing, Low Vision & Blindness, LBS1, Elementary Ed and Early Childhood. My student teaching experiences were specifically related to my majors (DHH and LVB).
- Being a brand new Special Education Teacher, I feel ISU has not prepared me to be the best teacher I can be. They did not go over enough assessments in Reading and Math and strategies to teach fluency, decoding, comprehension, etc. My district and burnt-out building mentor both cannot help me with IEPs, assessments, and direction with different strategies. I've had to utilize people in other districts, buy my own materials, and do a lot research, all of which has cost a lot of money and time. I spend 12 hours a day at school. I also didn't have enough experience teaching so many different grade levels with many different ability levels. The Woodcock Johnson is out of date and not utilized in the classroom. I wish (name of district) utilized it more than DIBELS. They need DRA, MAPS, and a district wide Math assessment. I have no direction and training on Fountas and Pinnell and other assessments I'm supposed to use.
- I got a lot out of traditional student teaching and am grateful I did not take part in PDS. I felt it was a good transition into teaching and really prepared me. I also was very lucky because I got a job in the school I student taught in.
- I think the answers to these questions depend on how many years prior to this year a person has been teaching. Some of us are new to the district, but we are not new to the field. I don't feel as though I need a mentoring program as much as a fresh out of college teacher might.

- I believe that a 1-1 mentoring program is best. I have seen them work. At my school, we have monthly meetings with all the new teachers where we discuss how it is going. The problem this has is that we have no guidance from experienced teachers. Also, we feel more isolated from the current staff. The new teachers are close with one another, but we still have to fight to fit in.

Data Analysis

In order to analyze the data for both first year teachers' perceptions of supports provided to them as well as their projections for continued futures in the teaching profession, a paired-sample t-test was run. Likewise, the paired-sample t-test was also used in order to identify which factor—voluntary mentoring, formal mentoring, 1:1 mentoring, teacher preparation, or peer impact had the strongest relationship with the feeling of support felt by first year teachers in public schools.

The correlation between teachers' perceived levels of support provided in their first year of teaching and their participation in voluntary mentoring, formal mentoring, 1:1 mentoring, a teacher preparation program, and/or peer impact was analyzed by inputting the data collected from the new teacher survey into the Statistical Packet for Social Sciences (SPSS) for Windows program. This program determined the correlation and statistical significance for each of the individual variables when paired with the level of mentoring support felt by new teachers. The outcome from the data entered into the SPSS program identified whether the variables (voluntary mentoring, formal mentoring, 1:1 mentoring, teacher preparation, or peer impact) have a statistically significant relationship with first year teachers' perceived level of support provided by their school and/or district. Tables were created through the SPSS program that outlined these results.

Total responses on the web-based survey regarding teachers' perceptions of the supports provided to them in their first year of teaching in a public school were computed and represented in Table 6. According to the data collected, having district mentors as well as having a new teacher in-service program both resulted in moderately strong correlations with the level of support felt by first year teachers. However, one resulted in a moderately strong positive association while the other resulted in a moderately strong negative association. The correlational coefficient between district mentors and level of support felt by new teachers was the highest, .675, making it was statistically significant at the .001 level. The new teacher in-service program and level of support felt by first year teachers had a -.519 correlational coefficient, which also made it statistically significant at the .001 level. The researchers had hypothesized that the first year teachers provided only with the new teacher in-service programs would feel less supported in their first year of teaching than those provided with a formal district mentor, and this negative association was confirmed by the data collected in the survey.

While the researchers expected to find a strong statistical significance in the correlation between having district mentors and feeling a higher level of support, they were surprised that the 1:1 mentoring, which they had assumed would provide new teachers with the greatest level of support, only had a correlational coefficient of .063 when compared to level of support felt by new teachers. This weak statistical significance could be attributed to the fact that participants in the survey may have become confused by the three different options for mentoring programs provided in Question 2 on the survey. The also may not have realized that they were able to select more than one mentoring program if applicable. Another factor that may have impacted this finding is the fact that all teachers new to the district in which the 1:1 mentoring is used are assigned a mentor regardless of previous experience and need for support. This was noted by one respondent when he/she commented, "I think the answers to these questions depend on how many years prior to this year a person has been teaching. Some of us are new to the district, but we are not new to the field. I don't feel as though I need a mentoring program as much as a fresh out of college teacher might."

Table 6: Paired Samples Correlations, Preparation and Support

Paired samples	N	Correlation	Sig.
Pair 1-PDS & Teacher Preparation Quality	32	.447	.010
Pair 2-Traditional & Teacher Preparation Quality	32	-.272	.132
Pair 3-Other & Teacher Preparation Quality	32	-.235	.195
Pair 4-Inservice & Level of Mentoring Support	32	-.519	.002
Pair 5-1:1 & Level of Mentoring Support	32	.063	.731
Pair 6-District & Level of Mentoring Support	32	.675	.000
Pair 7-Other & Level of Mentoring Support	32	-.446	.011

Question Two, *Please indicate the mentoring program(s) in which you are participating*, offered three different types of mentoring programs for participants to select from and also offered an "other" response. Written responses to Question Two in the survey were:

- No mentoring. Occasional new teacher programs.
- There are no mentoring programs in my district.
- I have both a district mentor and a building mentor.
- This is my third year teaching but first year at this school; I am not in an official mentoring program due to my unique program, but I am offered support whenever I ask.

These open-ended comments collected from participants who selected "other" were compared; similar themes were grouped collectively and further analyzed by the researchers. Outlier responses on the survey, such as comments one, two, and four, were recorded and examined as well. These comments suggest that some participants may not have been aware that additional support programs provided by the district were considered mentoring programs.

Correlations between type of teacher preparation and the respondents' rating of their teacher preparation quality were also included in the paired sample t-test outlined in Table 6. All correlations were statistically significant (at the .001 level) but only PDS teacher preparation resulted in a positive correlation at .447. Both Traditional teacher preparation and "Other" were negatively correlated at -

.272 and -.235 respectively. This confirms the researchers' hypothesis that teachers who participated in the more comprehensive PDS teacher preparation program would perceive that their experience better prepared them for a classroom of their own.

After determining the correlational coefficients for each individual variable when paired with perceived level of support and reviewing the responses to the open ended questions, the results from this survey supported the researchers' hypothesis. First year teachers in public schools will feel more supported when they are part of a district with a formal mentoring program and will feel better prepared when they participated in a rigorous teacher preparation program.

To analyze the correlation between what factor had been most beneficial to the respondents during their first year of teaching and the likelihood that the respondents would still be teaching in five years, a paired-sample t-test was used. These results are represented in Table 7. For this question, the respondents were given the options of Mentoring Program, Administrative Support, Pre-Service Teaching Preparation and Other (Please Specify Below). The "Other" responses were analyzed and coded to reflect what the respondents specified. Peer support was indicated by eight of the ten "Other" respondents as being most important during their first year of teaching in their current district. One response indicated a mentoring program that had not been identified in the survey and one response indicated a form of administrative support. "Peer Support" replaced the "Other" option and the other two responses were added to their respective options.

Table 7: Paired Samples Correlations, Support and Projection

Paired samples	N	Correlations	Significance
Pair 1-Mentoring & 5 Year Projection of Likelihood of Continued Teaching	32	-.185	.310
Pair 2-Admin Support & 5 Year Projection of Likelihood of Continued Teaching	32	.181	.322
Pair 3-Pre-service Prep & 5 Year Projection of Likelihood of Continued Teaching	32	.156	.393
Pair 4-Peer Support & 5 Year Projection of Likelihood of Continued Teaching	32	.108	.555

All correlations were statistically significant (at the .001 level) but mentoring and the likelihood of still teaching in five years was negative at -.185. This conflicted with the researchers' hypothesis that a positive perception of mentoring during the first year would positively affect the teachers' projections for their futures in teaching. Positive correlations were found between the likelihood of still teaching in five years and administrative support (.181), pre-service teaching experience (.156), and peer support (.108).

The impact of peer support on the future teaching projections of new teachers was not a factor the researchers had originally considered when conducting this study. However, it is clear from the data collected that peer support is an invaluable factor that plays a critical role in the retention of new teachers. This is demonstrated in the following participant's comment, "Being able to talk with experienced teachers in your department is the biggest key because they can provide insight into the specific lessons or subjects you will be covering. They can make suggestions that will work in your classroom and can help with evaluations and instruction."

Discussion/Conclusion

The majority of participants in this survey responded that it is "likely" or "very likely" that they will still be teaching in five years (81.3 %), yet Ingersoll and Smith (2003) have estimated that the attrition rate for new teachers is 40 to 50 percent after five years. This statistic is even more significant when considering the fact that both districts involved in the research were experiencing financial difficulties and all the first year teachers in the larger school district had received reduction in force notices (meaning that they were not being rehired for the next year) just days before the survey invitation was sent to them. It should be noted, however, that the response rate for the survey was only 24%. It is possible that the results were skewed by this low response rate.

Though the focus of the researchers was teacher preparation and mentoring programs, the importance of meeting and reflecting with peers was noted by 53.1% of respondents as being extremely important to their growth during their first year of teaching in their current district. The importance of peers was again noted by 25% of respondents when they were asked to indicate the factor that had been most beneficial to them during their first year of teaching. This support was also noted as a top motivation by Certo and Fox (2002) when they researched the reasons that teachers give for staying in their positions. This factor could prove to be especially important considering the fact that mentoring programs last only one to two years. The support of peers could prove to be the long-term factor that influences a teacher's decision to stay in the profession.

The factor that was identified by the highest percentage of respondents (34%) as being most beneficial to them during their first year of teaching was their mentoring program. In contrast to this, when mentoring was correlated with the projection of the likelihood of still teaching in five years, the result was a negative correlation of -.185. It could be possible that the teachers knew that the mentoring program was a temporary support and therefore did not consider mentoring to be an important factor when projecting five years into the future.

The teacher preparation program that provided the only positive correlation with teacher preparation quality was the PDS program (.447). However, when asked which factor had been most beneficial to the teachers during their first year of teaching in their current district, only 15.6% of respondents identified their pre-service teaching preparation as being most beneficial. Pre-service teacher preparation did have a positive correlation with the five year projection of the likelihood of continuing in the teaching profession, making this factor one to consider when looking into the concerns about teacher attrition.

The results of this research did not clearly identify any one factor as being the deciding factor for retaining teachers in the teaching profession. It does appear that mentoring has an immediate (though not long-term) effect on teachers and the perception of support that they have received. Administrative support, pre-service preparation, and peer support appear to support the longer term perceptions of support for first year teachers.

Implications

This research provided support for PDS programs and mentoring when surveying teachers who were in their first year of teaching in two public school districts in the Midwest region of the United States. Less clear from the research was the long term effects of mentoring for new teachers. The fact that 81.2% of the respondents projected that they would still be in the teaching profession in five years indicates that district support resources have positively impacted the perceptions of teachers in their first year of teaching. Considering the significant discrepancy between these teachers' five year projections of continuing in the teaching profession and the attrition rate found by Ingersoll and Smith (2003) of 40 to 50 percent, more research is needed as teachers progress from their first year of teaching to their fifth year of teaching. Most beneficial may be a longitudinal study that surveys the same teachers each year during this progression to evaluate how their perceptions of support are changing and/or evolving.

Other research that may be beneficial is in the area of mentoring. Currently, mentoring programs in the two districts where this research took place end after one or two years. The effects of longer term mentoring programs could be researched since this factor was the one most cited by respondents as being the most beneficial to them during their first year of teaching. Unfortunately, this research would need funding as mentors are often paid.

Peer support is an area that could be strengthened and researched with little financial cost to districts. Team building activities could be encouraged by administrators to bolster the rapport between new and experienced faculty members. In addition to strengthening peer relationships, this team building may also increase the perception of administrative support for teachers. These were two factors that were positively correlated to the five year projections of first year teachers continuing in the teaching profession with peer support yielding the strongest significance at .555.

A future study related to the area of peer support could examine whether or not providing collaborative teacher preparation time is effective for new teachers. The experiences of all teachers involved in the collaborative team could be collected through a reflective qualitative study and might indicate the specific issues that new teachers need addressed to make their first year in the teaching profession not only more manageable, but more productive for themselves and for their students as well. The experienced teachers in these teams might be able to target the most essential concerns with which new teachers need to grapple during their first year of teaching in order to work more effectively in the classroom, such as behavior management, grading, creating lesson plans, etc.

References

Certo, J. L., & Fox, J. E. (2002). Retaining quality teachers. *High School Journal.* *86*(1), 57-75. Retrieved from ERIC database.

Chubbuck, S. M., Clift, R. T., Allard, J., & Quinlan, J. (2001). Playing it safe as a novice teacher implications for programs for new teachers. *Journal of Teacher Education 52*(5), 365-376. doi: 10.1177/0022487101052005003

Dinsmore, J., & Wenger, K. (2006). Relationships in preservice teacher preparation: From cohorts to communities. *Teacher Education Quarterly, 33*(1), 57-75. Retrieved from EBSCO database.

Feiman-Nemser, S. (2001). From preparation to practice: Designing a continuum to strengthen and sustain teaching. *Teachers College Record, 103*(6), 1013-1055. Retrieved from ERIC database.

Feiman-Nemser, S. (2003). What new teachers need to learn. *Educational Leadership, 60* (8), 25-29. Retrieved from EBSCO database.

Fresko, B. & Alhija, F. N. (2009). When intentions and reality clash: Inherent implementation difficulties of an induction program for new teachers. *Teaching and Teacher Education 25*, 278-284. Retrieved from EBSCO database.

Fry, S. W. (2007). First-year teachers and induction support: Ups, downs, and in-betweens. *The Qualitative Report 12*(2), 216-237. Retrieved from EBSCO database.

Gonzalez, L, Stallone Brown, M., & Slate, J.R. (2008). Teachers who left the teaching profession: A qualitative understanding. *The Qualitative Report 13* (1), 1-11. Retrieved from EBSCO database.

Herbert, K., & Ramsey, M. (2004). Teacher turnover and shortages of qualified teachers in Texas public school districts. Austin, TX: Texas State Board for Educator Certification.

Illinois school report card (2009). Retrieved November 10,2009 from http://webprod.isbe.net/ereportcard/publicsite/getsearchcriteria.aspx

Illinois State Board of Education. (2001). *Educator supply and demand.* Springfield, IL.

Ingersoll, R.M. (1999). The problem of under-qualified teachers in American secondary schools. *Education Researcher, 28*(2), 26-37.

Ingersoll, R. (2001). Teacher turnover and teacher shortages: An organizational analysis. *American Education Research Journal, 38*(3), 499-534.

Ingersoll, R. (2002). The teacher shortage: A case of wrong diagnosis and wrong prescription. *NASSP Bulletin, 86*(631), 16-31. Retrieved from ERIC database.

Ingersoll, R. M., & Smith, T. M. (2003). The wrong solution to the teacher shortage. *Educational Leadership, 60*(60), 30-33. Retrieved from EBSCO database.

Kelley, L. M. (2004). Why induction matters. *Journal of Teacher Education 55*(5), 438-448. doi: 10.1177/0022487104269653

Latham, N. I., & Vogt, W. P. (2007). Do professional development schools reduce teacher attrition? Evidence from a longitudinal study of 1,000 graduates. *Journal of Teacher Education, 58*(2), 152-167. doi: 10.1177/0022487106297840

National Education Association (NEA). (2002). Attracting and keeping quality teachers. Retrieved September 21, 2009, from http://www.nea.org/teachershortage/index.html

National Education Association (NEA). (2003a, October). Attracting and keeping quality teachers. Retrieved September 21, 2009, from http://www.nea.com/teachershortage

National Education Association (NEA). (2003b, October). Meeting the challenges of recruitment and retention. Retrieved September 21, 2009, from http://www.nea.org/teachershortage/recruitmentguide.html www.nea.org

Ridley, D. S., Hurwitz, S., Hackett, M. R. D., & Miller, K. K. (2005). Comparing PDS and campus-based preservice teacher preparation: Is PDS-based preparation really better?. *Journal of Teacher Education 56*(1), 46-56. doi: 10.117/0022487104272098

Smith, T. M., & Ingersoll, R. M. (2004). What are the effects of induction and mentoring on beginning teacher turnover?. *American Education Research Journal 41*(3), 681-714. Retrieved from EBSCO database.

Tusin, L. F. (1995, February 21). *Success in the first year of teaching: Effects of a clinical experience program.* Paper presented at the annual meeting of the Association of Teacher Educators, Detroit, MI. Retrieved from ERIC database.

Valencia, S. W., Martin, S. D., Place, N. A., & Grossman, P. (2009). Complex interactions in student teaching lost opportunities for learning. *Journal of Teacher Education 60*(3), 304-322. doi: 10.1177/0022487109336543

Weiss, E. M., & Weiss, S. G. (1999). Beginning teacher induction. ERIC Digest. *ERIC Clearinghouse on Teaching and Teacher Education.* Retrieved from ERIC database.

CPSIA information can be obtained at www.ICGtesting.com
Printed in the USA
LVOW02s1454100913

351818LV00001B/1/P